IMAGES
of America

MOON TOWNSHIP

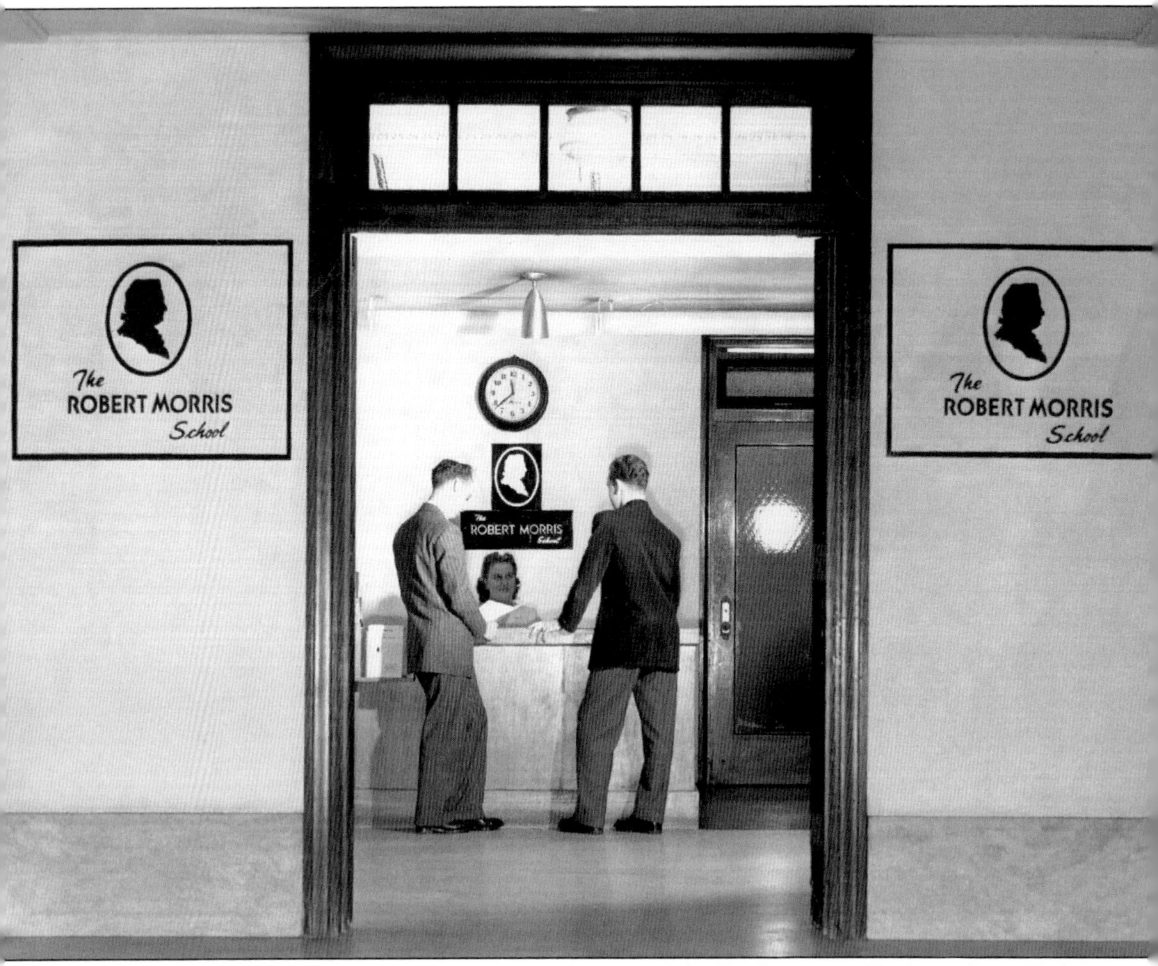

Named after early Pennsylvania senator and signer of the Declaration of Independence Robert Morris, Robert Morris University had modest roots as an accounting school. The school was founded by Andrew Blass out of a demand for more accountants in the workforce. The Robert Morris school became part of Moon Township's history in 1962 when 230 acres were purchased to accommodate the school's expanding student base. Today Robert Morris University continues to shape Moon Township and its development. (Courtesy Robert Morris University.)

On the cover: The congregation of Sharon Community Presbyterian Church gathers for a group photograph. The church is the oldest church in Moon Township and is responsible for the growth of the village of Carnot growing up around it. Carnot later became a major crossroads in old Moon Township and continues today to be a major intersection along the township's major commercial district—University Boulevard. Carnot was once home to a general store, a blacksmith's shop, and a simple barbershop. (Courtesy Sharon Community Presbyterian Church.)

IMAGES
of America

MOON TOWNSHIP

Mark Berton

ARCADIA
PUBLISHING

ISBN 978-0-7385-5484-6

Published by Arcadia Publishing
Charleston SC, Chicago IL, Portsmouth NH, San Francisco CA

Printed in the United States of America

Library of Congress Catalog Card Number: 2007926417

For all general information contact Arcadia Publishing at:
Telephone 843-853-2070
Fax 843-853-0044
E-mail sales@arcadiapublishing.com
For customer service and orders:
Toll-Free 1-888-313-2665

Visit us on the Internet at www.arcadiapublishing.com

For Marilyn Bates—poet, teacher, and friend

Contents

ACKNOWLEDGMENTS

Moon Township is an extremely diverse community with a plethora of people from all walks of life. Some families in Moon can trace their lineage back to the early days of the township's settlement. Others are new, settling here for the first time in one of the township's new planned residential developments. Still others live in one of the neighboring communities that once were Moon and have since splintered off. What makes the Moon community special, however, is its willingness to come together to help with this book.

Firstly, I would like to thank Marjorie Johnson of the Crescent-Shousetown Area Historical Association. Johnson's late husband, Eliot, documented much of Crescent's history, and his work was integral to this book.

I would also like to thank Nancy Mills for opening up her home and personal history to me.

I thank the Meanors, Clyde and Ruth, whose history in Moon is long and rich with stories, and Dr. Dale Gass.

Other individuals and organizations that also played a part in putting this book together include Pittsburgh International Airport, Robert Morris University, Sharon Community Presbyterian Church, St. Margaret Mary Catholic Church, and Coraopolis-Moon Masonic Lodge 674.

I would also like to thank the Township of Moon, supervisors Cindy Johnston and Mike Hopper, and anyone that I may have left out who helped make this endeavor possible.

INTRODUCTION

The history of Moon Township goes back to the early days of Allegheny County itself. Many attempts to compile the history of Moon Township have resulted in startlingly detailed composites of individual families from the early days of the township's settlement. Other bits and pieces of the township's history reside in personal archives of the descendants of these founding families, the churches they attended, and the organizations they belonged to.

Despite the fact that Moon Township's history is the longest in Allegheny County, Moon Township is unique in that its history continues as the families that reside here continue to evolve. These families, once known by long distinguished surnames, now yield to the new families, families made up of the enormous businesses, corporations, and social institutions that have taken the old rural landscape of this bustling township and are sculpting them into a Moon Township with a history that will be written by future hands. Entities such as at Pittsburgh International Airport, Robert Morris University, Moon Area School District, and the municipal government of Moon Township all are playing a part in shaping the future of Moon Township. Other community entities such as Sharon Community Presbyterian Church, St. Philip's Episcopal Church, and St. Margaret Mary Parish led the township's population, spiritually.

Compiling a history of Moon Township in one book is a challenging feat because the history of Moon Township could actually fill several books, one for each of the municipalities that have since broken away from the original Moon landmass. Each of these municipalities contains parts of Moon's history. Yet each grew in its own direction from common roots. This book features Moon Township by today's borders, and, to a lesser degree, Crescent Township, which broke away from Moon. Combined, the two townships make up the current Moon Area School District. The depictions of Crescent are by no means comprehensive and are shown here only as a means to enhance the reader's understanding of how Moon came to be the township it is today.

One

The First Township in Allegheny County

Moon Township has the unique distinction of being the first township in Allegheny County, a county that over the years has amassed more than 130 municipal entities. *The History of the Erection of Allegheny County, Its Townships, Boroughs and Cities*, a 1914 work written by J. McKees Boal and produced by the Union Fidelity Title Insurance Company of Pittsburgh, cites the date of Moon Township's formation as December 16, 1788. The township was, at that time, formed by the court of quarter sessions and was an enormous tract of land that was 143 square miles in total. However, the sheer volume of land in early Moon made governance difficult. Lack of infrastructure, reliance on poorly maintained dirt trails, and an untamed western Pennsylvania wilderness made traveling in Moon trying. Early Moon residents often could not report to their assigned polling places for elections.

In reaction, Moon was slowly whittled down into smaller municipalities. The *History of Allegheny County*, published by A. Warner Company in 1889, describes the early Moon Township as "broken and hilly, but well adapted to farming, which is the principal pursuit." According to this source, many of Moon's early residents were "Tomahawk Claim" settlers and of Scotch nationality. From Moon Township, Fayette Township was formed in 1790; Findlay Township in 1820; and Crescent Township in 1855. By the early 1900s, Moon Township had a population of 1,526 people, according to the 13th U.S. census, a number that would double by 1940 and continue to grow to its present number of more than 27,000 people.

Because of its rugged roots, Moon Township's people grew from a handful of founding families whose names continue to mark the land that they helped found. The names of Vance, Meek, Springer, Mercer, and Shouse still have meaning in the municipalities that used to be old Moon Township. Local landmarks such as Shousetown, Stoops Ferry, and Vanceport all share the names of these forefathers of Moon Township.

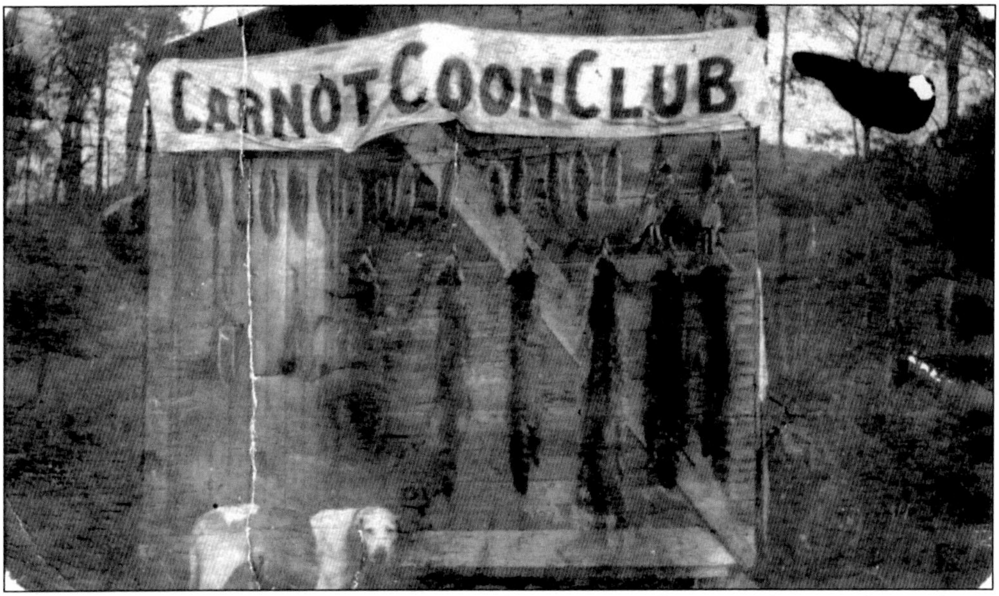

The history of Moon Township can be traced back to the 1700s; however, photographic evidence of its history only goes back to the dawn of the 20th century. While settlements arose in and around Moon far earlier, Moon's rugged, backwoods nature is evident in this photograph of the Carnot Coon Club. (Courtesy the Meanor family.)

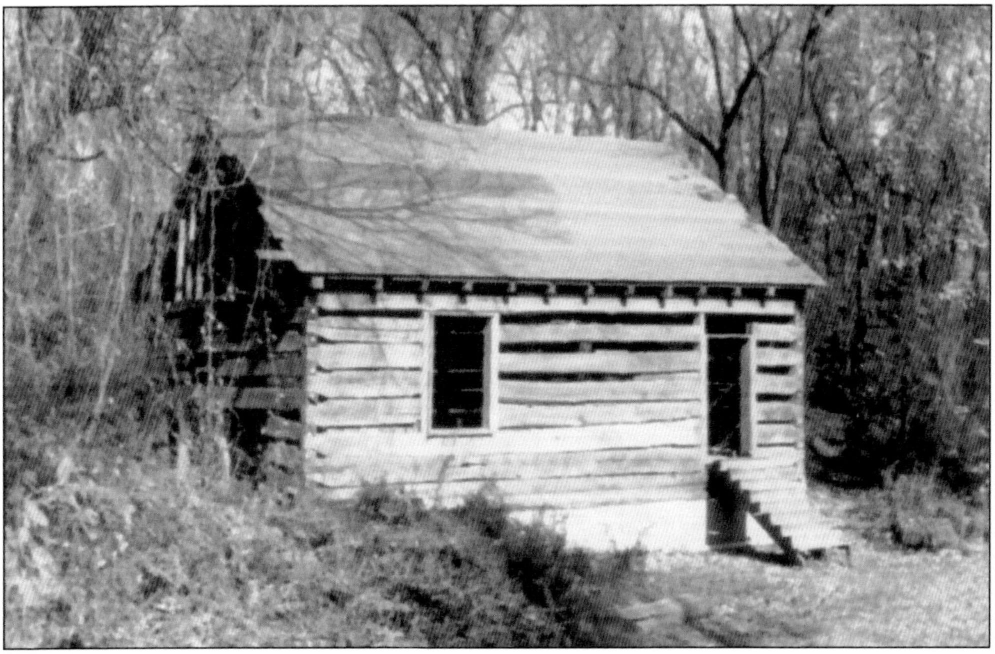

Coventry Cabin is a 150-year-old log cabin owned by John Coventry. The cabin was moved from neighboring Washington County to Moon's Robin Hill Park. Prior to the move, each log was meticulously numbered. The cabin took eight years to reassemble and was rebuilt by the old Moon Historical Society. The cabin was a tool for students to learn about the history of the township. (Courtesy Eliot and Marjorie Johnson and the Crescent-Shousetown Area Historic Association.)

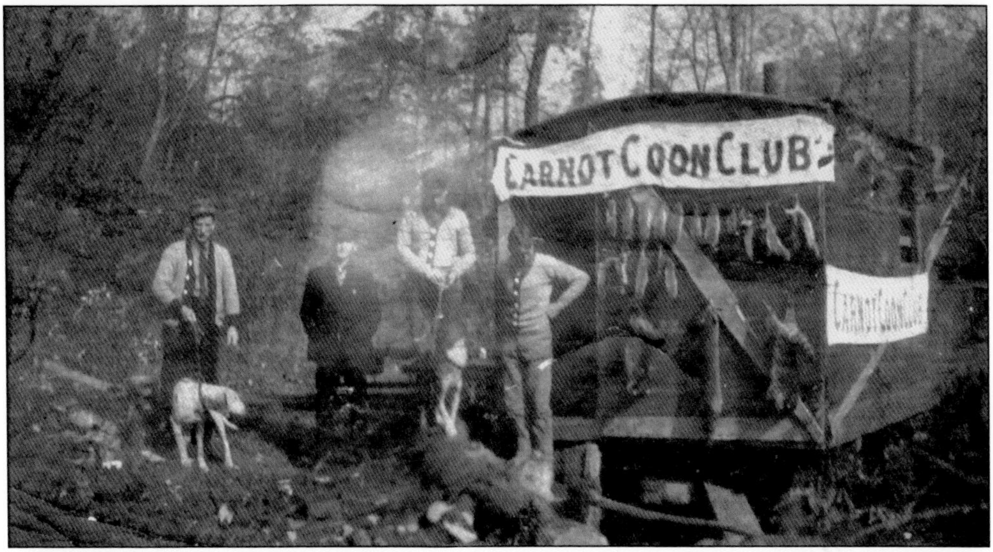

Living off the land was how old Moon Township residents survived. According to the *History of Allegheny County* published in 1876, agriculture was cited as being the predominant occupation of Moon residents. Raccoon hunting was a pastime for early residents. Coon clubs continue to exist today, but in predominantly rural areas of the country. (Courtesy the Meanor family.)

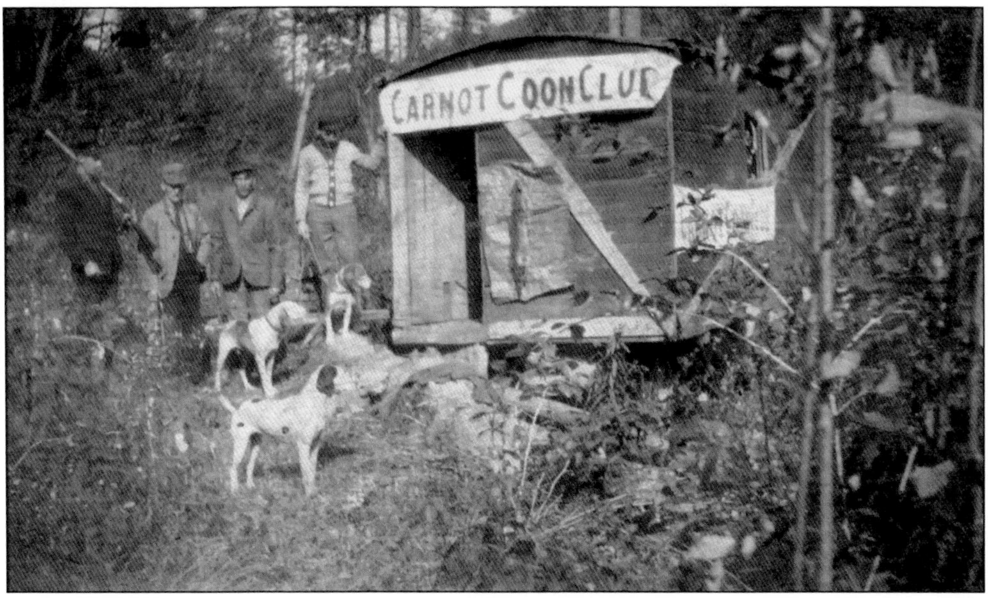

Raccoon hunting is a nocturnal sport that follows the sleep cycle of raccoons. Hunters would gather in posses with their hounds and track the coons. The aim was to tree the raccoons, or chase them into a tree, which effectively cornered the animal. Raccoons were not hunted for food, but rather for their pelts or as trophies. (Courtesy the Meanor family.)

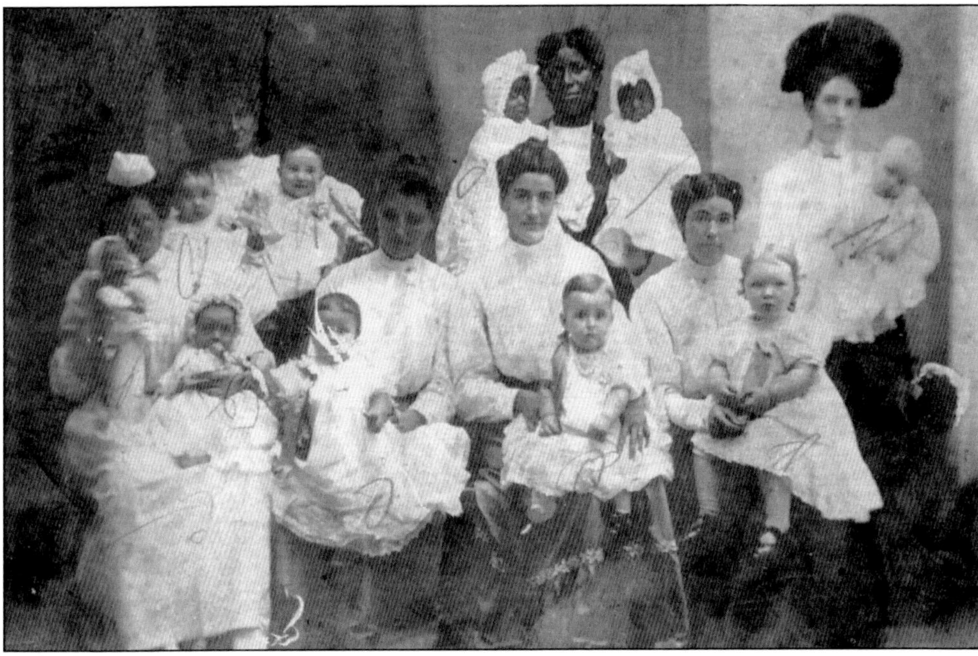

This photograph, taken on the Springer Farm, shows what are believed to be nannies looking over the Springer children. The Springer family in Moon can be traced back to Mathias and Matthew Springer, who settled in after their service in the Revolutionary War in 1785. Descendants of the brothers still reside in Moon Township today. (Courtesy Nancy Mills.)

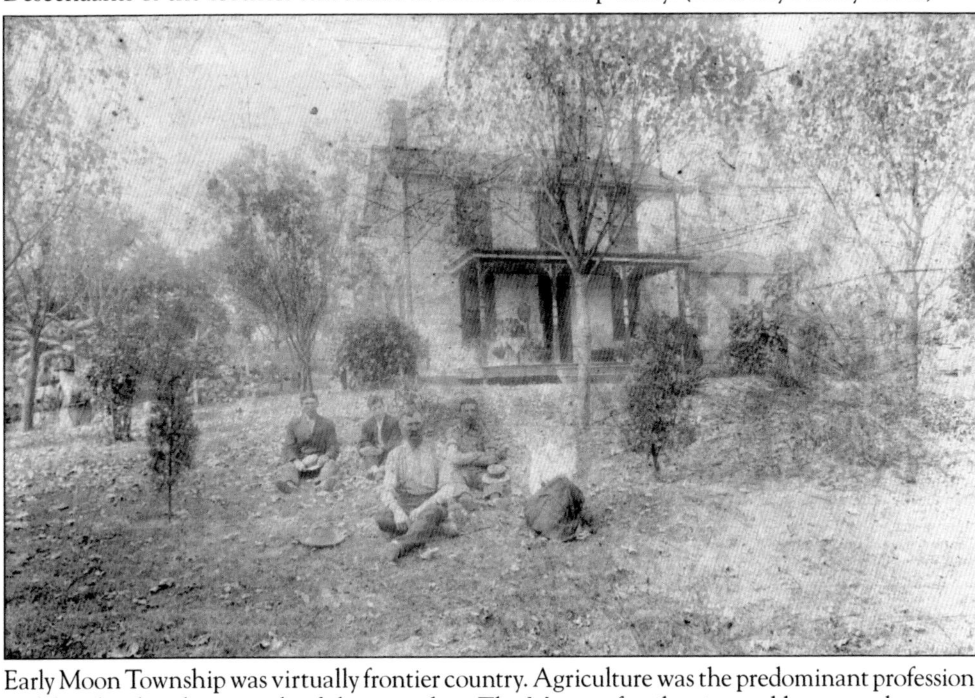

Early Moon Township was virtually frontier country. Agriculture was the predominant profession, and farmland took up much of the township. The Meanor family, pictured here, can be traced back to these early days of Moon. Samuel Meanor had three sons and a daughter. He died in 1892. Relatives of the Meanor family still reside in Moon today. (Courtesy the Meanor family.)

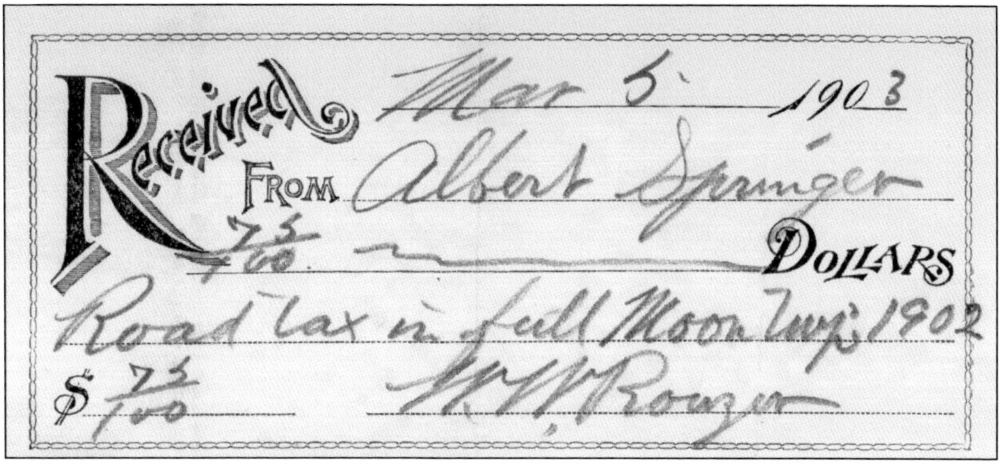

Received Mar 5 1903
From Albert Springer
75/100 Dollars
Road tax in full Moon Twp; 1902
$ 75/100 W. W. Rouzer

This receipt for road taxes is dated 1903 and is in the amount of 75¢. However, with a population of less than 1,500 and roads that were so deplorable they were partially responsible for those who did live in Moon to petition the court of quarter sessions in 1855 to break off and form their own municipality. On November 17 of that same year, Crescent Township was erected. (Courtesy Nancy Mills.)

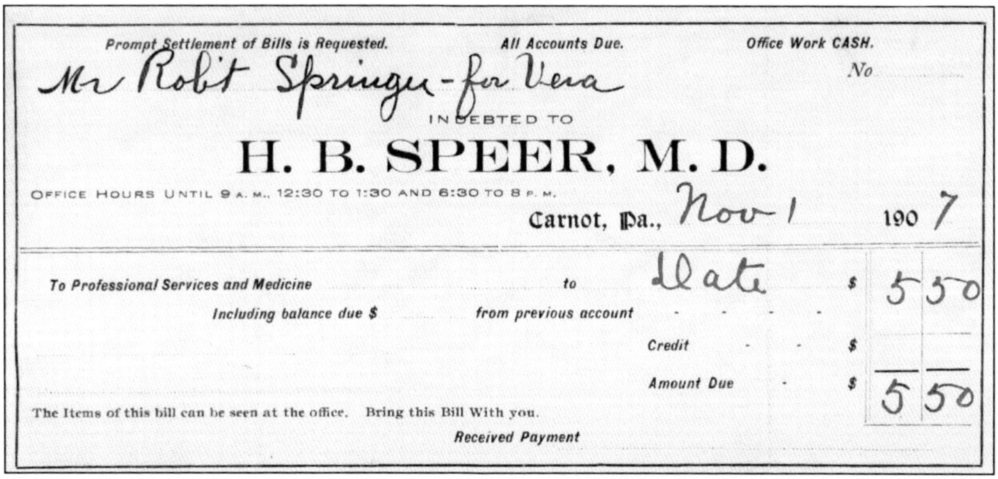

Prompt Settlement of Bills is Requested. All Accounts Due. Office Work CASH.
Mr Robt Springer - for Vera No
INDEBTED TO
H. B. SPEER, M. D.
OFFICE HOURS UNTIL 9 A. M., 12:30 TO 1:30 AND 6:30 TO 8 P. M.
Carnot, Pa., Nov 1 1907

To Professional Services and Medicine to date	$	5 50
Including balance due $ from previous account		
Credit	$	
Amount Due	$	5 50

The Items of this bill can be seen at the office. Bring this Bill With you.
Received Payment

The Springer family has been in Moon for more than 220 years. This receipt for medical services to Vera Springer from 1907 lists H. B. Speer's office in Carnot. Carnot is now a historic part of Moon Township. While it no longer has the prominence it held at the beginning of the 20th century, local residents know Carnot as more of a general neighborhood or district rather than as a village. (Courtesy Nancy Mills.)

Carnot had its own postmark, as this letter from 1900 shows. Prior to 1900, Moon had five post offices: Moon, Beers, Stoops, Montours, and Tipps. Both Montours and Tipps were discontinued before 1886. Carnot has been preserved by township officials by way of a historic overlay district designation. New buildings in the district must conform to a stricter set of design specifications than in other regularly zoned portions of the township. (Courtesy Nancy Mills.)

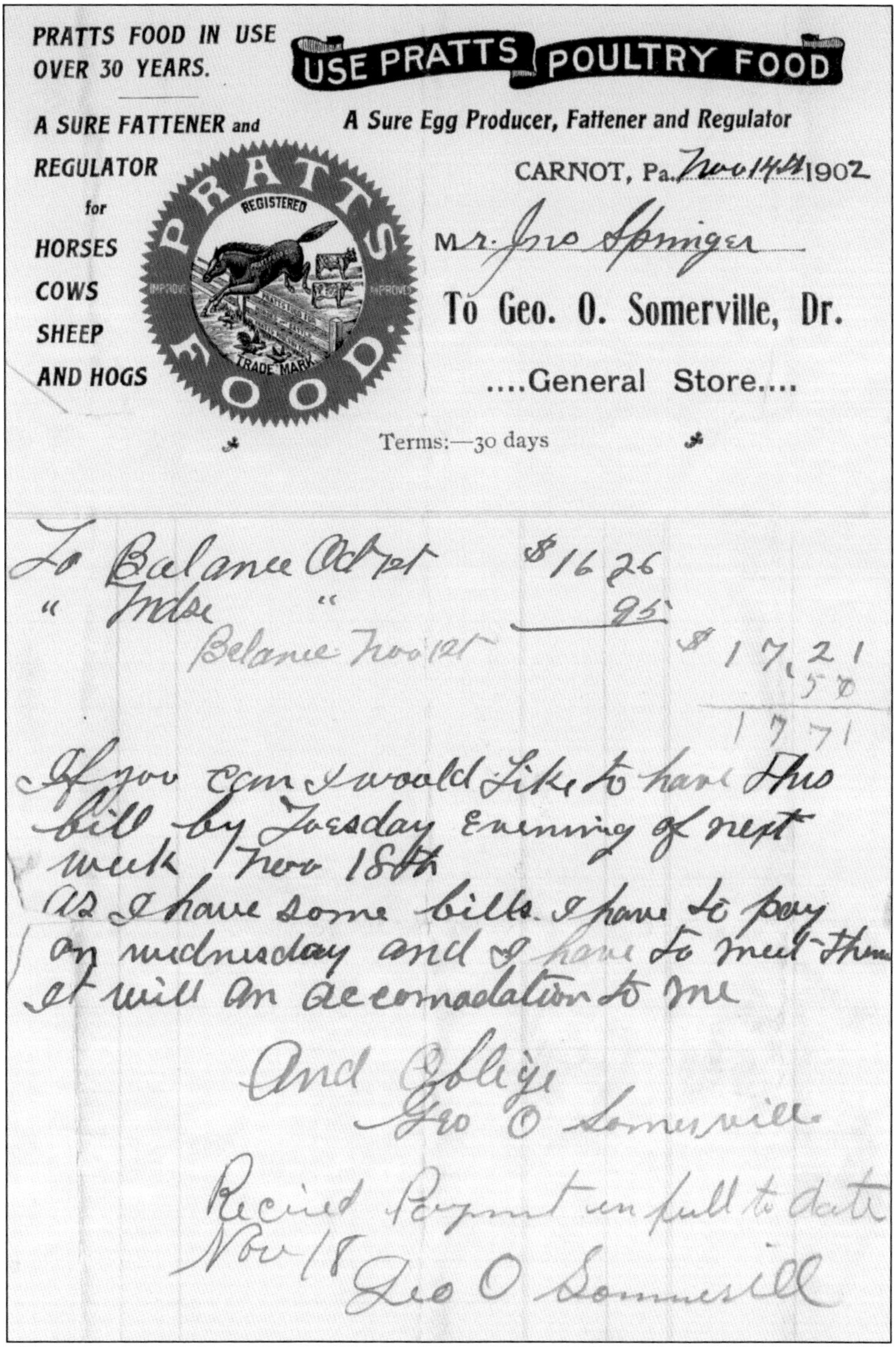
PRATTS FOOD IN USE OVER 30 YEARS.

USE PRATTS POULTRY FOOD

A SURE FATTENER and REGULATOR for HORSES COWS SHEEP AND HOGS

PRATTS FOOD REGISTERED TRADE MARK

A Sure Egg Producer, Fattener and Regulator

CARNOT, Pa. Nov 14th 1902

Mr. Jno Springer

To Geo. O. Somerville, Dr.

....General Store....

Terms:—30 days

To Balance Oct 1st $16 26
" Mdse " 95
Balance Nov 1st $17.21
.50
17 71

If you can I would Like to have this bill by Tuesday Evening of next week Nov 18th as I have some bills I have to pay on Wednesday and I have to meet them it will an accomadation to me

And Oblige
Geo O Somerville

Recivd Payment in full to date
Nov 18 Geo O Somerville

The Springer family has been a part of Moon Township since its earliest roots after the Springer brothers, Mathias and Michael, were awarded 800 acres in land grants for Revolutionary War service. Mathias's son Joseph, one of 10 children, developed a portion of the land bequeathed to him by his father into a farm of more than 1,000 acres. This receipt, dated 1902, is for agricultural products from the Somerville General Store. (Courtesy Nancy Mills.)

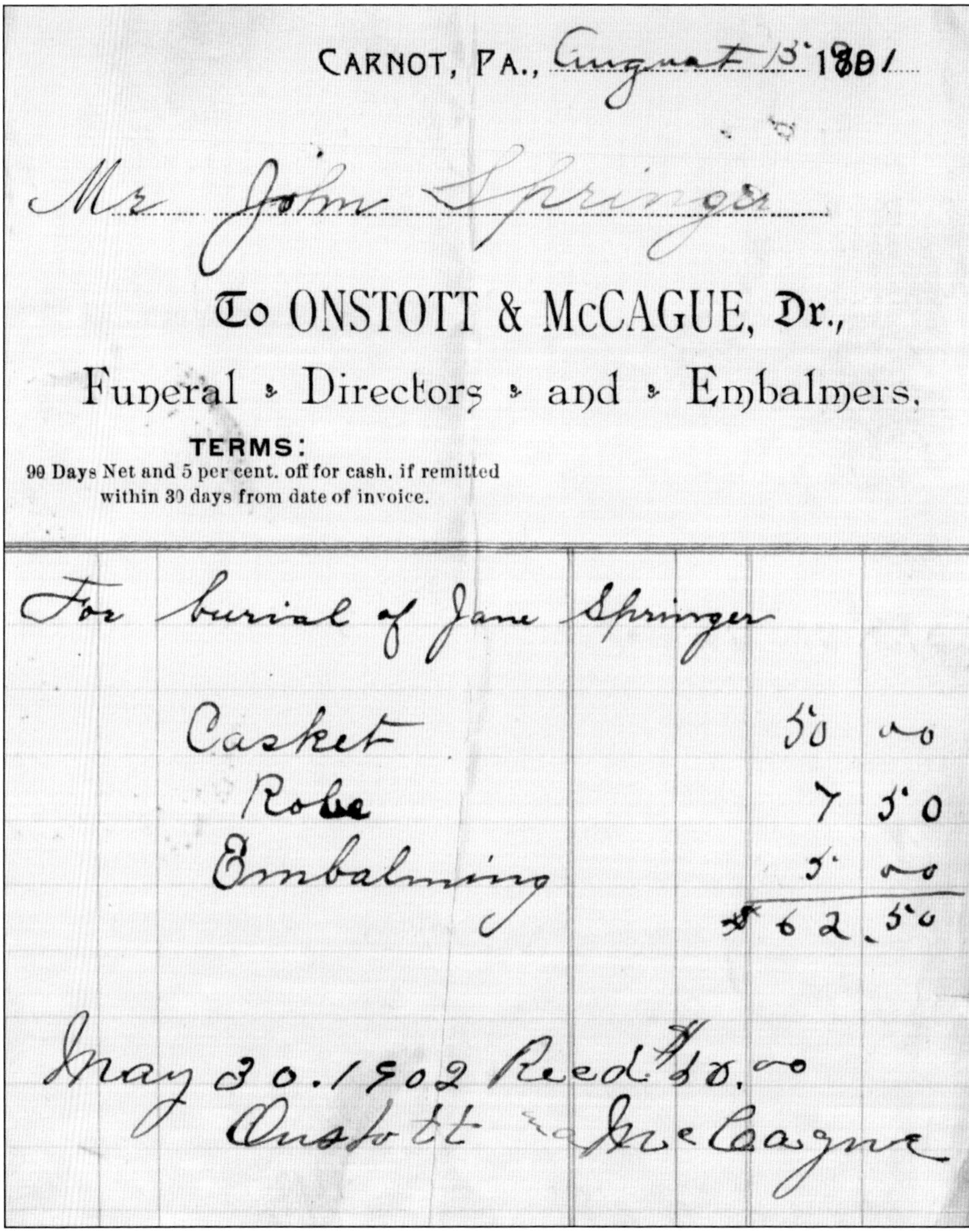

CARNOT, PA., August 15 1901

Mr John Springer

To ONSTOTT & McCAGUE, Dr.,

Funeral Directors and Embalmers.

TERMS:
90 Days Net and 5 per cent. off for cash, if remitted within 30 days from date of invoice.

For burial of Jane Springer

Casket	50	00
Robe	7	50
Embalming	5	00
	$62	50

May 30. 1902 Recd $50.00
Onstott & McCague

The Springer family was very large, as were many of the early families of Moon Township. This receipt for burial of James Springer does not specify which James Springer or John Springer the services were for. Published accounts of the Springer family lineage cite James Leander Springer's death as 1909. He is outlived by his father, John, who lived until 1917 according to the Moon Bicentennial Book. (Courtesy Nancy Mills.)

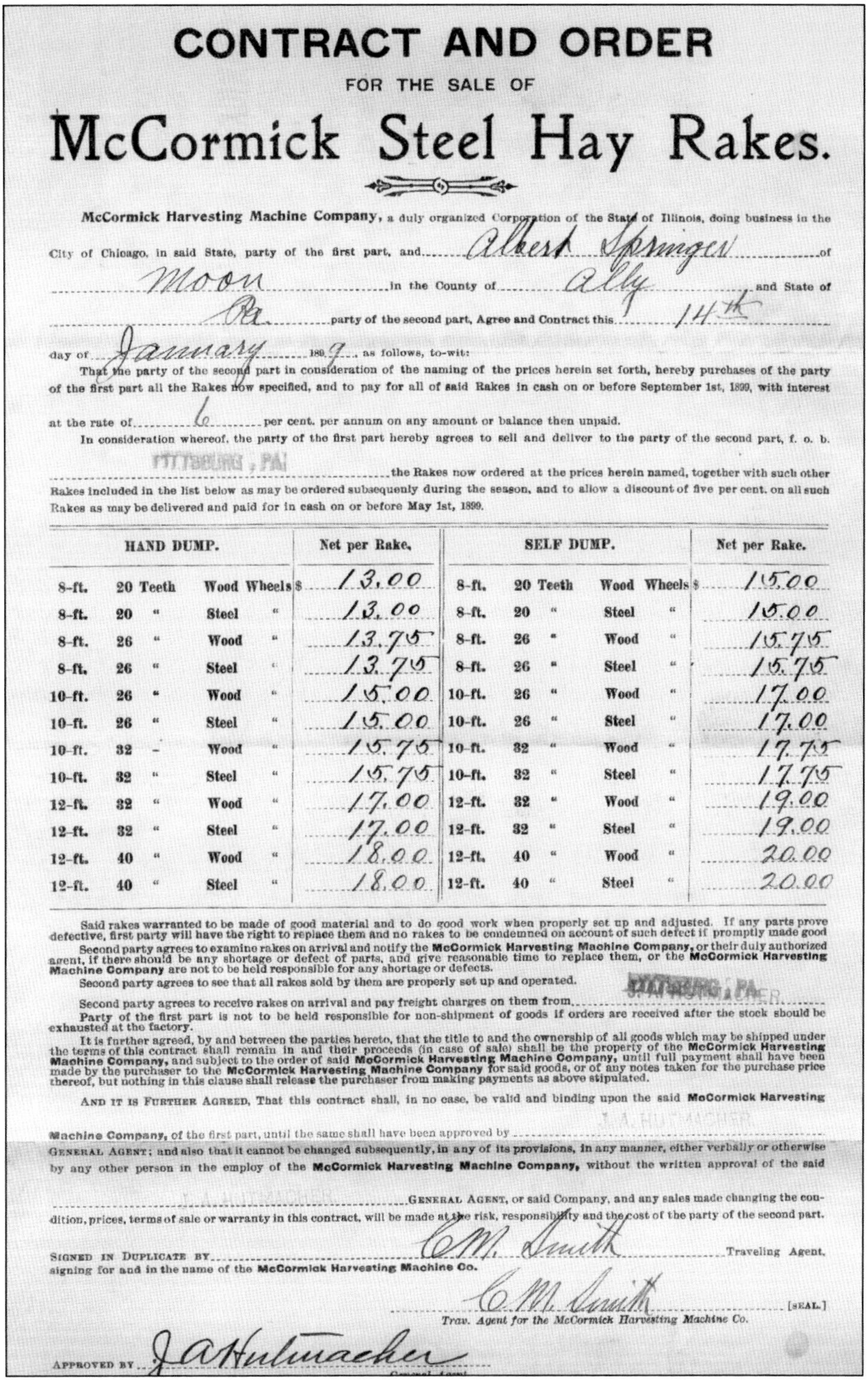

CONTRACT AND ORDER

FOR THE SALE OF

McCormick Steel Hay Rakes.

McCormick Harvesting Machine Company, a duly organized Corporation of the State of Illinois, doing business in the City of Chicago, in said State, party of the first part, and Albert Springer of Moon in the County of Ally and State of Pa. party of the second part, Agree and Contract this 14th day of January 1899, as follows, to-wit:

That the party of the second part in consideration of the naming of the prices herein set forth, hereby purchases of the party of the first part all the Rakes now specified, and to pay for all of said Rakes in cash on or before September 1st, 1899, with interest at the rate of 6 per cent. per annum on any amount or balance then unpaid.

In consideration whereof, the party of the first part hereby agrees to sell and deliver to the party of the second part, f. o. b. PITTSBURG, PA. the Rakes now ordered at the prices herein named, together with such other Rakes included in the list below as may be ordered subsequenly during the season, and to allow a discount of five per cent. on all such Rakes as may be delivered and paid for in cash on or before May 1st, 1899.

HAND DUMP.				Net per Rake.	SELF DUMP.				Net per Rake.
8-ft.	20	Teeth	Wood Wheels	$ 13.00	8-ft.	20	Teeth	Wood Wheels	$ 15.00
8-ft.	20	"	Steel "	13.00	8-ft.	20	"	Steel "	15.00
8-ft.	26	"	Wood "	13.75	8-ft.	26	"	Wood "	15.75
8-ft.	26	"	Steel "	13.75	8-ft.	26	"	Steel "	15.75
10-ft.	26	"	Wood "	15.00	10-ft.	26	"	Wood "	17.00
10-ft.	26	"	Steel "	15.00	10-ft.	26	"	Steel "	17.00
10-ft.	32	"	Wood "	15.75	10-ft.	32	"	Wood "	17.75
10-ft.	32	"	Steel "	15.75	10-ft.	32	"	Steel "	17.75
12-ft.	32	"	Wood "	17.00	12-ft.	32	"	Wood "	19.00
12-ft.	32	"	Steel "	17.00	12-ft.	32	"	Steel "	19.00
12-ft.	40	"	Wood "	18.00	12-ft.	40	"	Wood "	20.00
12-ft.	40	"	Steel "	18.00	12-ft.	40	"	Steel "	20.00

Said rakes warranted to be made of good material and to do good work when properly set up and adjusted. If any parts prove defective, first party will have the right to replace them and no rakes to be condemned on account of such defect if promptly made good

Second party agrees to examine rakes on arrival and notify the **McCormick Harvesting Machine Company**, or their duly authorized agent, if there should be any shortage or defect of parts, and give reasonable time to replace them, or the **McCormick Harvesting Machine Company** are not to be held responsible for any shortage or defects.

Second party agrees to see that all rakes sold by them are properly set up and operated.

Second party agrees to receive rakes on arrival and pay freight charges on them from PITTSBURG, PA.

Party of the first part is not to be held responsible for non-shipment of goods if orders are received after the stock should be exhausted at the factory.

It is further agreed, by and between the parties hereto, that the title to and the ownership of all goods which may be shipped under the terms of this contract shall remain in and their proceeds (in case of sale) shall be the property of the **McCormick Harvesting Machine Company**, and subject to the order of said **McCormick Harvesting Machine Company**, until full payment shall have been made by the purchaser to the **McCormick Harvesting Machine Company** for said goods, or of any notes taken for the purchase price thereof, but nothing in this clause shall release the purchaser from making payments as above stipulated.

And it is Further Agreed, That this contract shall, in no case, be valid and binding upon the said **McCormick Harvesting Machine Company**, of the first part, until the same shall have been approved by J. A. HUTMACHER General Agent; and also that it cannot be changed subsequently, in any of its provisions, in any manner, either verbally or otherwise by any other person in the employ of the **McCormick Harvesting Machine Company**, without the written approval of the said J. A. HUTMACHER General Agent, or said Company, and any sales made changing the condition, prices, terms of sale or warranty in this contract, will be made at the risk, responsibility and the cost of the party of the second part.

Signed in Duplicate by C. M. Smith Traveling Agent, signing for and in the name of the **McCormick Harvesting Machine Co.**

C. M. Smith [SEAL.]
Trav. Agent for the McCormick Harvesting Machine Co.

Approved by J. A. Hutmacher
General Agent.

Albert Springer also ran a family farm. He was a son of James Leander Springer. This receipt for steel hay rakes is from 1899. Albert served on the Moon School Board and raised six children, all of whom went on to live out their lives in Moon Township. (Courtesy Nancy Mills.)

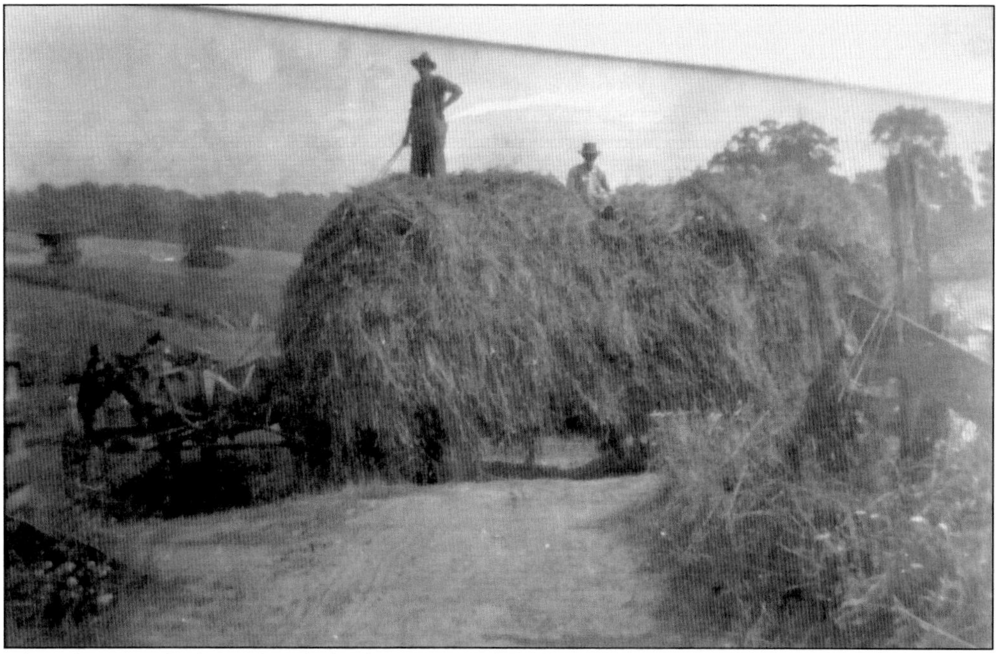

This photograph shows hay bales being moved by horse-drawn carts. The photograph comes from a direct descendant of the Springer family, and it is generally accepted that this is part of one of the Springer farms. However, the people in the photograph are unidentified and the date is not specified on the photograph either. (Courtesy Nancy Mills.)

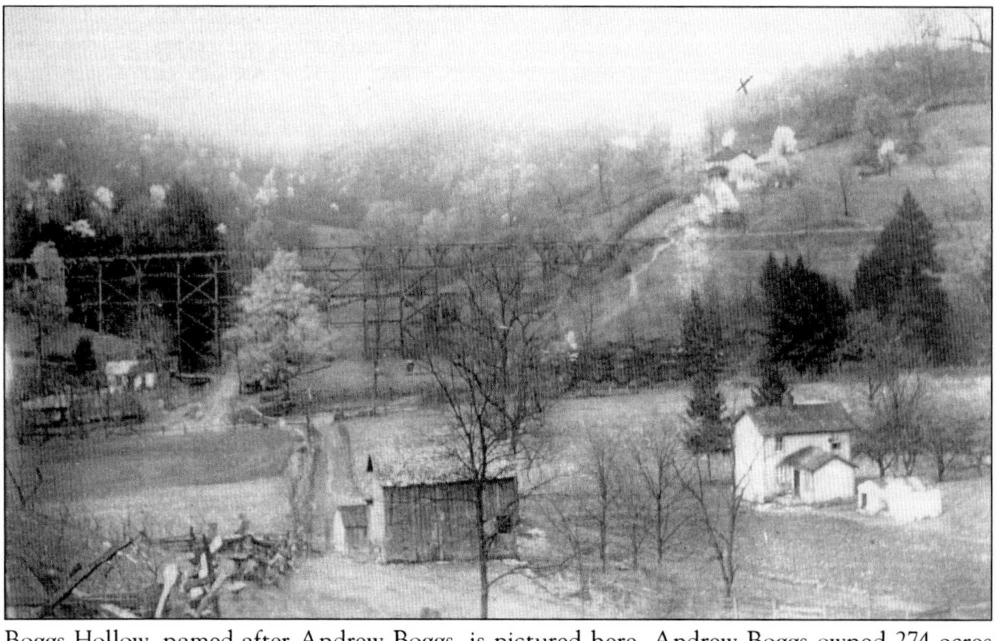

Boggs Hollow, named after Andrew Boggs, is pictured here. Andrew Boggs owned 274 acres in Moon Township. In 1862, the property was sold to Thomas Seaton Guy, who sold the property seven years later to Capt. William Stoops. Stoops set up a ferry service along the river and transported people across the Ohio River between Moon and Sewickley. (Courtesy Nancy Mills.)

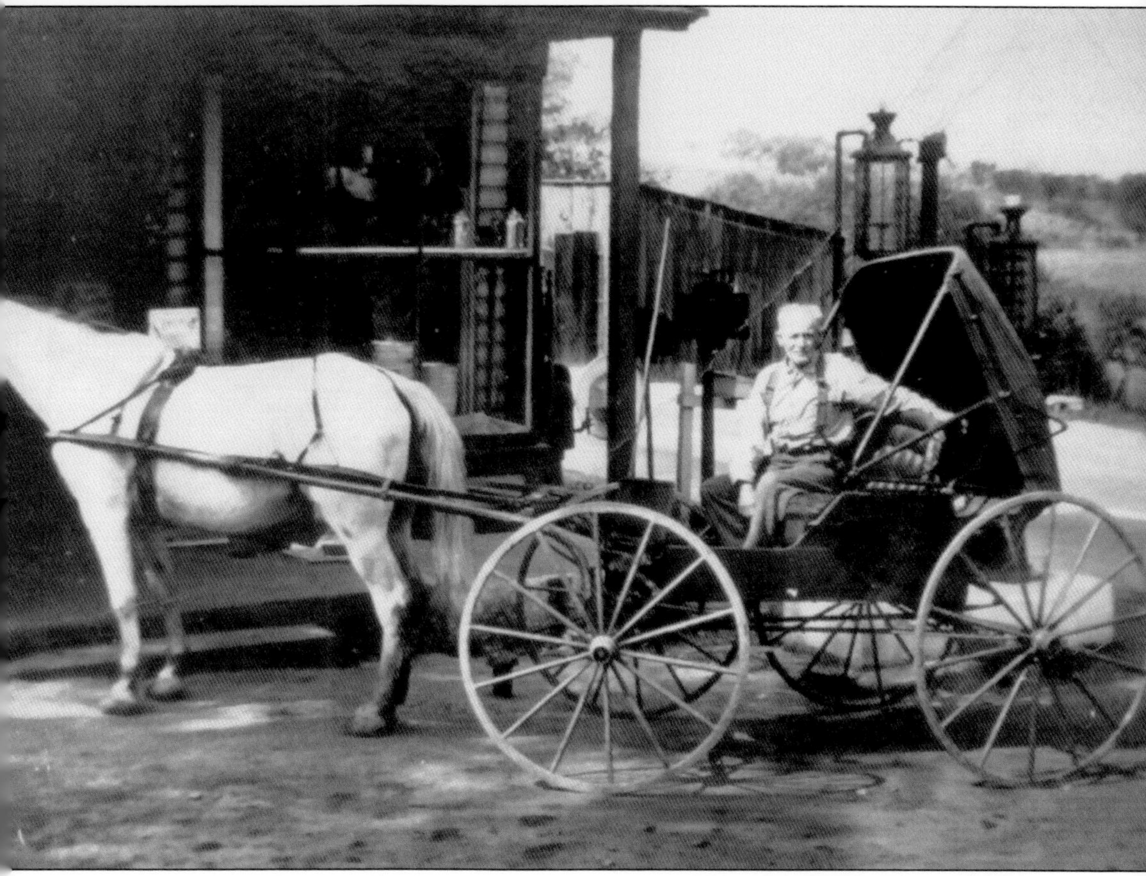

The Parry family can be traced back to 1871 in Moon. Henry Harrison, pictured here, was born on July 24, 1864. The family business was farming, and their land was once part of the original 416-acre Joshua Meek land grant. Henry H. Parry, who went on to become a house painter, had four children—two sons and two daughters. This photograph shows Parry in front of Lee Realty at the intersection of Brodhead and Carnot Roads. (Courtesy the Meanor family.)

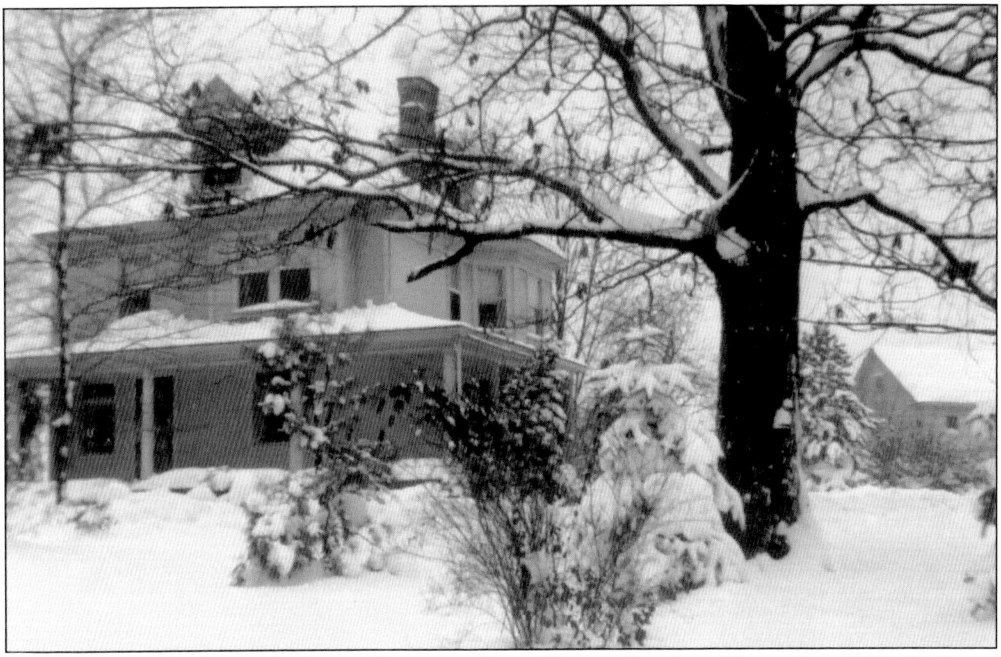

This photograph shows the Parry Homestead on Sharon Road in November 1950. Built on land purchased from the Neely family, the home was built in the early 1900s. Henry Parry's son George moved into the home with his wife in 1936, and they remained there for the remainder of their lives. (Courtesy the Meanor family.)

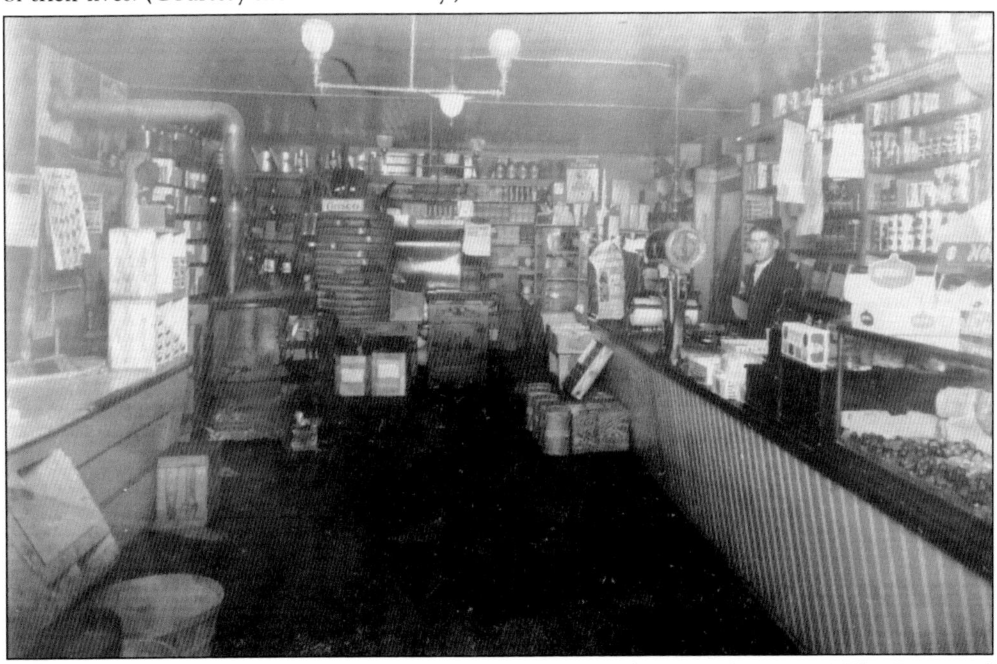

This photograph of Roy Meanor in the S. S. Meanor general store is from 1916. The Parry and Meanor families were united in 1950 when Clyde Meanor married Ruth Parry. The S. S. Meanor General Merchandise Store was located on Stoops Ferry Road. Members of the Meanor family still reside in Moon Township today. (Courtesy the Meanor family.)

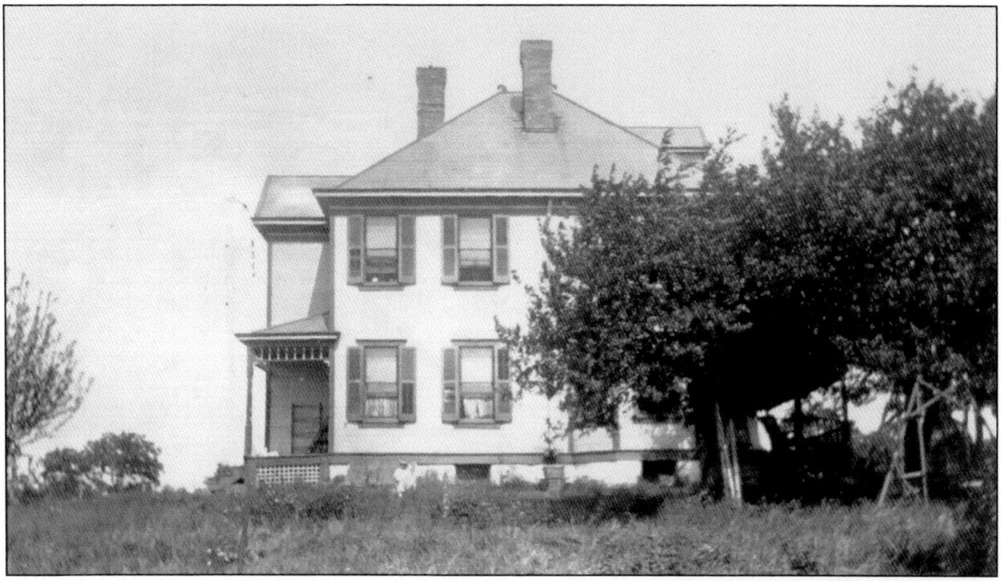

The Charles Andrew Dally house was torn down to make way for Carnot Oil Change and later became part of West Hills Shopping Center, which at the time of this writing is being considered as a site for a future Wal-Mart. The family members were devout members of Sharon Community Presbyterian Church, and C. A. Dally was a member of the Moon Township School Board. (Courtesy the Meanor family.)

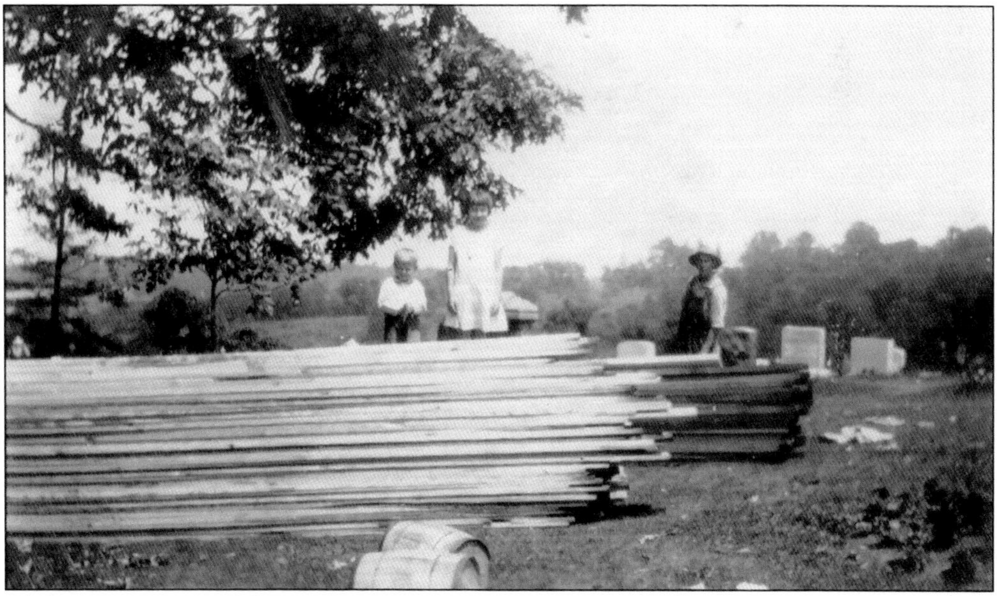

Clyde T. Meanor and his sister Virginia stand on a wood pile in the cemetery of Sharon Community Presbyterian Church. The wood was used to rebuild the church after a 1929 tornado struck. Clyde went on to be a World War II veteran. The family lived in Carnot. (Courtesy Sharon Community Presbyterian Church.)

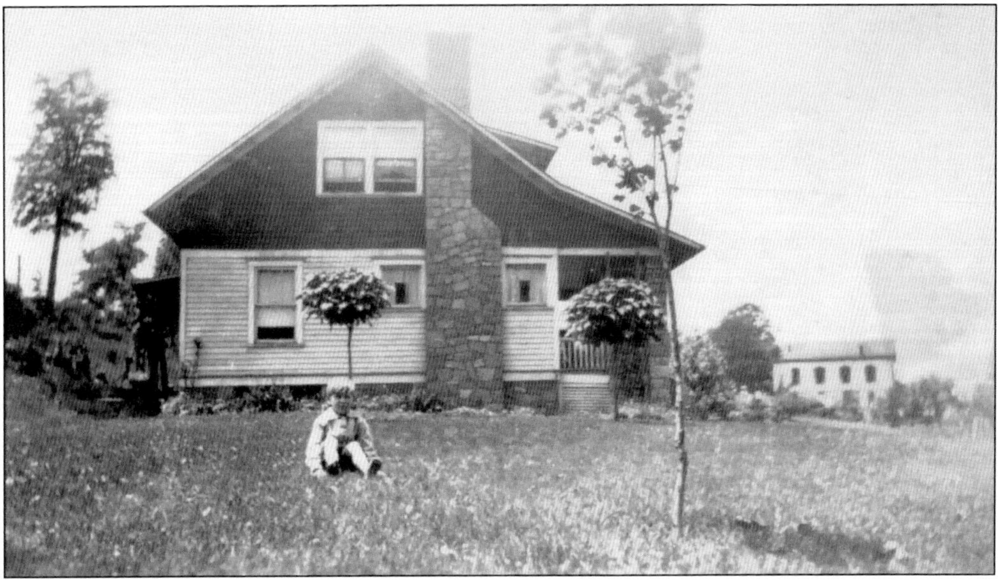

Pictured here is the Meanor house along Beaver Grade Road. Clyde T. Meanor is shown as a child. He grew up in the Somerville house, which was torn down to make way for a gas station. He married his wife, Ruth, and they still reside in Moon Township today. (Courtesy the Meanor family.)

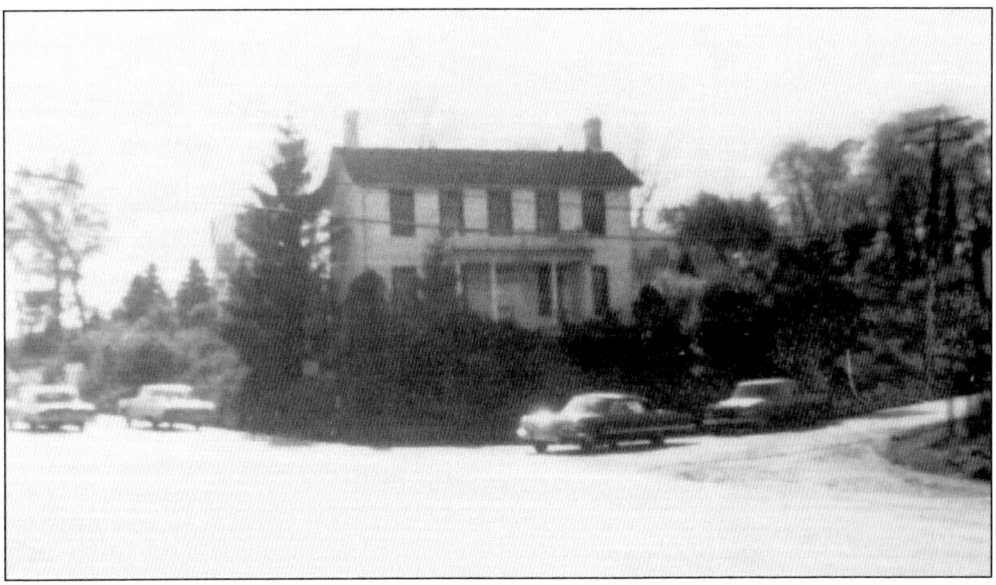

The Somerville property was purchased by Clyde J. Meanor in 1947 and located at the corner of Beers School and Moon Clinton Roads. Beers School Road is now known as University Boulevard, and the house is long gone. It was demolished in 1968 to make way for a gas station. (Courtesy the Meanor family.)

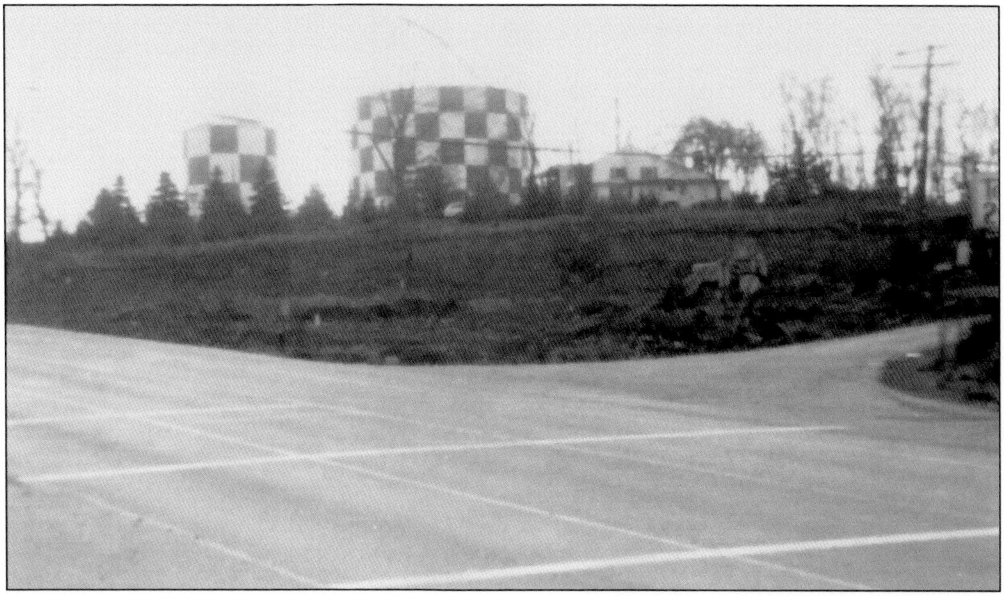

This 1968 photograph shows the old Meanor house completely razed. Township water tanks were constructed atop the knoll, and the Meanors moved into the house visible to the right of the tanks. The house was removed to construct a Texaco gas station. The site is directly across the street from Sharon Community Presbyterian Church. (Courtesy the Meanor family.)

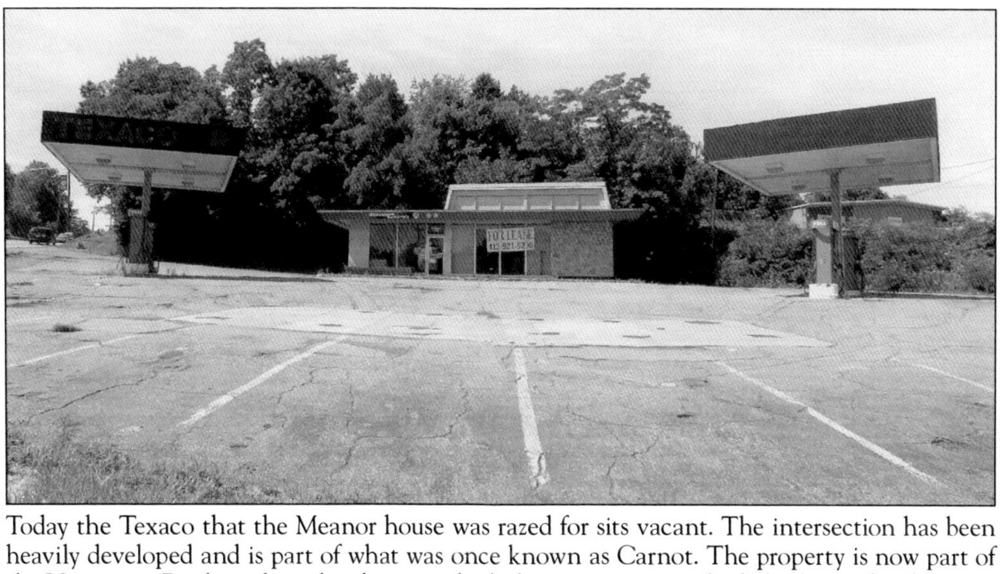

Today the Texaco that the Meanor house was razed for sits vacant. The intersection has been heavily developed and is part of what was once known as Carnot. The property is now part of the University Boulevard overlay district, which dictates strict standards for future development along Moon's most vibrant business corridor. (Photograph by Mark Berton.)

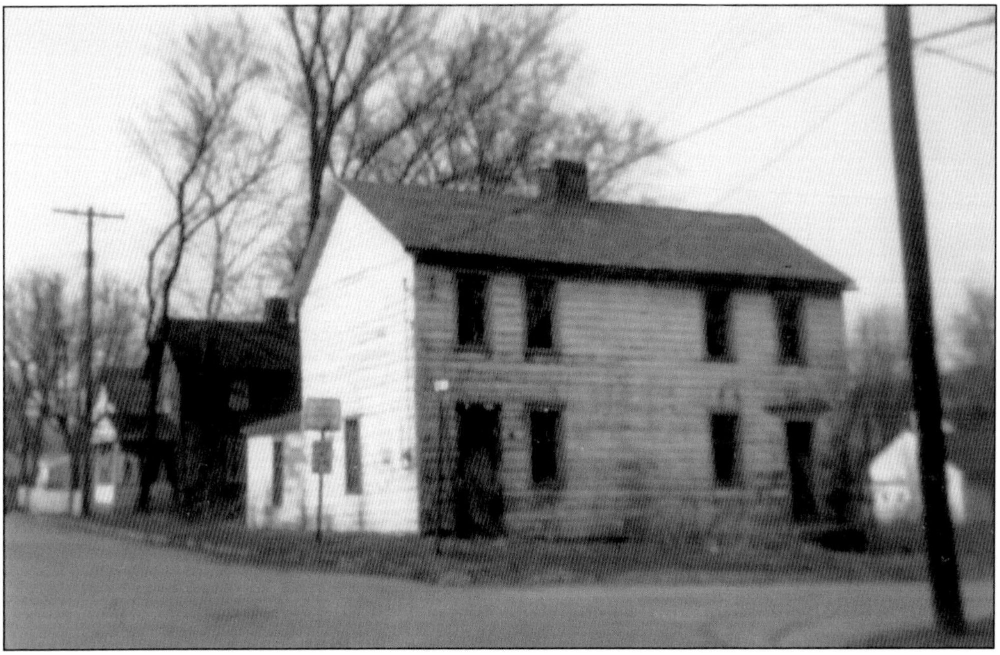

Pictured here is the John G. Keim house, which is situated at Main and Ferry Streets in Shousetown. Shousetown was a community in what is now Crescent Township. The house stood from 1841 to 1972. Shousetown was named after Peter Shouse, a local boatbuilder. (Courtesy Eliot and Marjorie Johnson and the Crescent-Shousetown Area Historic Association.)

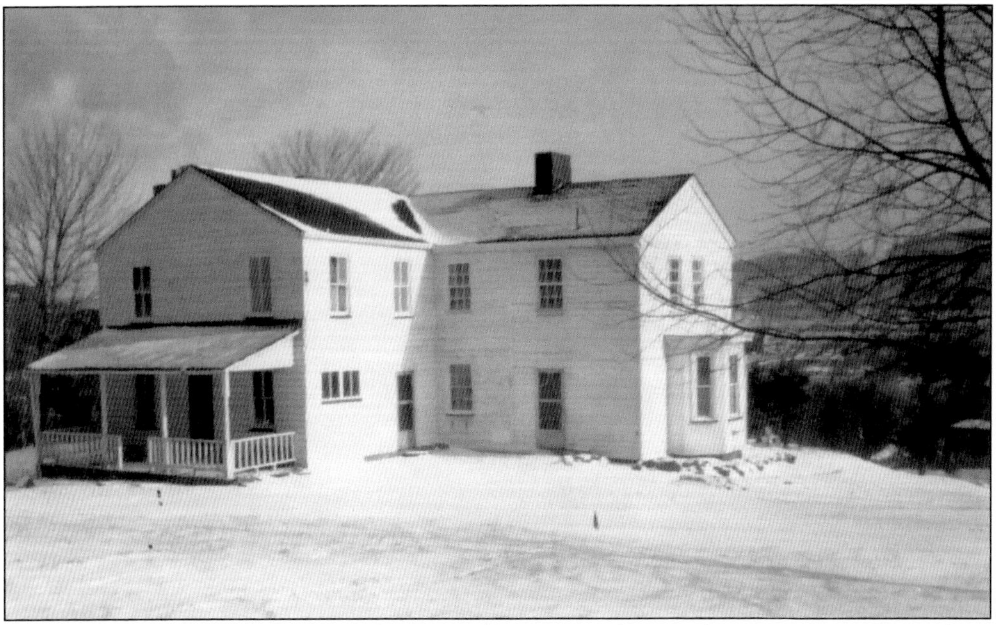

This photograph shows the home of Capt. William B. Anderson who was an active steamboat captain during the Civil War. The river played an integral role in the development of early Moon and later Crescent Townships. Anderson died in November 1897. A collection of his letters to his wife, Louisa, is maintained by Ohio State University. (Courtesy Eliot and Marjorie Johnson and the Crescent-Shousetown Area Historic Association.)

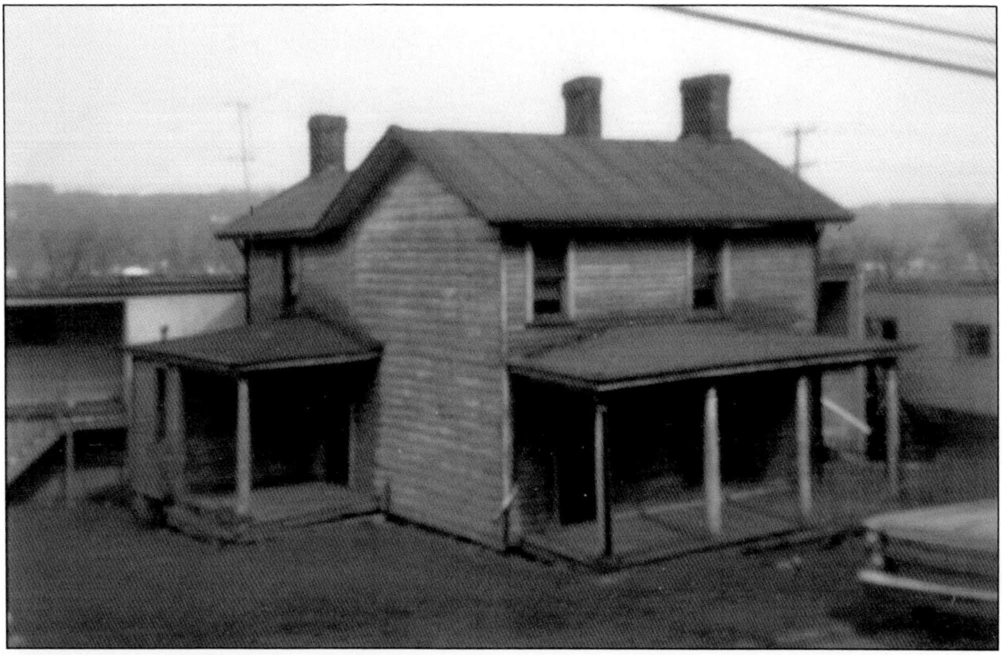

The Edna Heidler house along Prospect Street in Crescent Township was believed to be the oldest house in the township. The property was acquired from a land grant. The house was torn down in 1980. (Courtesy Eliot and Marjorie Johnson and the Crescent-Shousetown Area Historic Association.)

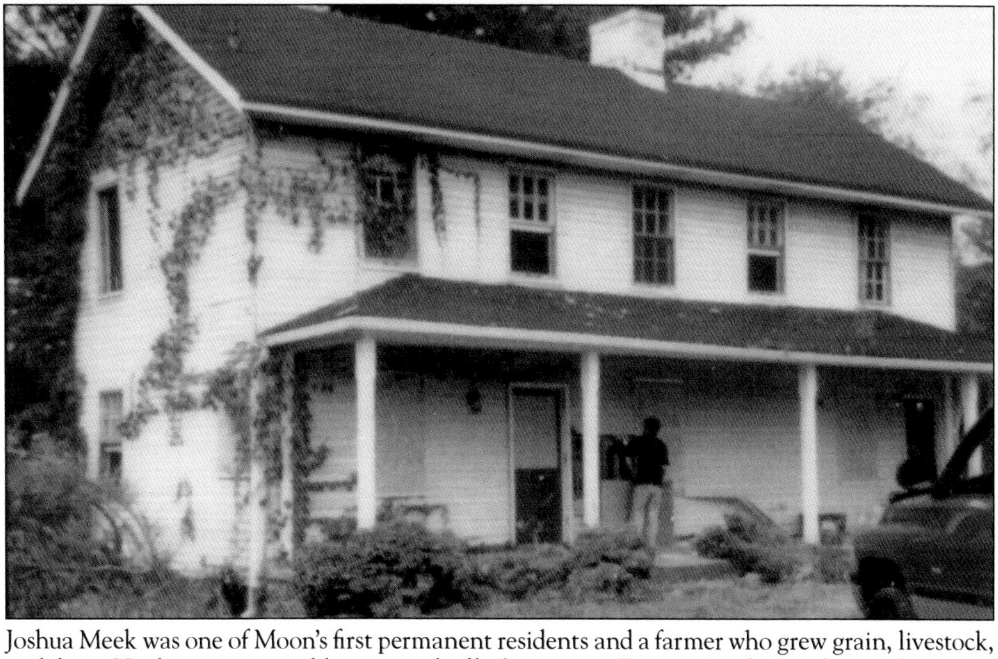

Joshua Meek was one of Moon's first permanent residents and a farmer who grew grain, livestock, and fruit. His house, pictured here, stood off what is now Beaver Grade Road near the Forest Glen condominium complex. The house stood until the fall of 2000—just five years shy of its 200th anniversary—when it was razed amid much controversy to make way for a 60-unit housing complex.

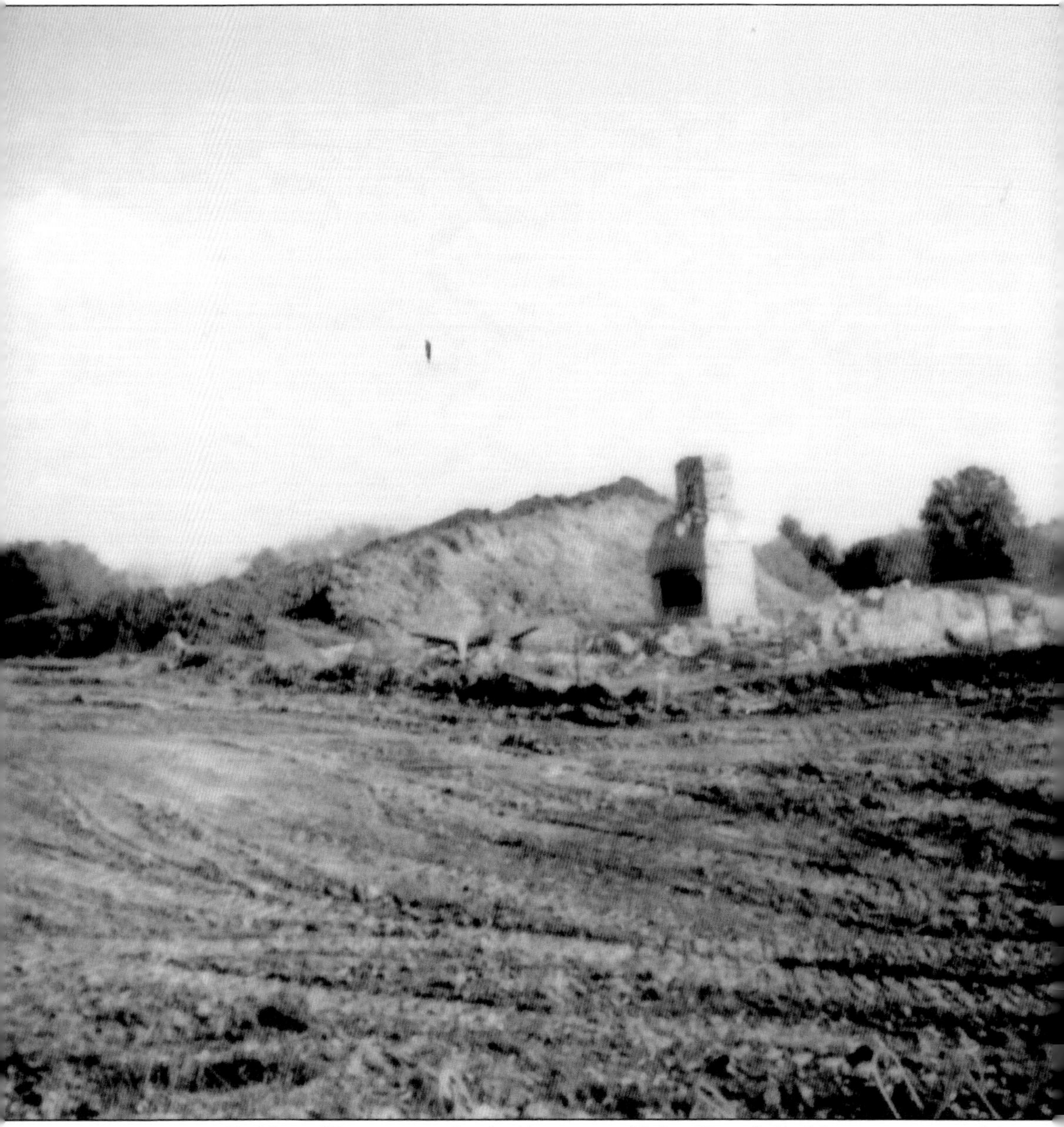

Community Builders of Boston was the developer on a $2.2 million federal housing project that destroyed the nearly 200-year-old Meek house. The state historical and museum commission recommended that demolition be delayed and a stop-work order was issued by the Moon Township building inspector. Both issues were ignored by the developer, and by October 2000, when this photograph was taken, all that remained of the Meek house was the fireplace. (Courtesy Eliot and Marjorie Johnson and the Crescent-Shousetown Area Historic Association.)

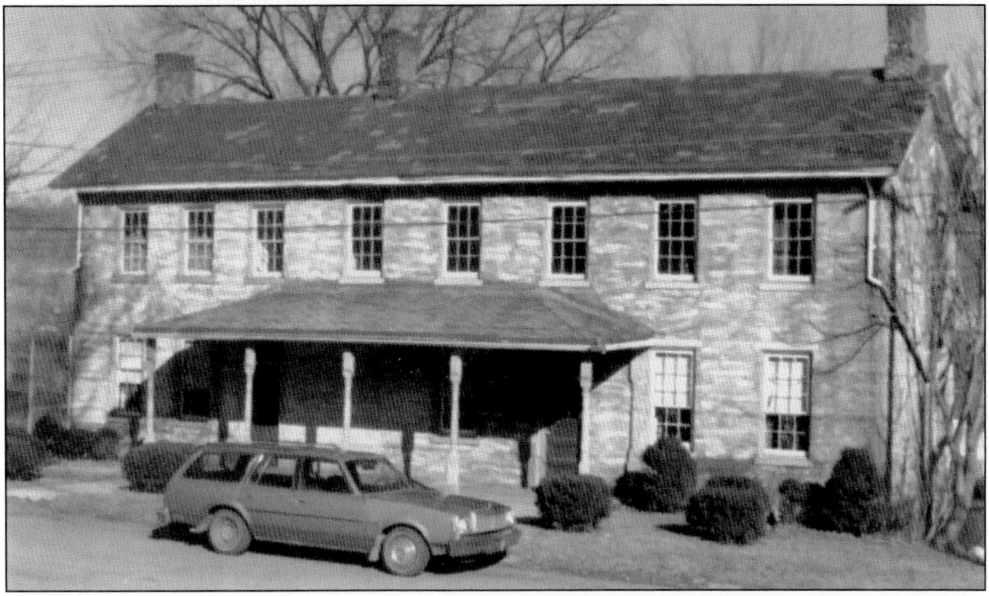

Peter Shouse came to Moon in 1827 and helped build the first steamboat that sailed the Ohio River. This photograph from December 17, 1984, shows the Shouse house. In 1985, an application was submitted to place the property on the National Register of Historic Places. Shouse continued the boatbuilding business in Shousetown until 1837, when he passed the business on to his brother Samuel and brother-in-law Ezra Porter. (Courtesy Eliot and Marjorie Johnson and the Crescent-Shousetown Area Historic Association.)

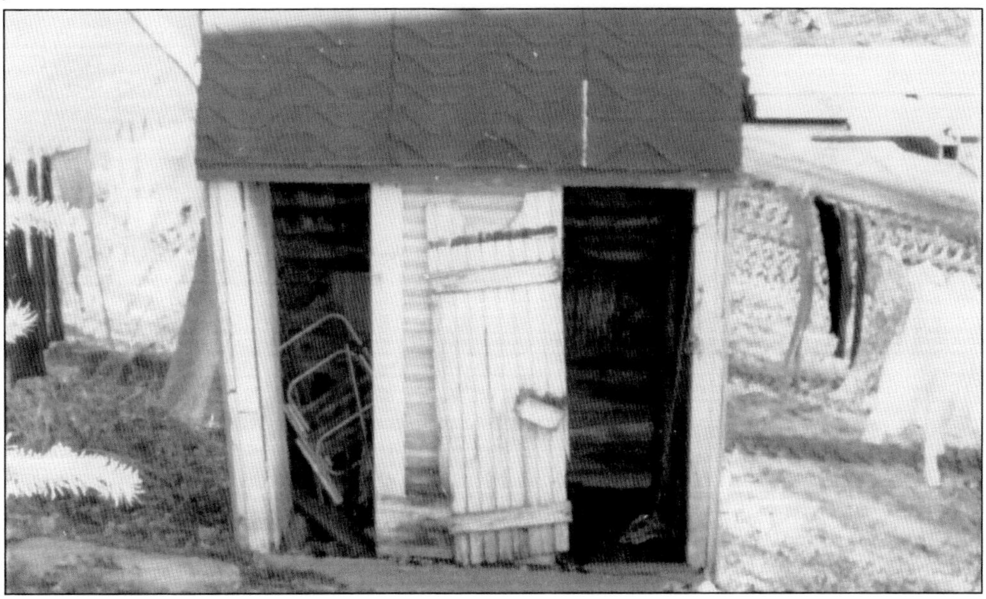

Behind the Shouse house stood the last outhouse in Glenwillard. This photograph from December 1984 documents a bit of history that is not frequently considered. Shousetown was described as "exceedingly small" in the *History of the Erection of Allegheny County, Its Townships, Boroughs and Cities*. The town had two churches, a schoolhouse, a post office, and two stores, according to the same account. (Courtesy Eliot and Marjorie Johnson and the Crescent-Shousetown Area Historic Association.)

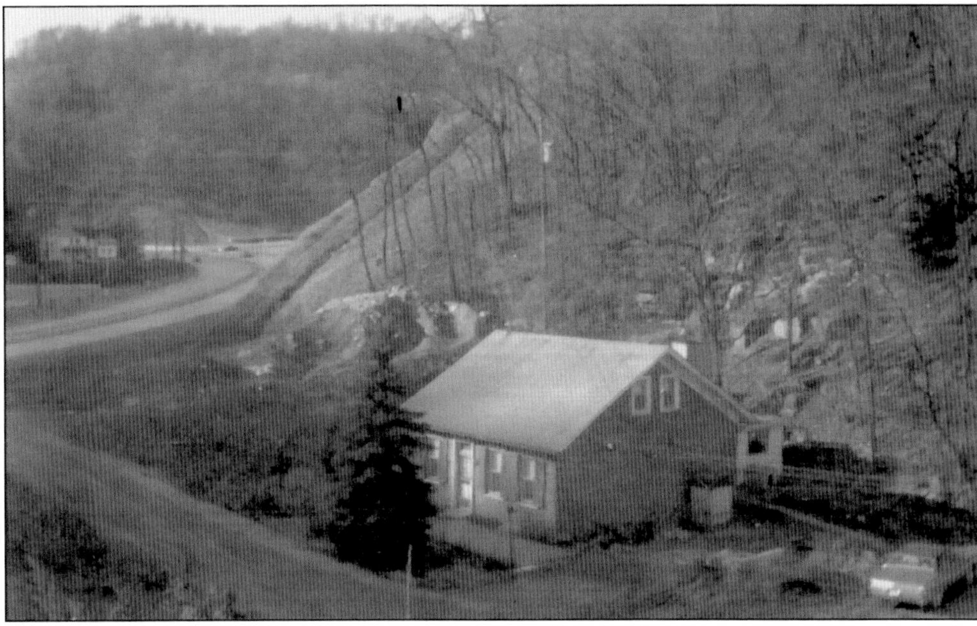

Stoops Ferry was started by Capt. William Stoops, who would take passengers across the Ohio River to Sewickley. When the Sewickley Bridge was built in 1911, the ferry stop became a railroad stop. The Pittsburgh and Lake Erie Railroad ran along the southwest side of the riverbanks and generated more traffic for Moon Township. (Courtesy Eliot and Marjorie Johnson and the Crescent-Shousetown Area Historic Association.)

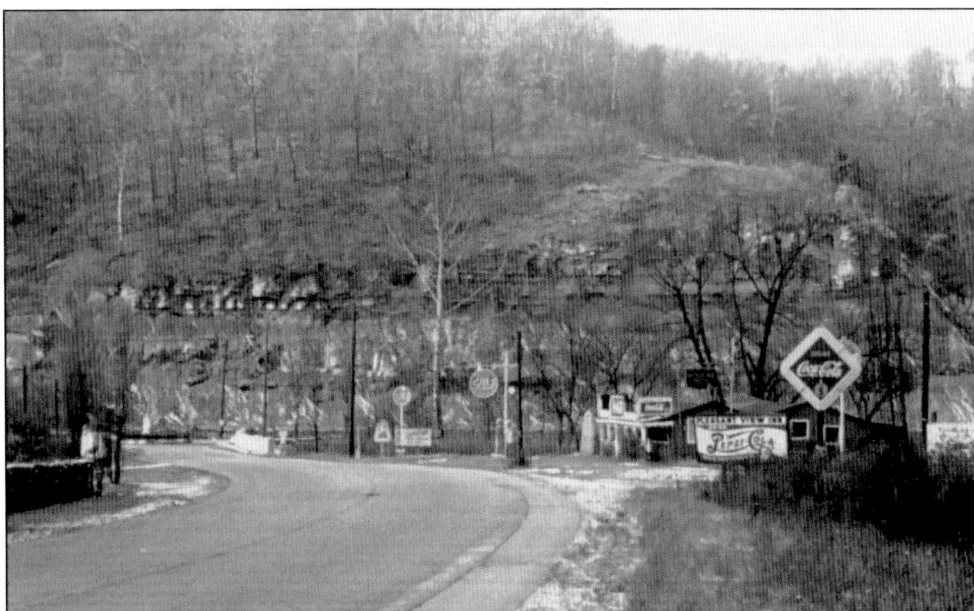

As the traffic flow increased, Stoops Ferry grew to be more than just a ferry stop—it became a landmark. While it does not officially exist on the map, natives of Moon know exactly where Stoops Ferry was. Stoops Ferry is the first sight people see when they enter Moon via the Sewickley Bridge on their way to the airport. (Courtesy Eliot and Marjorie Johnson and the Crescent-Shousetown Area Historic Association.)

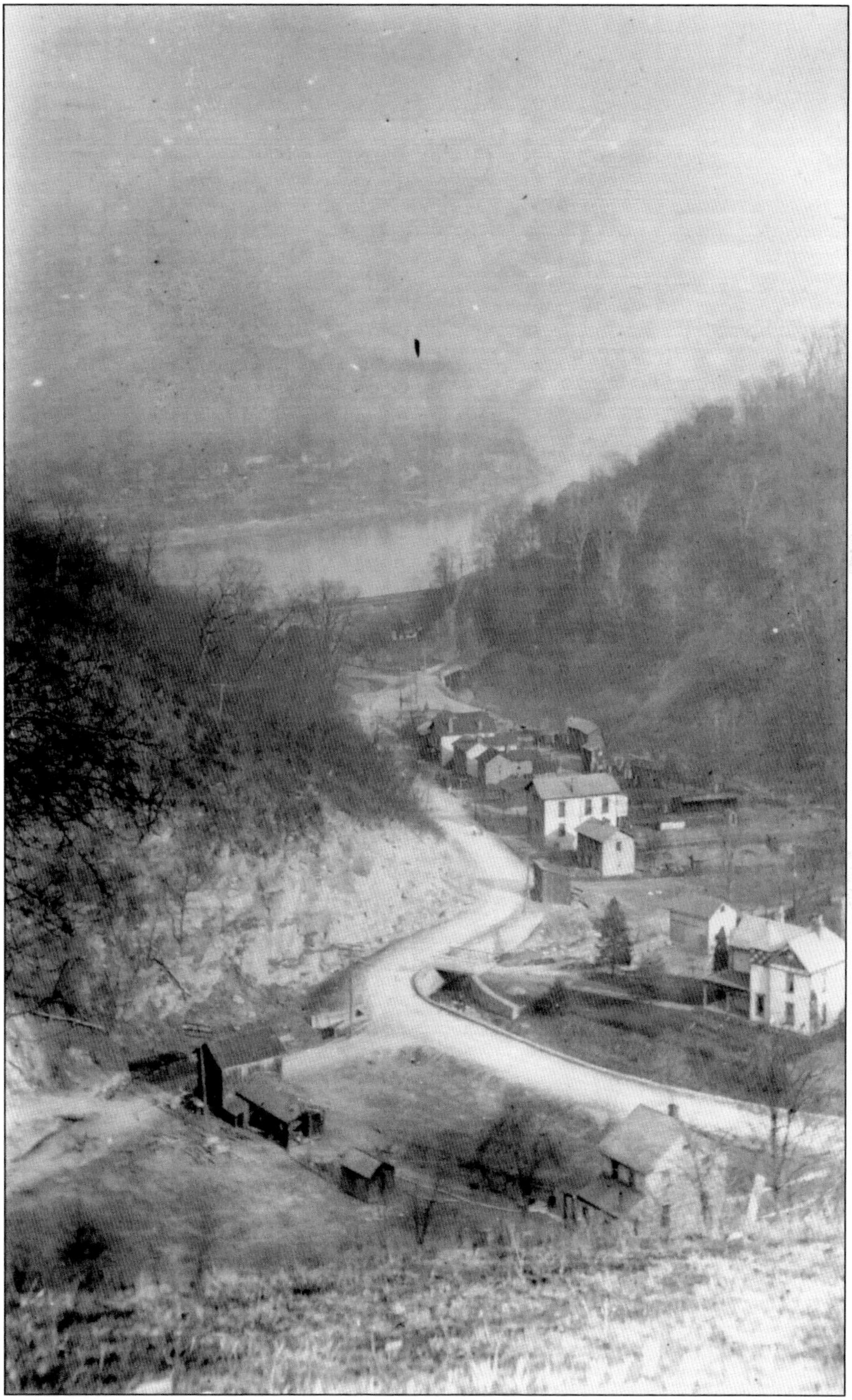

Seen from this vantage point, Stoops Ferry's proximity to the Ohio River is clearly visible. Capt. William Stoops died across the river in Sewickley in 1879. In 1884, Jeremiah Meek bought the property from Stoops's widow. The ferry was located along the path of a Native American trail that crossed the river. (Courtesy Dr. Dale Gass.)

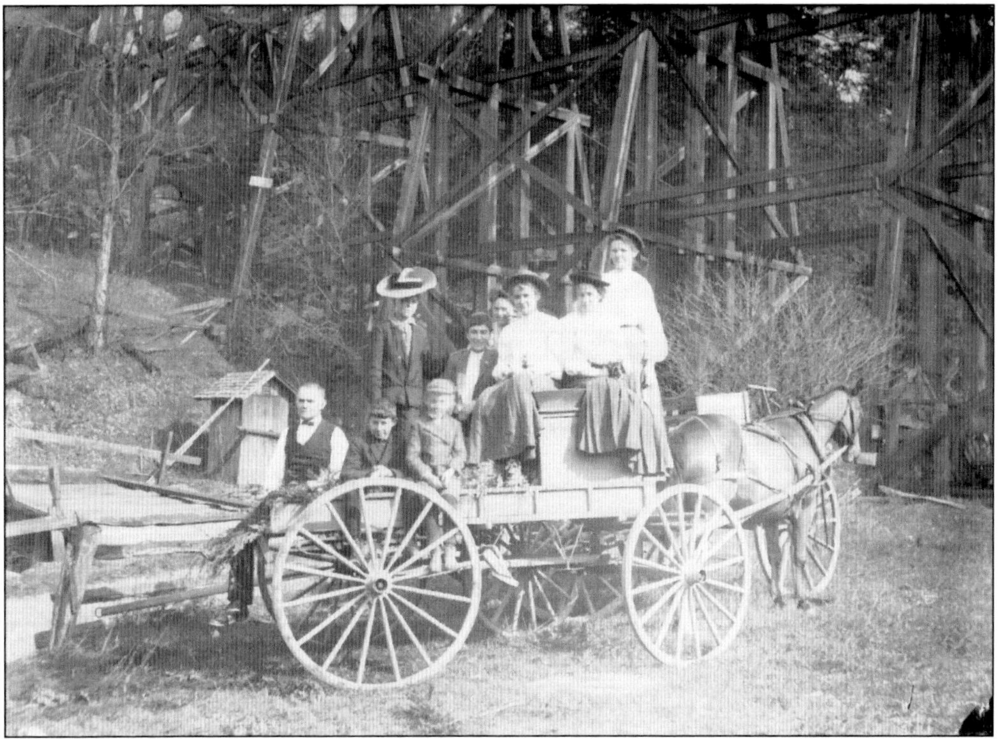

Horse-drawn carriages were common in early-20th-century Moon Township. This undated photograph shows a family located near a trestle near Flaugherty Run. Deplorable road conditions in early Moon Township made traveling difficult. (Courtesy Dr. Dale Gass.)

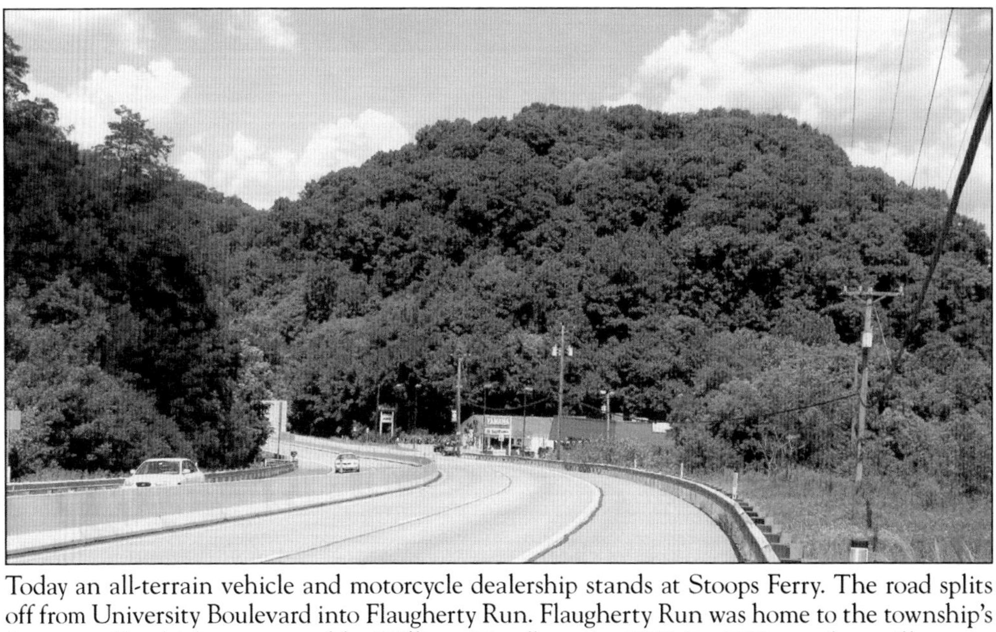

Today an all-terrain vehicle and motorcycle dealership stands at Stoops Ferry. The road splits off from University Boulevard into Flaugherty Run. Flaugherty Run was home to the township's first sawmill, which was started by William Woodburn in 1807. By 1833, another mill was in operation, this one powered by water. (Photograph by Mark Berton.)

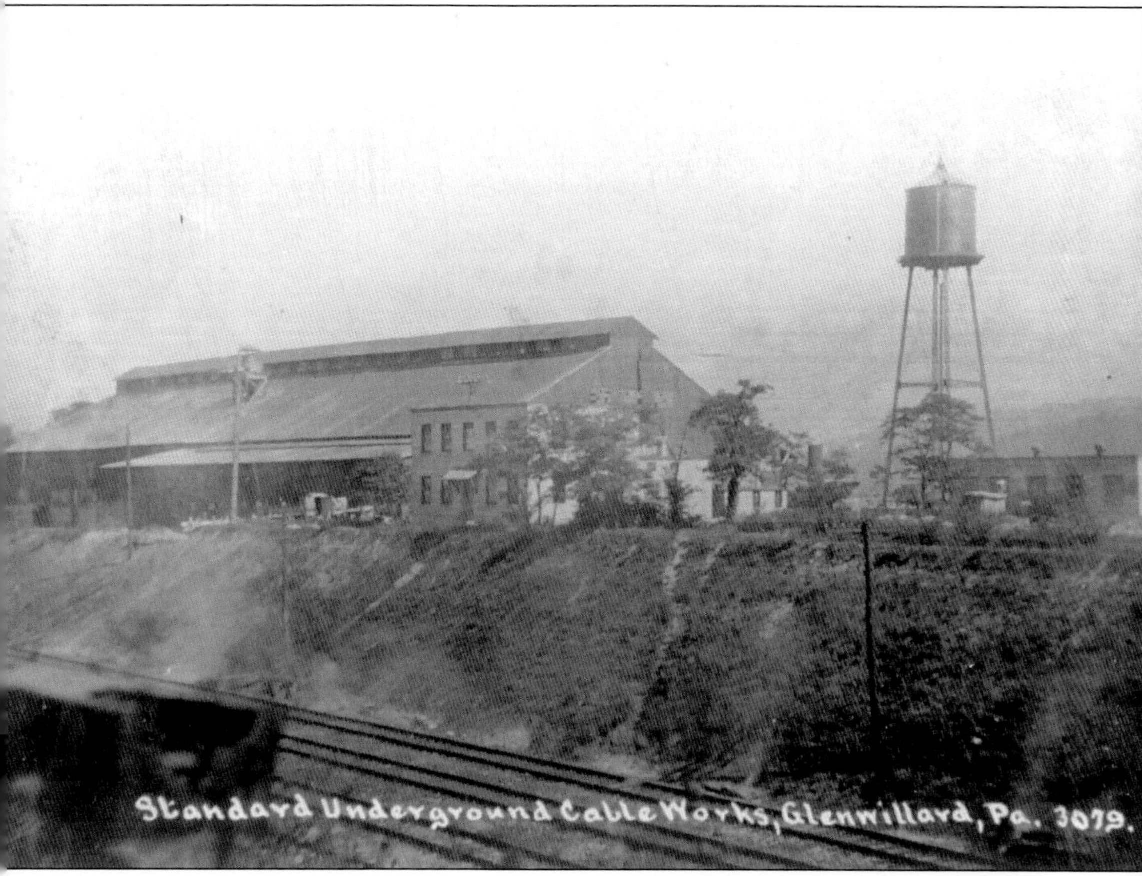

Being close to a river does not mean the riverboat industry was the only show in town. The Standard Underground Cable Works of Glenwillard, shown here, was one of many industries represented in the area. The company made underground, aerial-to-submarine cables and conduit. Moon and Crescent were home to the railroad, coal mining, and shipbuilding industries. Today Moon's major businesses are more service oriented than manufacturing. (Courtesy Eliot and Marjorie Johnson and the Crescent-Shousetown Area Historic Association.)

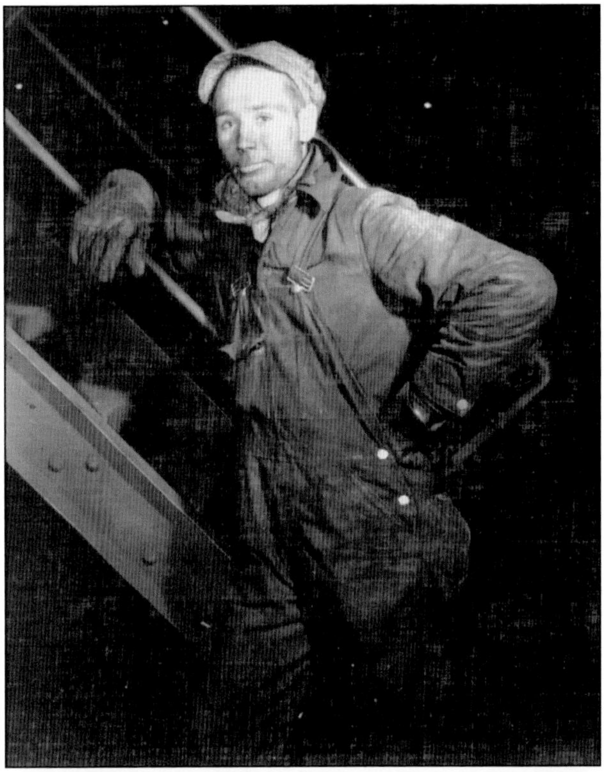

The railroads in Moon served not only passengers but also the burgeoning coal mining industry in the region. The Montour Railroad existed to serve the Imperial Coal Company. This railroad was later taken over by Pittsburgh and Lake Erie Railroad Company. In the mid-1980s, the rights-of-way leftover from these railroads were acquired by the Montour Trail Council and converted to a passive recreation trail. Pictured here is an unidentified Pittsburgh Coal Company miner. (Courtesy Carnegie Library of Pittsburgh.)

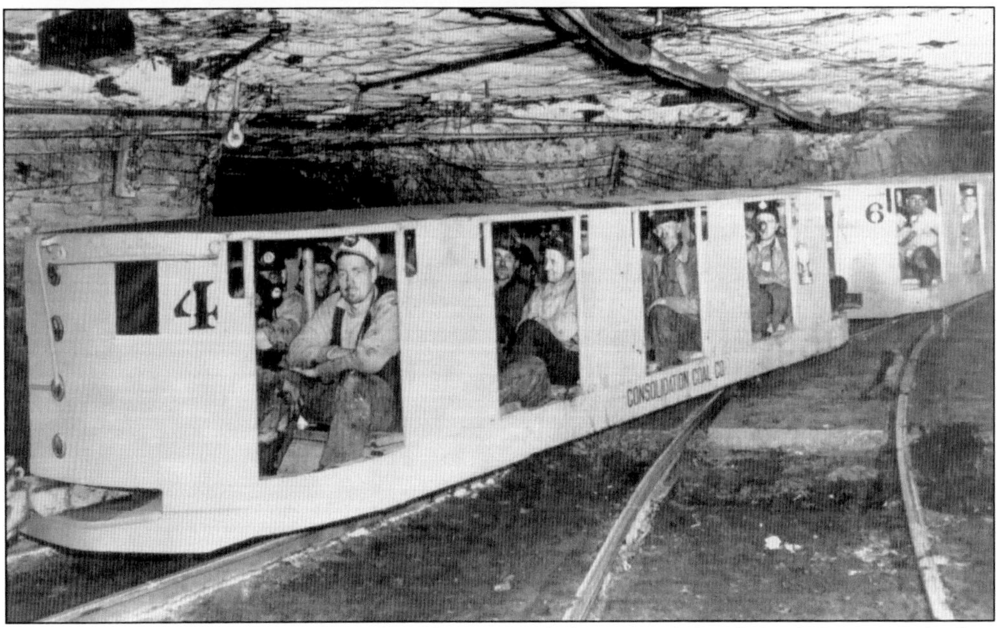

Coal mining was prevalent in nearby Clinton, and the Consolidated Coal Company built a railroad that ran through Moon. Coal from these mines was instrumental in producing coke of Pittsburgh's steel industry. This 1947 photograph shows Consolidated Coal miners in safety-oriented "man-trip" cars. Consolidated Coal ran trains through Moon as recently as 1983. (Courtesy Carnegie Library of Pittsburgh.)

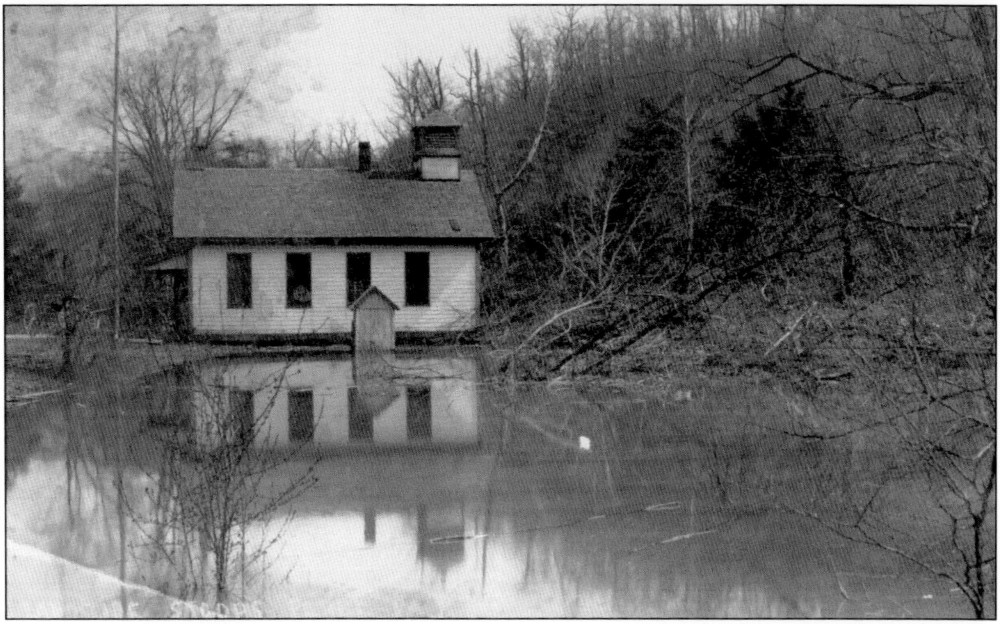

Stoops Ferry sat at the base of the Narrows Run ravine, which was a traditional Native American canoe link connecting two popular Native American trails. A one-room schoolhouse was built at Stoops Ferry and suffered the effects of a landslide. This undated photograph shows how the slide brought debris right up to the rear of the school and its outhouse. (Courtesy Eliot and Marjorie Johnson and the Crescent-Shousetown Area Historic Association.)

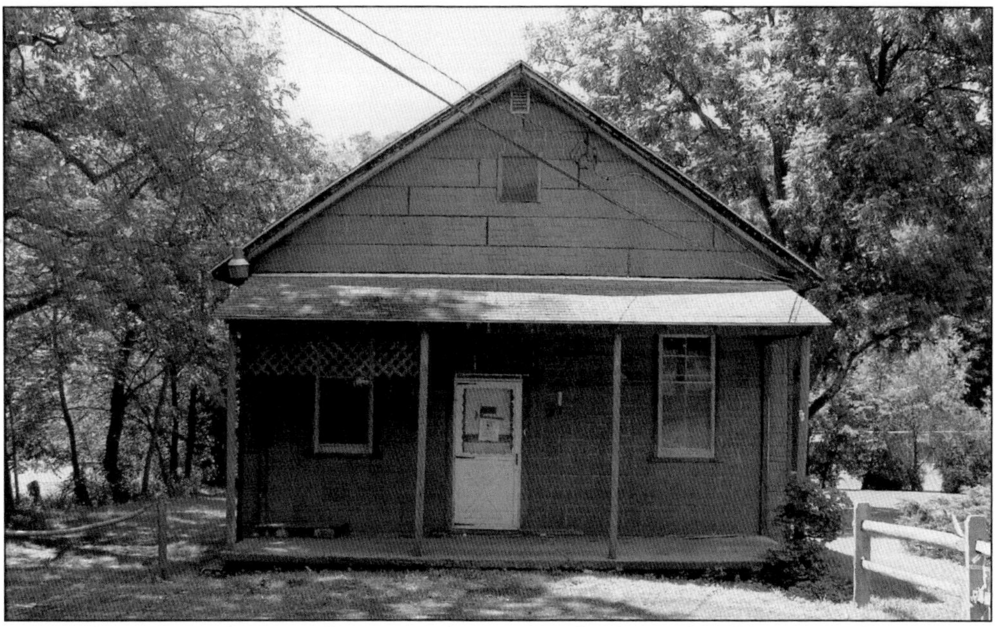

Prior to burning to the ground in 1880, the Boggs School was the oldest schoolhouse in the township. It was rebuilt that same year and still stands today. In 2006, a Friends of Boggs School group cleaned the site up and made efforts to preserve the property, which was renovated into a single-family home. The house stands along Boggs School Road on property owned by Andrew Boggs at one time. (Photograph by Mark Berton.)

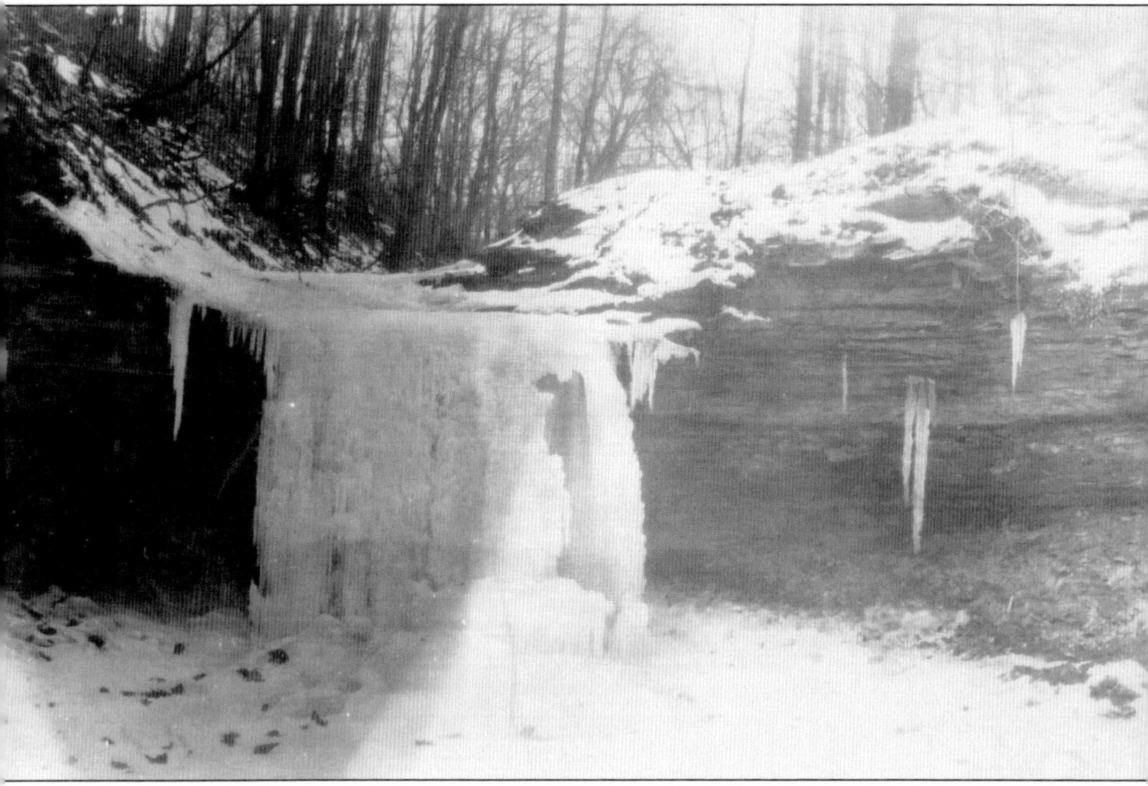

The steep topography of Moon Township makes for unique natural occurrences. This waterfall along Narrow's Run Road (now part of University Boulevard) is frozen over in this 1930s shot. The same topography is known for slides, slippages, and sometimes flooding. Moon Township also has fallen victim to tornadoes through the years. Because of its proximity to the airport, Moon Township is home to a National Weather Service Station. (Courtesy the Meanor family.)

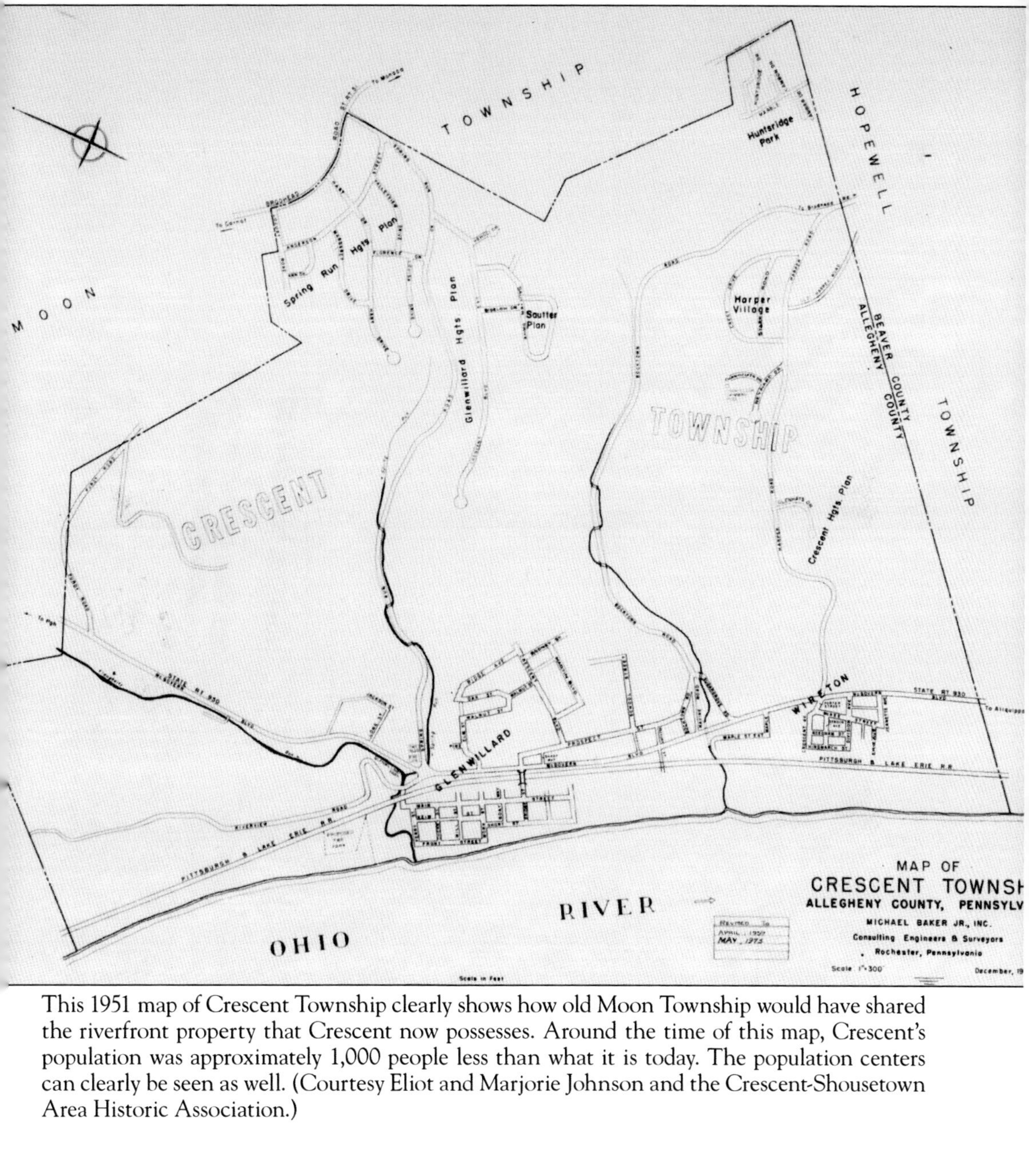

This 1951 map of Crescent Township clearly shows how old Moon Township would have shared the riverfront property that Crescent now possesses. Around the time of this map, Crescent's population was approximately 1,000 people less than what it is today. The population centers can clearly be seen as well. (Courtesy Eliot and Marjorie Johnson and the Crescent-Shousetown Area Historic Association.)

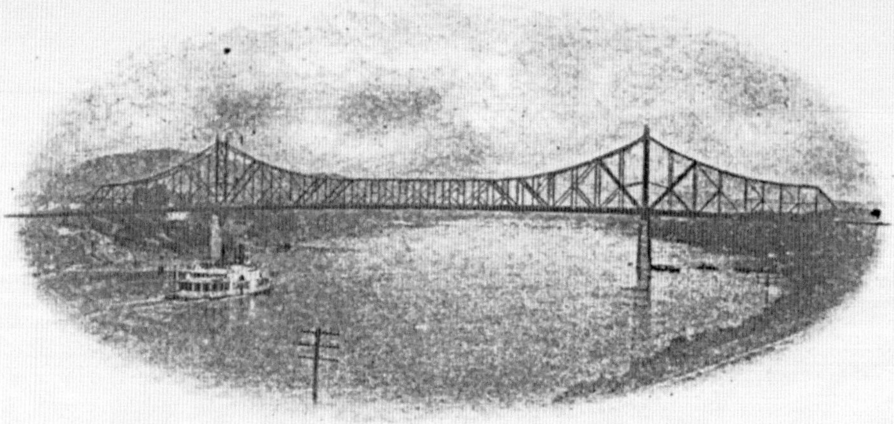

The honor of your presence is requested

at the

Opening Celebration

of the

Allegheny County Ohio River Bridge

Connecting Sewickley and Coraopolis,

Tuesday, September Nineteenth, 1911.

At 1:30 o'clock P. M.

Gilbert A. Hays, Chairman,
Sewickley Committee.

E. C. Dithrich, Chairman,
Coraopolis Committee.

Take Pittsburgh & Lake Erie Railroad to Coraopolis or Stoop's Ferry; Pennsylvania Lines to Sewickley.

On September 19, 1911, the Sewickley Bridge was opened for traffic. This, along with another bridge crossing upriver in neighboring Beaver County, effectively put the river ferry business out of business. Stoops Ferry was taken over by the Pennsylvania and Lake Erie Railroad, which kept the location relevant as the township grew. (Courtesy Eliot and Marjorie Johnson and the Crescent-Shousetown Area Historic Association.)

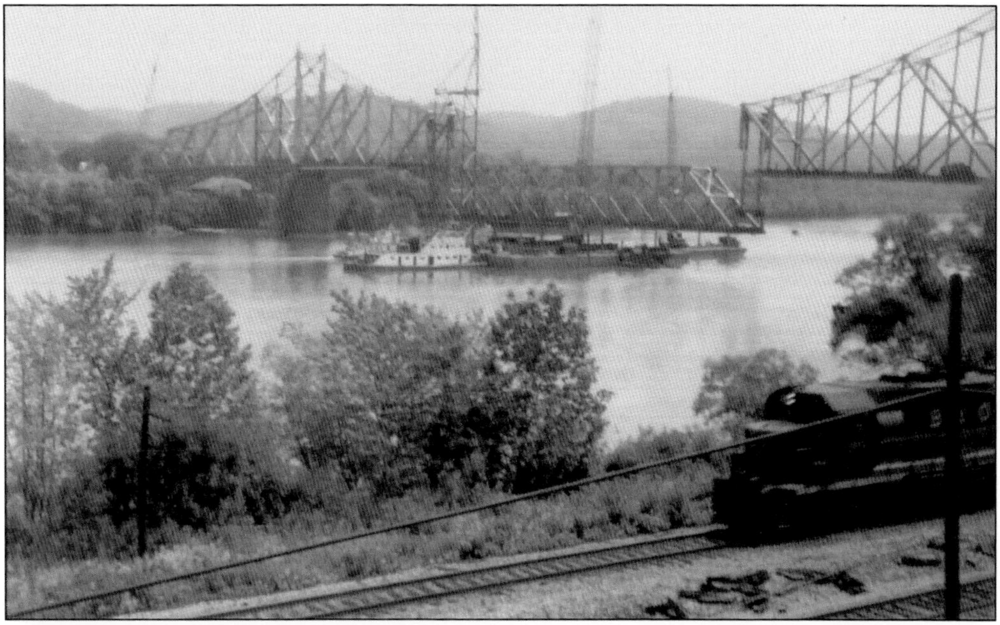

In 1980, the Sewickley Bridge was restored after inspections in the 1970s revealed the structure to be significantly deteriorated. On July 9, the center span was lowered onto barges situated on the river below. The endeavor took 10 one-inch cables to lower the 350-foot span. The span was only about a fifth of the total span, which is estimated to be about 1,850 feet long. (Courtesy Eliot and Marjorie Johnson and the Crescent-Shousetown Area Historic Association.)

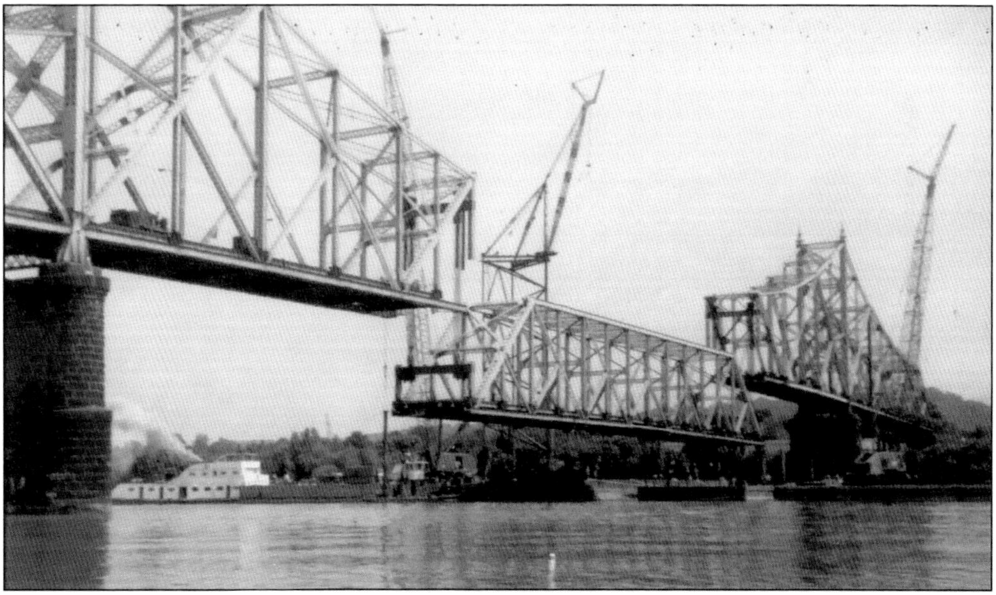

The 800 tons of center span took the American Bridge Division of U.S. Steel two and one-half hours to lower onto barges below. Traffic was stopped on the bridge for four hours while the work was performed. The $7.9 million project was studied by a group from Carnegie-Mellon University, and it was estimated that losing the bridge rather than repairing it would cost the region $4.2 million each year in lost time and miscellaneous expenses. (Courtesy Eliot and Marjorie Johnson and the Crescent-Shousetown Area Historic Association.)

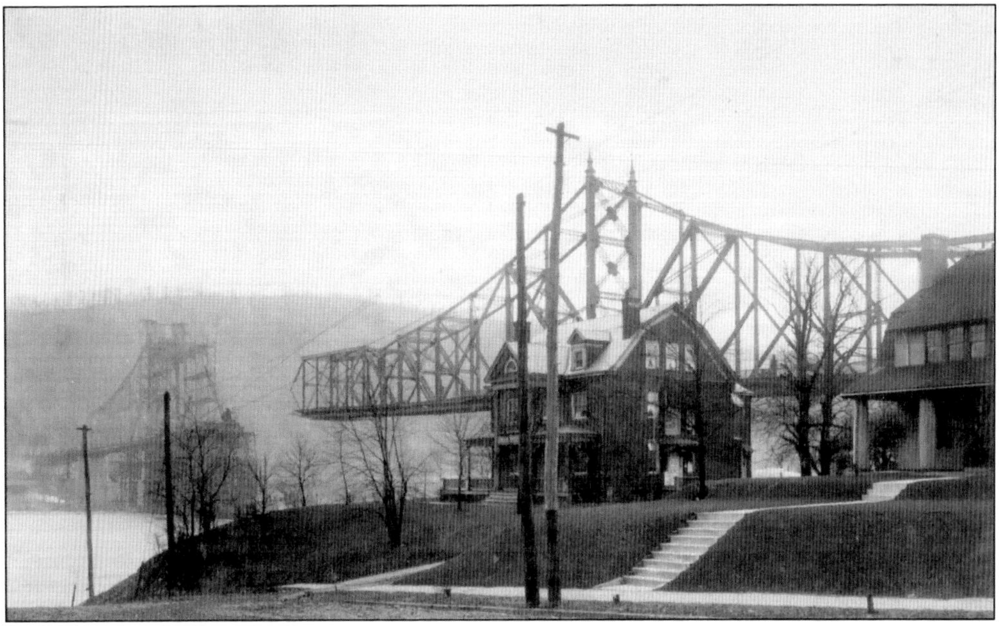

This 1911 photograph of the Sewickley Bridge in mid-construction shows Moon Township in the background. Today several of the original finials that adorned the tops of the bridge supports stand as memorials in parks around the county. One is at Broad and Walnut Streets in Sewickley, one is at the old Sewickley train station, and one is at Station Square in downtown Pittsburgh. (Courtesy Carnegie Library of Pittsburgh.)

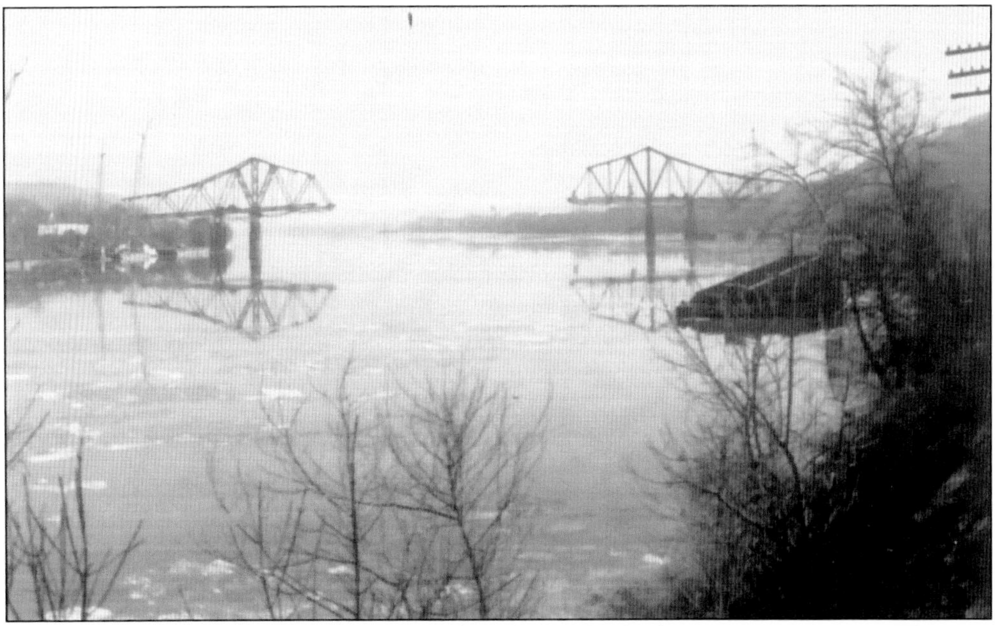

This 1980 photograph from Moon Township shows the bridge sans center span. The new Sewickley Bridge contains 4,500 tons of steel. It has 28 feet of roadway and a five-foot sidewalk. The steel came from the upriver Ambridge U.S. Steel plant. The new bridge used the piers from the old bridge, which saved the project an estimated year of construction. (Courtesy Eliot and Marjorie Johnson and the Crescent-Shousetown Area Historic Association.)

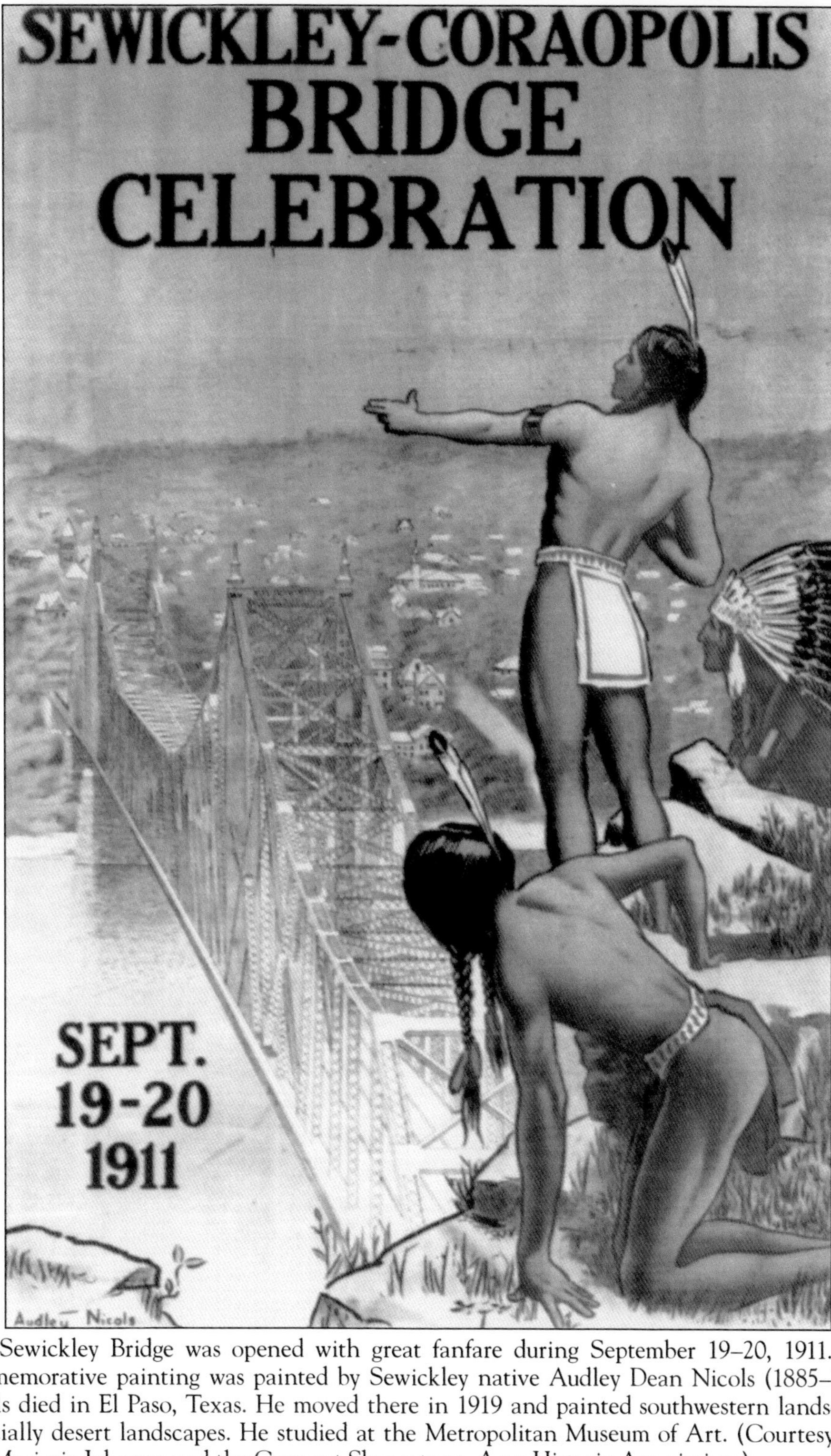

The Sewickley Bridge was opened with great fanfare during September 19–20, 1911. This commemorative painting was painted by Sewickley native Audley Dean Nicols (1885–1941). Nicols died in El Paso, Texas. He moved there in 1919 and painted southwestern landscapes, especially desert landscapes. He studied at the Metropolitan Museum of Art. (Courtesy Eliot and Marjorie Johnson and the Crescent-Shousetown Area Historic Association.)

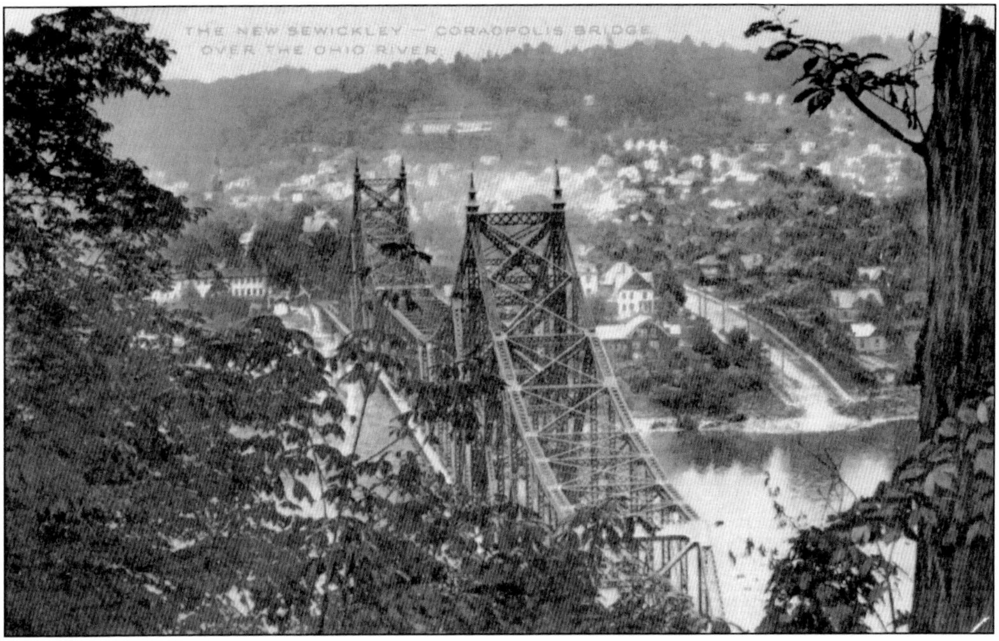

This undated postcard shows the Sewickley Bridge viewed from the Moon Township side. The small nooks and crannies of the bridge's structure made the original bridge hard to paint and maintain. The new bridge was designed to withstand the elements better than the old bridge, including a drainage system for the sidewalk. (Courtesy Dr. Dale Gass.)

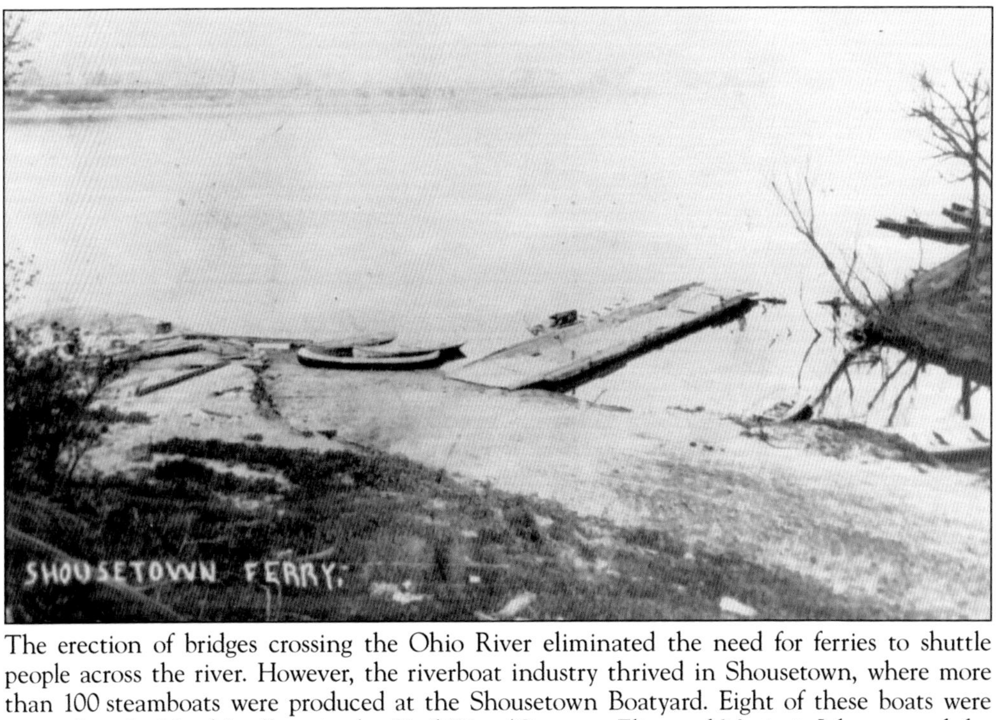

The erection of bridges crossing the Ohio River eliminated the need for ferries to shuttle people across the river. However, the riverboat industry thrived in Shousetown, where more than 100 steamboats were produced at the Shousetown Boatyard. Eight of these boats were integral to the North's efforts in the Civil War. (Courtesy Eliot and Marjorie Johnson and the Crescent-Shousetown Area Historic Association.)

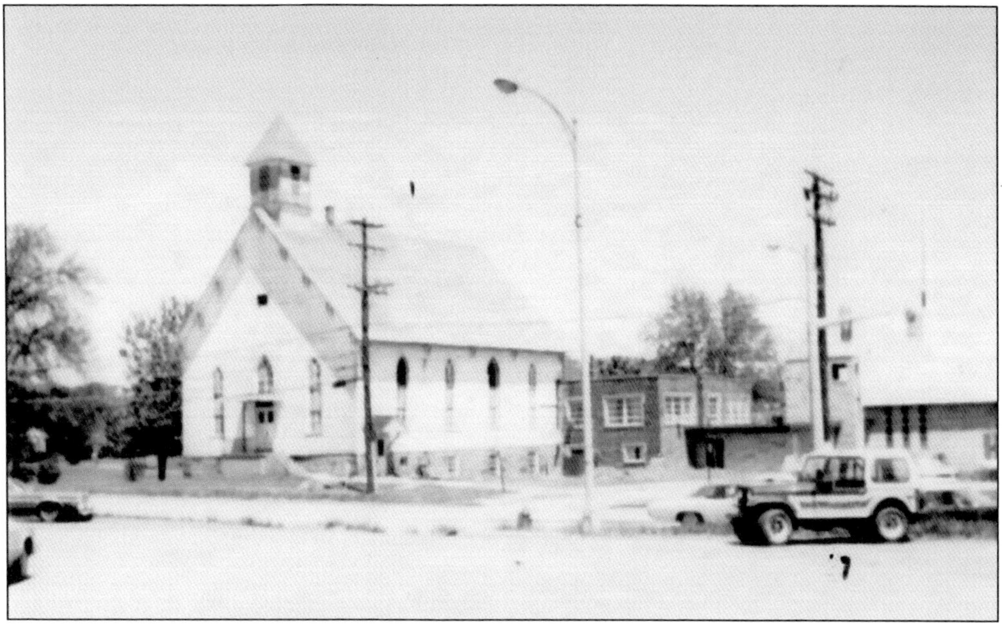

Mount Carmel United Presbyterian Church stood at Brodhead Road and Kennedy Boulevard. Built in 1871, the church stood until 1977 in Hopewell, which also was part of old Moon Township. James Jordon, Moon's first constable and Revolutionary War veteran, was among the first recorded elders of the church. (Courtesy Eliot and Marjorie Johnson and the Crescent-Shousetown Area Historic Association.)

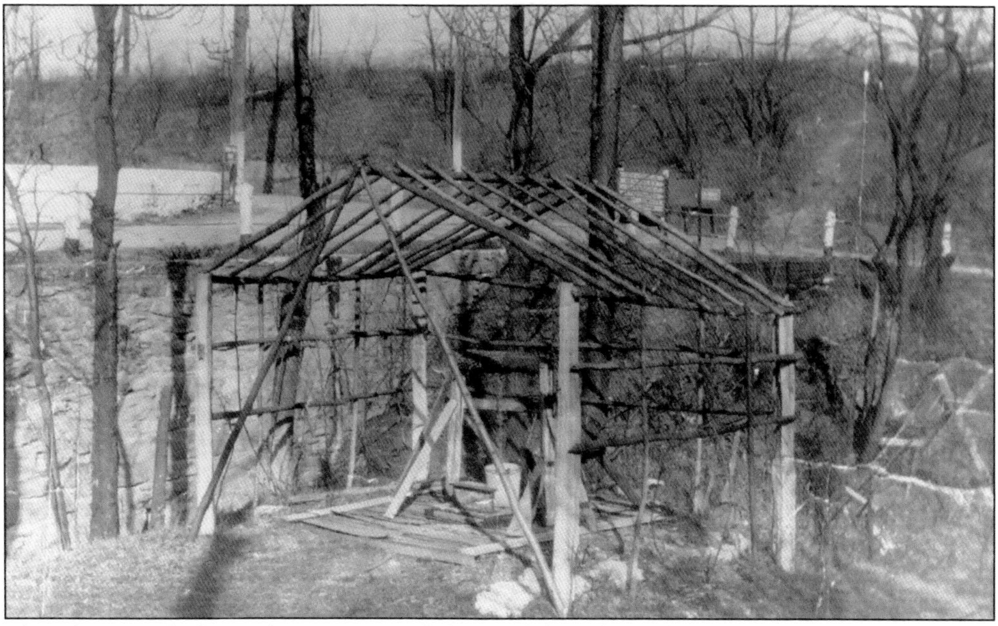

This photograph shows the remaining skeleton of the John Gilcrist property. The photograph lists the location as Stoops Ferry—Shousetown, but it is more accurately in Shousetown. The structure no longer exists but is a good example of the size and style of the cabins that peppered the early Moon Township topography. (Courtesy Eliot and Marjorie Johnson and the Crescent-Shousetown Area Historic Association.)

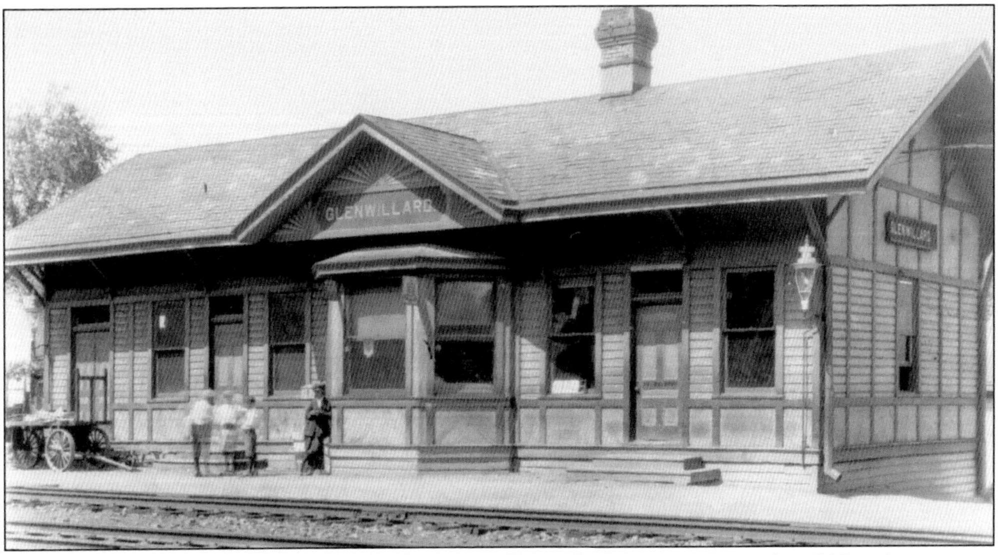

The Glenwillard Train Station was built in 1918. From the station, it was a brief 15-mile trip into the city of Pittsburgh. The station served the Pittsburgh and Lake Erie Railroad. Built in 1877, the railroad was designed to link Pittsburgh to Youngstown, Ohio. On February 24, 1879, passenger service commenced. (Courtesy Eliot and Marjorie Johnson and the Crescent-Shousetown Area Historic Association.)

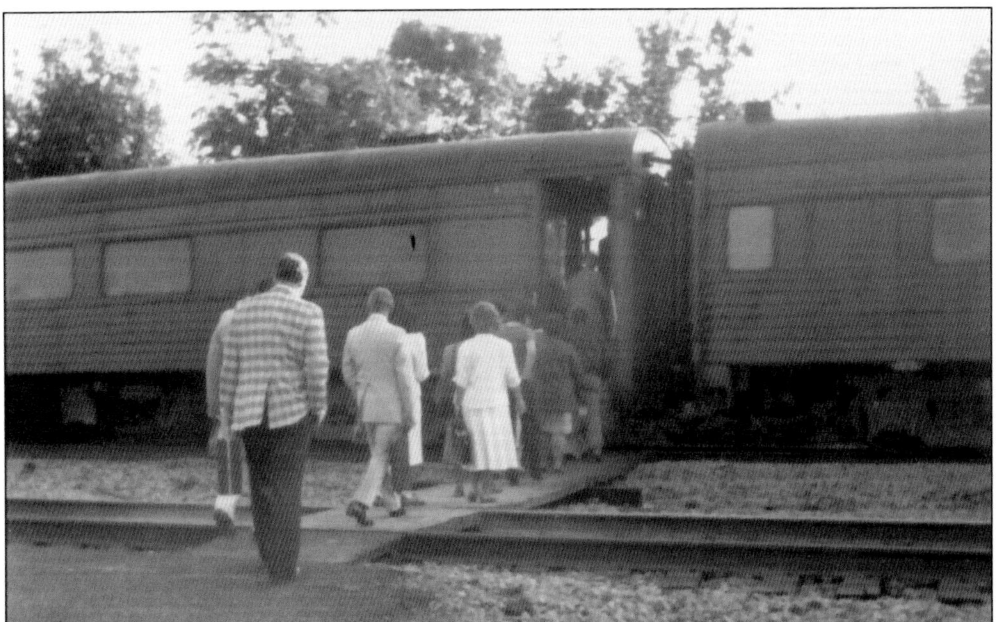

Commuter rail service ran steady into the mid-1980s. This photograph shows passengers boarding the 7:00 a.m. Pittsburgh inbound train in June 1985. The commuter service was terminated one month later in July 1985. The closure of the Pittsburgh and Lake Erie Railroad boosted neighboring Beaver County Transit Authority patronage by 130,000 in the two years following the closure. (Courtesy Eliot and Marjorie Johnson and the Crescent-Shousetown Area Historic Association.)

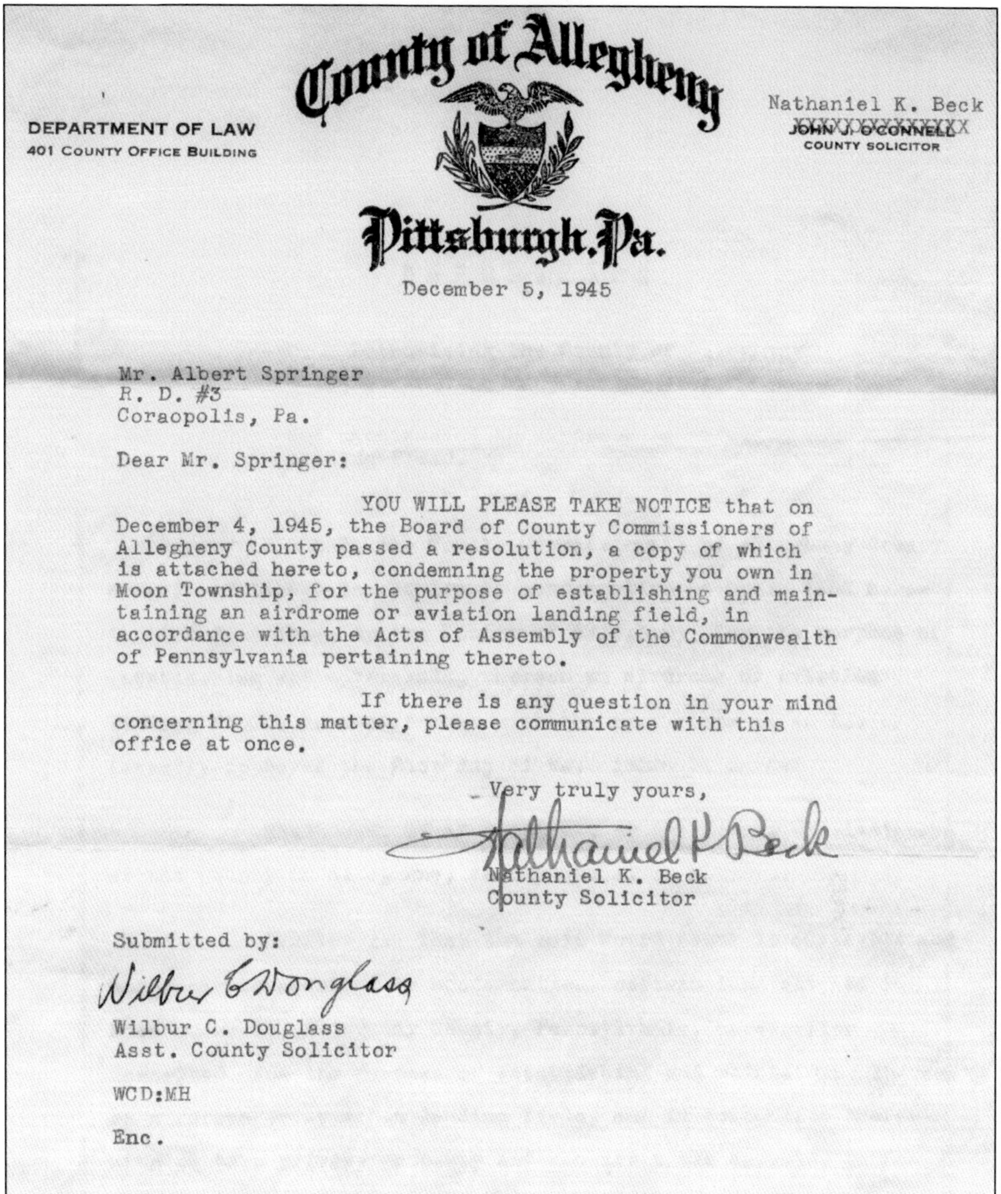

County of Allegheny
Pittsburgh, Pa.

DEPARTMENT OF LAW
401 COUNTY OFFICE BUILDING

Nathaniel K. Beck
~~JOHN J. O'CONNELL~~
COUNTY SOLICITOR

December 5, 1945

Mr. Albert Springer
R. D. #3
Coraopolis, Pa.

Dear Mr. Springer:

YOU WILL PLEASE TAKE NOTICE that on December 4, 1945, the Board of County Commissioners of Allegheny County passed a resolution, a copy of which is attached hereto, condemning the property you own in Moon Township, for the purpose of establishing and maintaining an airdrome or aviation landing field, in accordance with the Acts of Assembly of the Commonwealth of Pennsylvania pertaining thereto.

If there is any question in your mind concerning this matter, please communicate with this office at once.

Very truly yours,

Nathaniel K. Beck

Nathaniel K. Beck
County Solicitor

Submitted by:

Wilbur C. Douglass

Wilbur C. Douglass
Asst. County Solicitor

WCD:MH

Enc.

On December 4, 1945, Albert Springer received a letter from the Allegheny County solicitor that a portion of his property would be taken by eminent domain in anticipation of building the future Greater Pittsburgh International Airport. The Springer farm can be traced back to Revolutionary War land grants awarded to Mathias and Michael Springer. The two owned a combined 800 acres in adjacent tracts. (Courtesy Nancy Mills.)

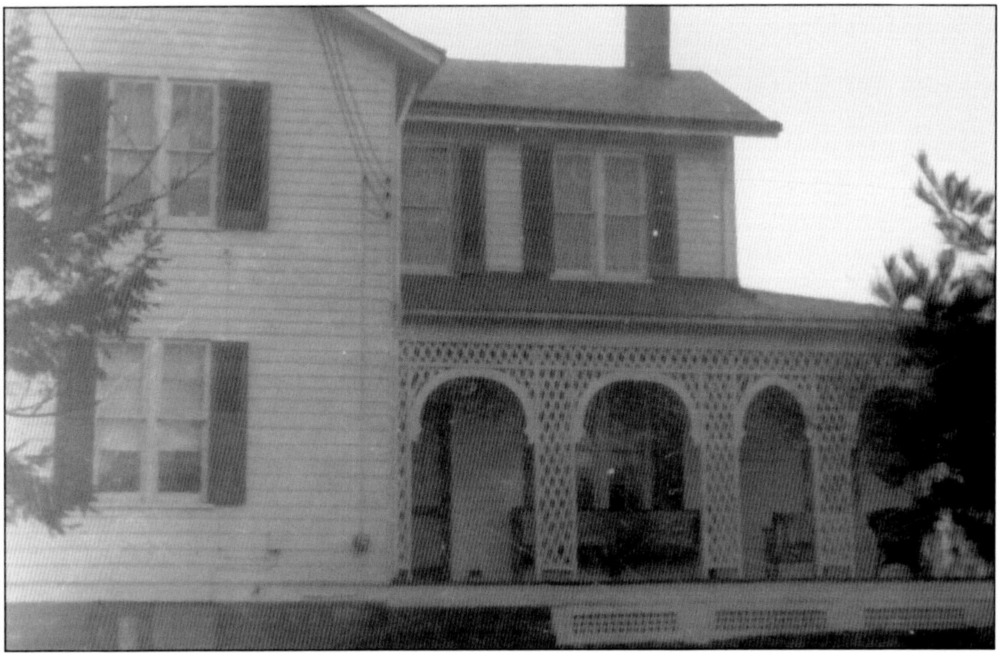

The Springer house, part of the Albert Springer farm, was razed to make way for Greater Pittsburgh International Airport. Descendants of the Springer family state that a TWA aircraft hangar was erected at the approximate site of this house. TWA declared bankruptcy in 2001 and was absorbed by American Airlines. (Courtesy Nancy Mills.)

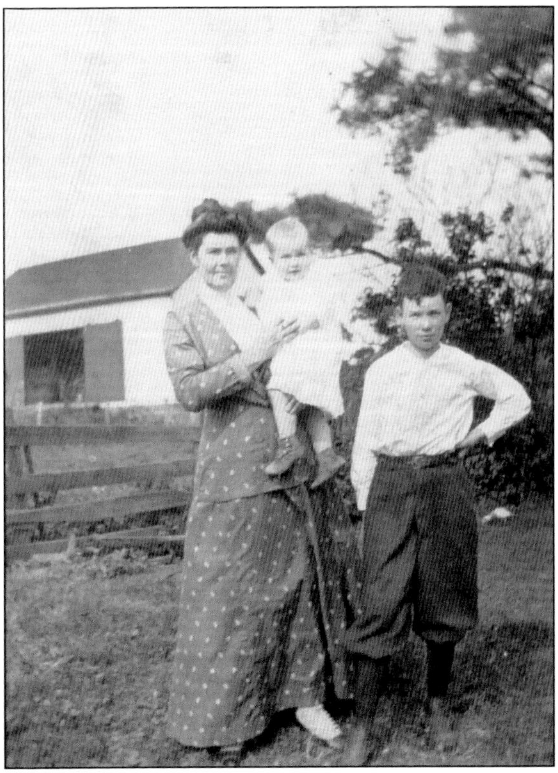

Pictured here are Ella Springer, holding Eleanor Springer, and John Springer on the Springer farm around 1915. The family was eventually displaced to make way for the Greater Pittsburgh International Airport. John remained in Moon Township and raised a family and worked for Martin Wise, Inc. (Courtesy Nancy Mills.)

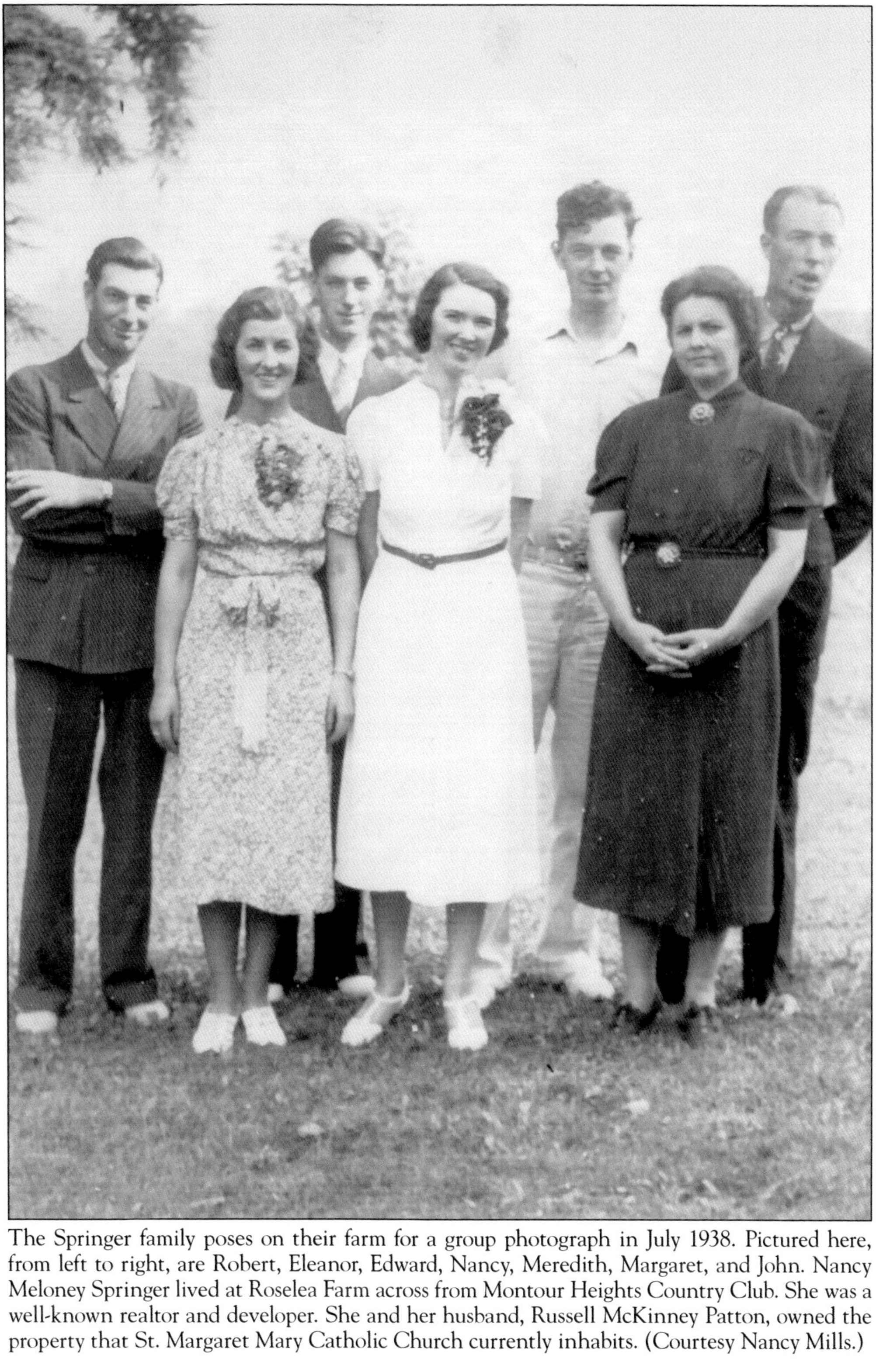

The Springer family poses on their farm for a group photograph in July 1938. Pictured here, from left to right, are Robert, Eleanor, Edward, Nancy, Meredith, Margaret, and John. Nancy Meloney Springer lived at Roselea Farm across from Montour Heights Country Club. She was a well-known realtor and developer. She and her husband, Russell McKinney Patton, owned the property that St. Margaret Mary Catholic Church currently inhabits. (Courtesy Nancy Mills.)

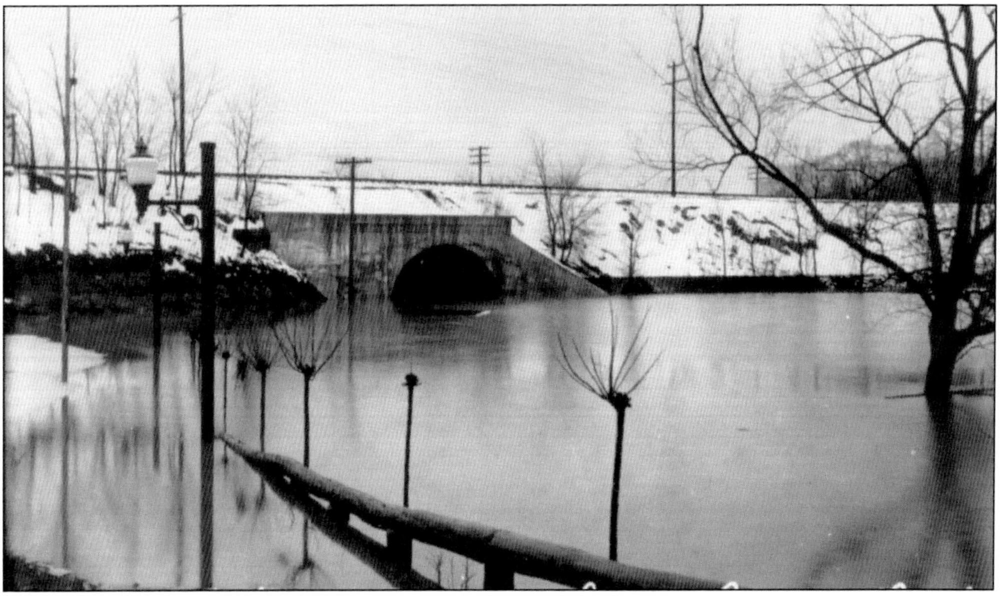

This March 18, 1936, photograph of the Glenwillard Auto Tunnel shows the results of the great flood of 1936. Water levels in downtown Pittsburgh rose to 46 feet and resulted in more than 3,000 injuries. The note on the photograph states that the water level reached 53.2 feet at the dam. The river has a series of locks and dams to ensure a constant minimum nine-foot shipping channel. (Courtesy Eliot and Marjorie Johnson and the Crescent-Shousetown Area Historic Association.)

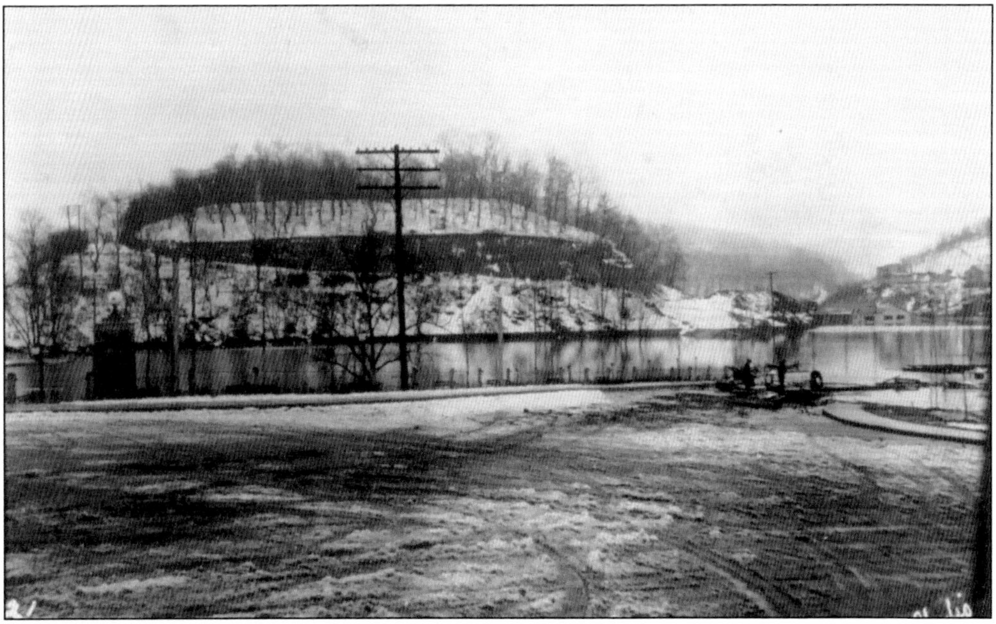

This photograph also shows the results of the flood at Shouse Park in Glenwillard. The St. Patrick's Day flood of 1936 was caused by fast-melting snow and heavy rains coupled with an already swollen river. It took five days for the water to recede to normal levels. The flood caused about $250 million worth of damage. (Courtesy Eliot and Marjorie Johnson and the Crescent-Shousetown Area Historic Association.)

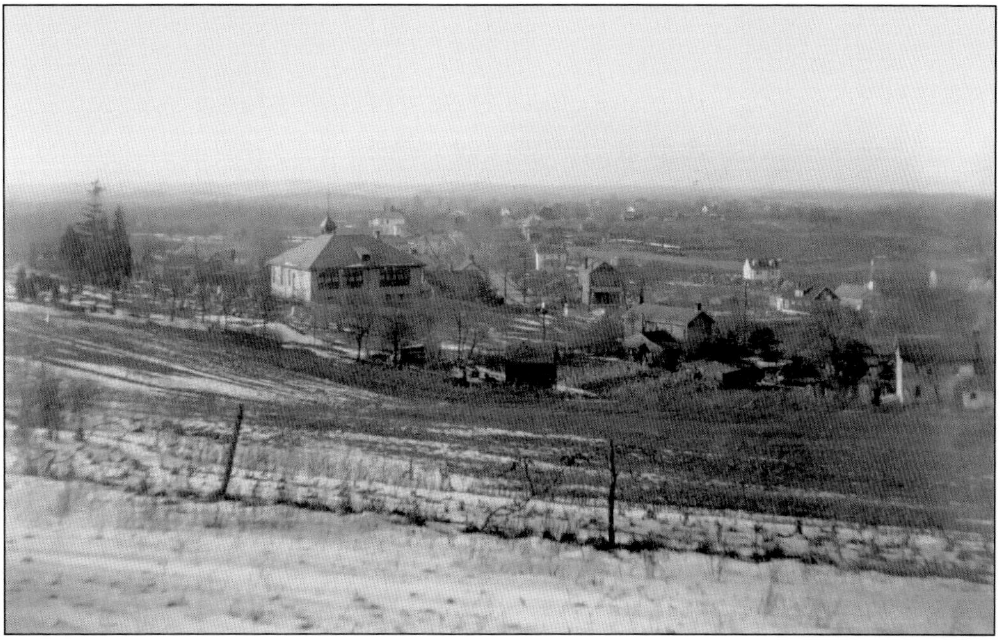

High above the flood plains was the village of Carnot, which was the heart of old Moon Township. The intersection of Beers School (now University Boulevard) and Brodhead/Beaver Grade Roads has been an integral intersection throughout Moon's history. The vantage point in this photograph is virtually unrecognizable today because of all the development. (Courtesy Dr. Dale Gass.)

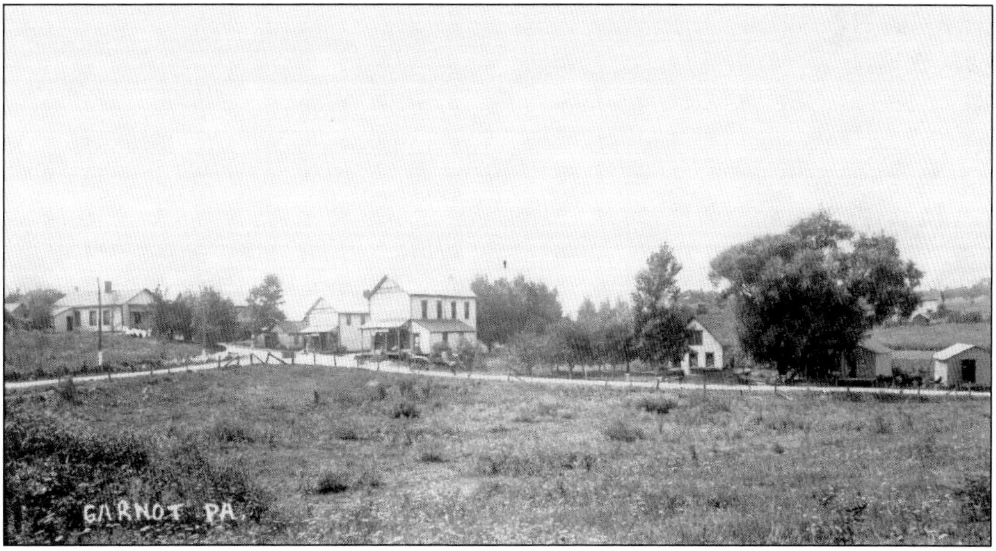

Originally known as Sharon, Carnot was and is still today the commercial business district of Moon Township. While much of the open land in this undated photograph is now shopping centers and fast-food restaurants, in early-20th-century Moon, the business district was comprised of a grocery store, a general store, and a real estate company. (Courtesy Dr. Dale Gass.)

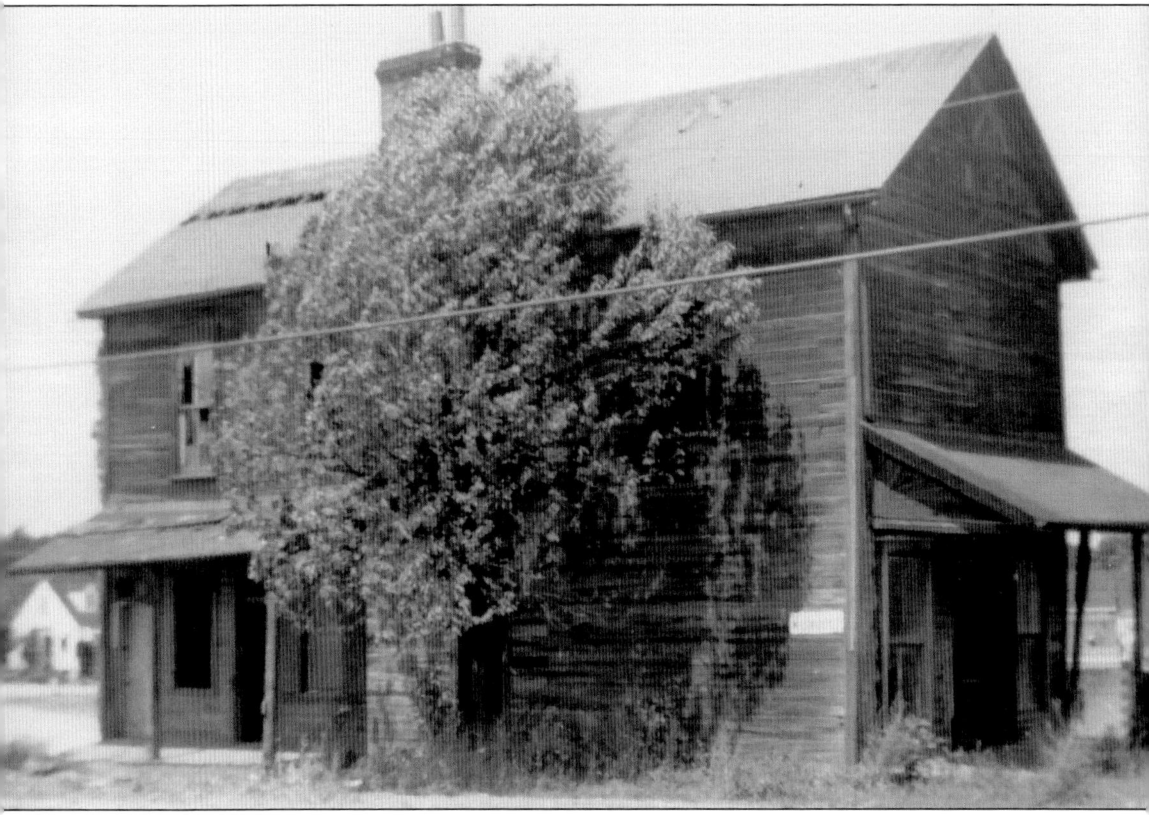

This house stood in Carnot until 1957, when it was razed to make way for the Narrows Run and Beers School Road widening. Narrows Run Road and Beers School Road were unified into University Boulevard, and a zoning overlay district dictates the future development that will take place along the road well into the future. Building projects in the overlay district will be held to a higher standard as the corridor is one of the main entryways into Moon.

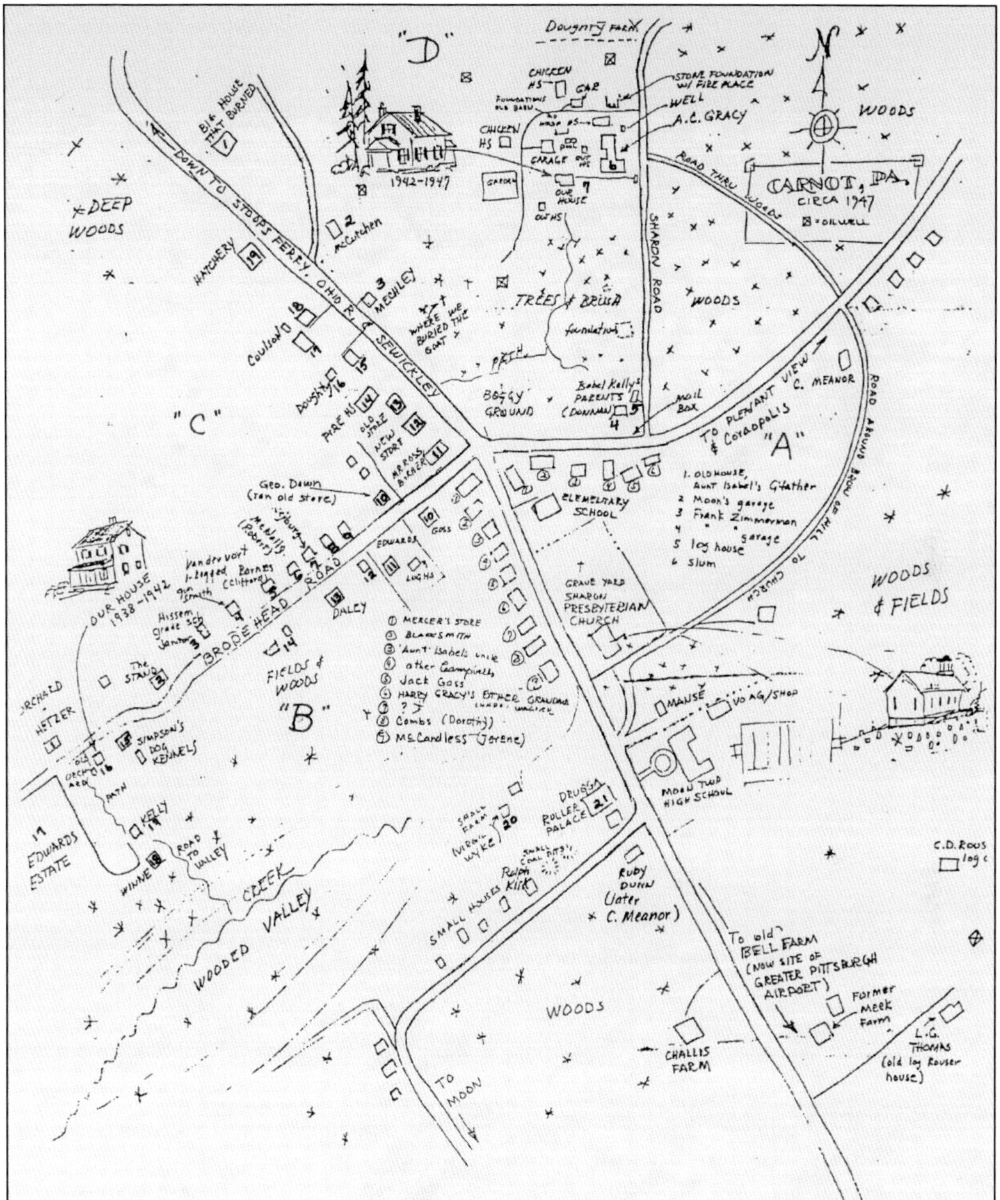

CARNOT AREA – 1947
Drawn by R. Campbell

This 1947 map of Moon Township's Carnot area was drawn by hand by R. Campbell and shows just how much of old Moon Township still existed even as the Greater Pittsburgh International Airport was being constructed just a few miles away. Businesses such as a blacksmith stood amid several farms. Oil wells peppered the topography as well. This map shows how much Carnot grew in a short period of time. Most of the property in the lower left quadrant was razed to make way for West Hills Shopping Center, which was purchased by Wal-Mart in January 2007. Wal-Mart's plans for the site have yet to be announced. (Courtesy Dr. Dale Gass.)

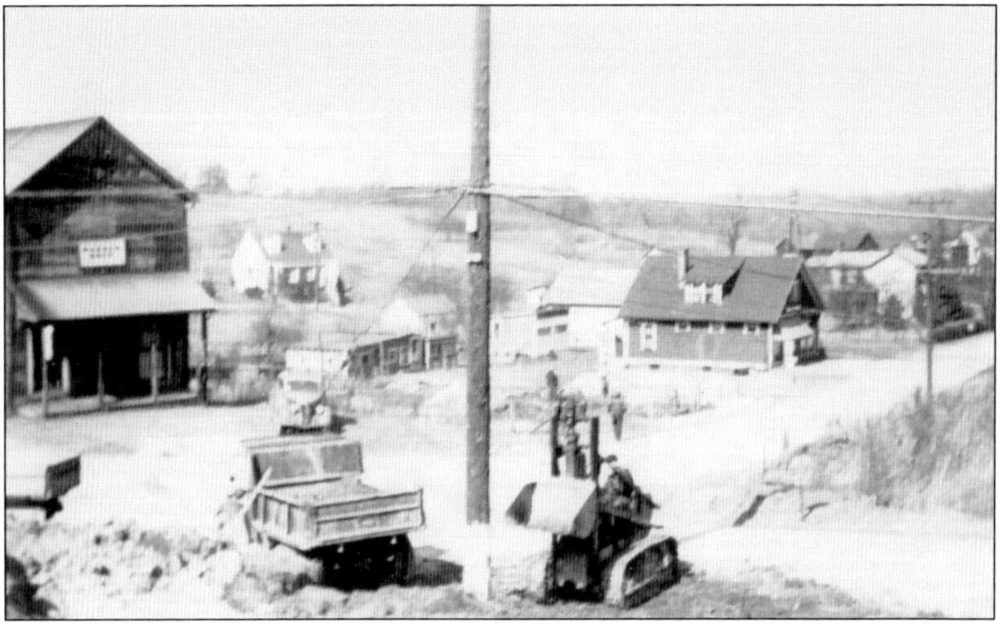

This photograph shows the road widening at Carnot. The major structure in the photograph was a barbershop. A major shopping center and grocery store now occupy the property across the road from where this photograph was taken. Moon Township's growth was less focused in this part of the township than it is today. The Carnot area is located in an overlay district, which will guide future growth and development. (Courtesy Dr. Dale Gass.)

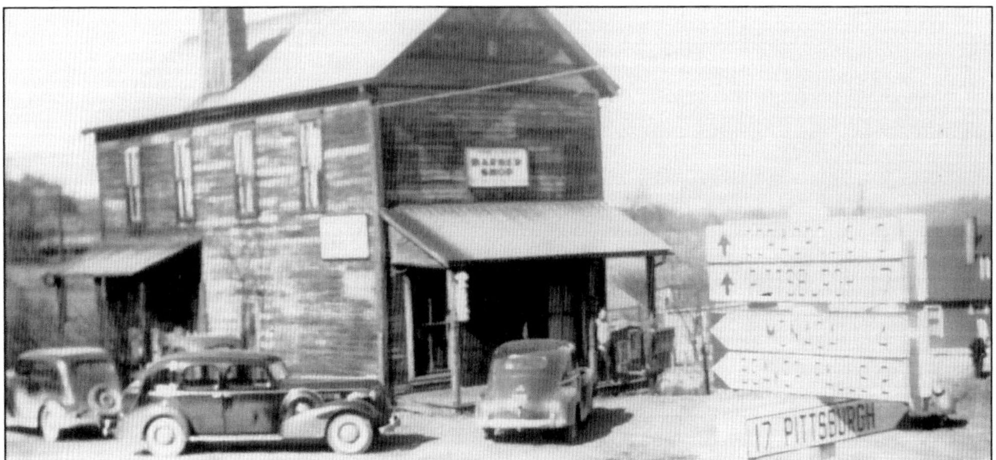

This 1940s photograph shows a barbershop in Carnot and an old-style signpost pointing the way to Pittsburgh. This route would have taken travelers toward Sewickley to Ohio River Boulevard. The Roth Barber Shop was demolished along with most of the other main street–style establishments in Carnot. Some of these buildings existed until 1989 before being torn down. (Courtesy Dr. Dale Gass.)

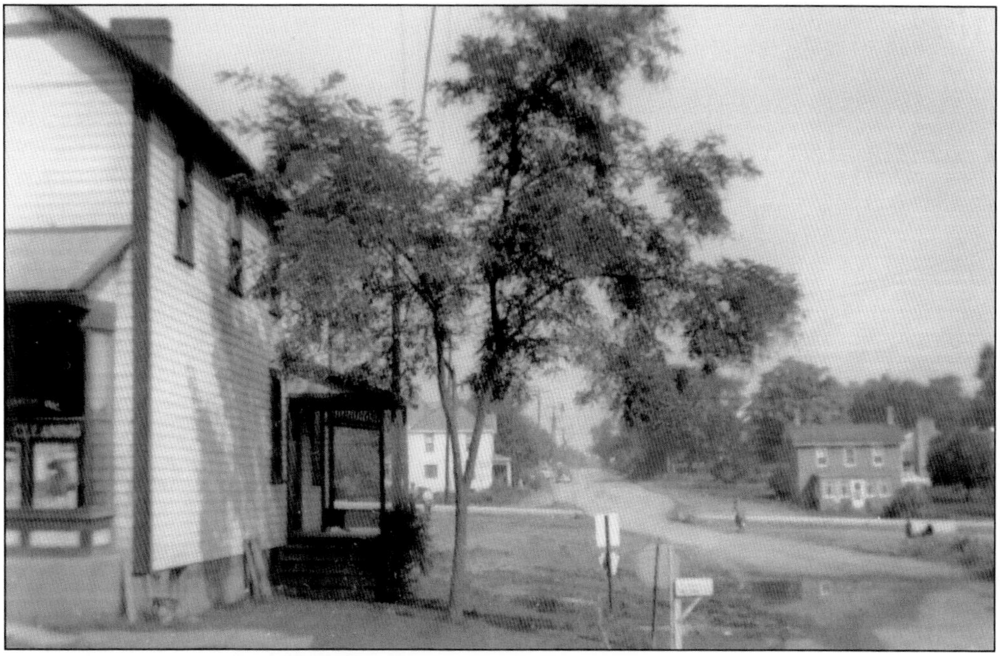

The building on the left of this photograph is the Mercer cleaning store. It was originally part of Sharon Presbyterian Church and was the church's parsonage. It was later converted to a general store, then a cleaning store. Later it became a real estate office. It was razed in 1989 and was one of the final pieces of Carnot's past to be erased. (Courtesy Dr. Dale Gass.)

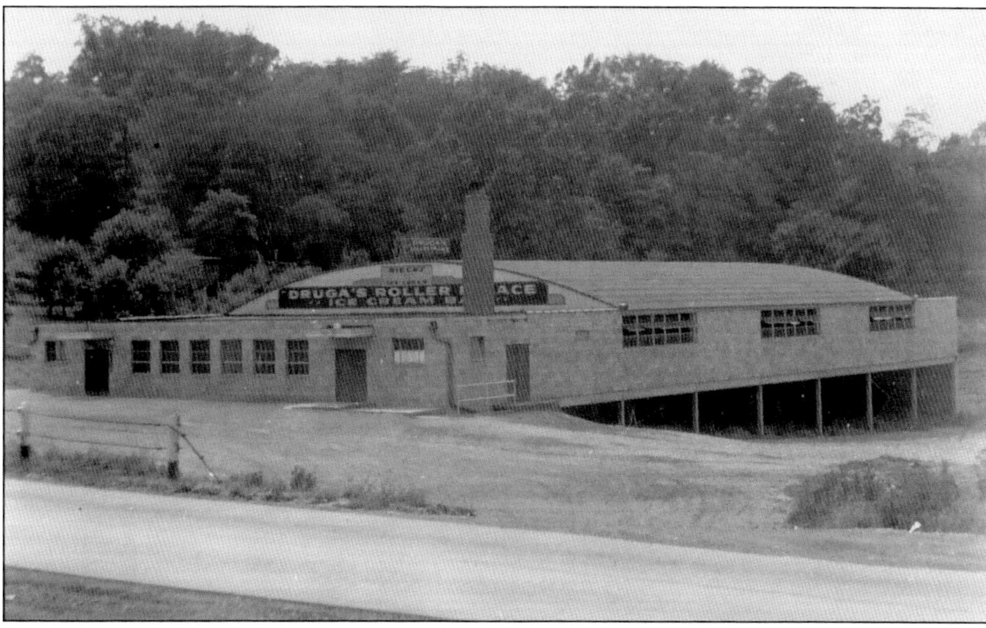

Druga's Roller Palace was a local staple for young Moon residents looking for something to do on a Friday night. The location also served as an early center of worship for St. Margaret Mary Catholic Church. The fees for renting the roller rink out were covered by Catholic society rummage and bake sales. Other fund-raisers helped this small group of women cover the cost of giving their children a Catholic education. (Courtesy Dr. Dale Gass.)

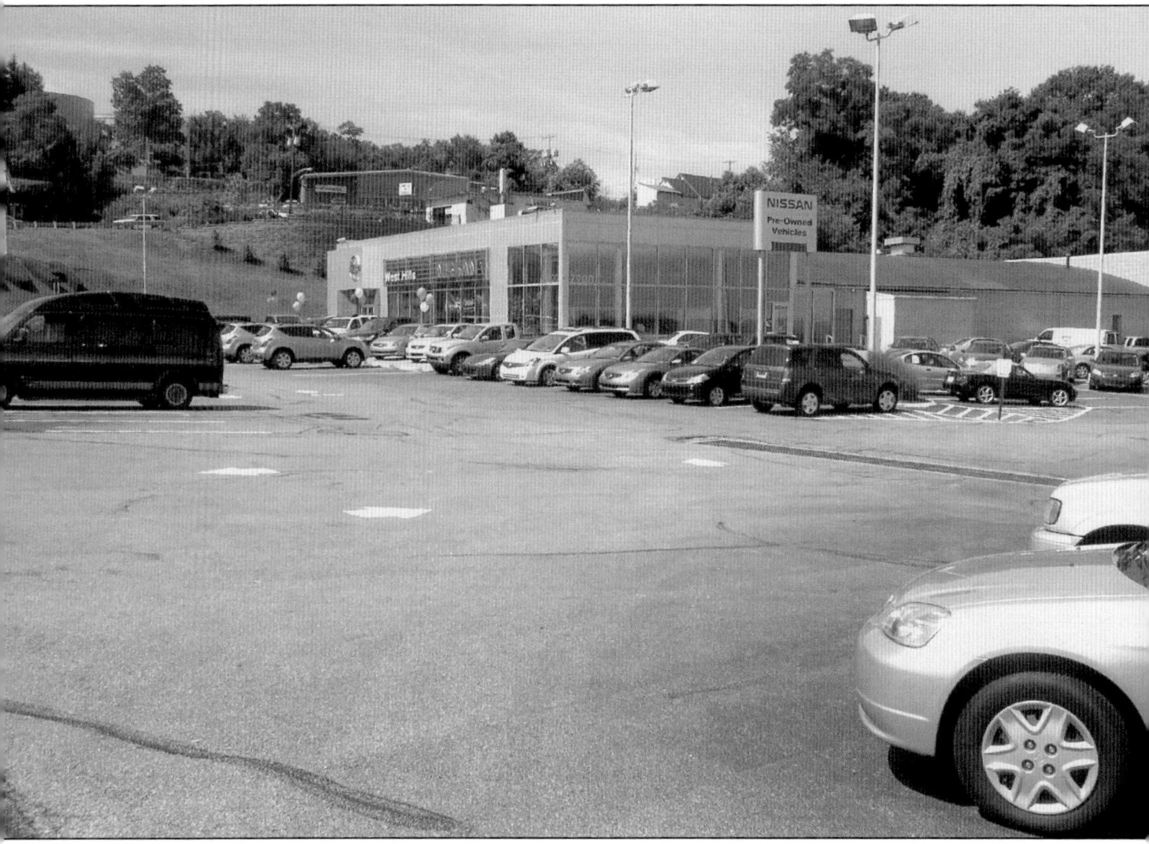

Today the roller rink property is home to West Hills Nissan, one of nearly a dozen car dealerships that line University Boulevard. Development along Moon's main business corridor promises to change the Carnot area even more as several remnant buildings will be razed in 2007 to make way for a Walgreen's Drugstore. (Photograph by Mark Berton.)

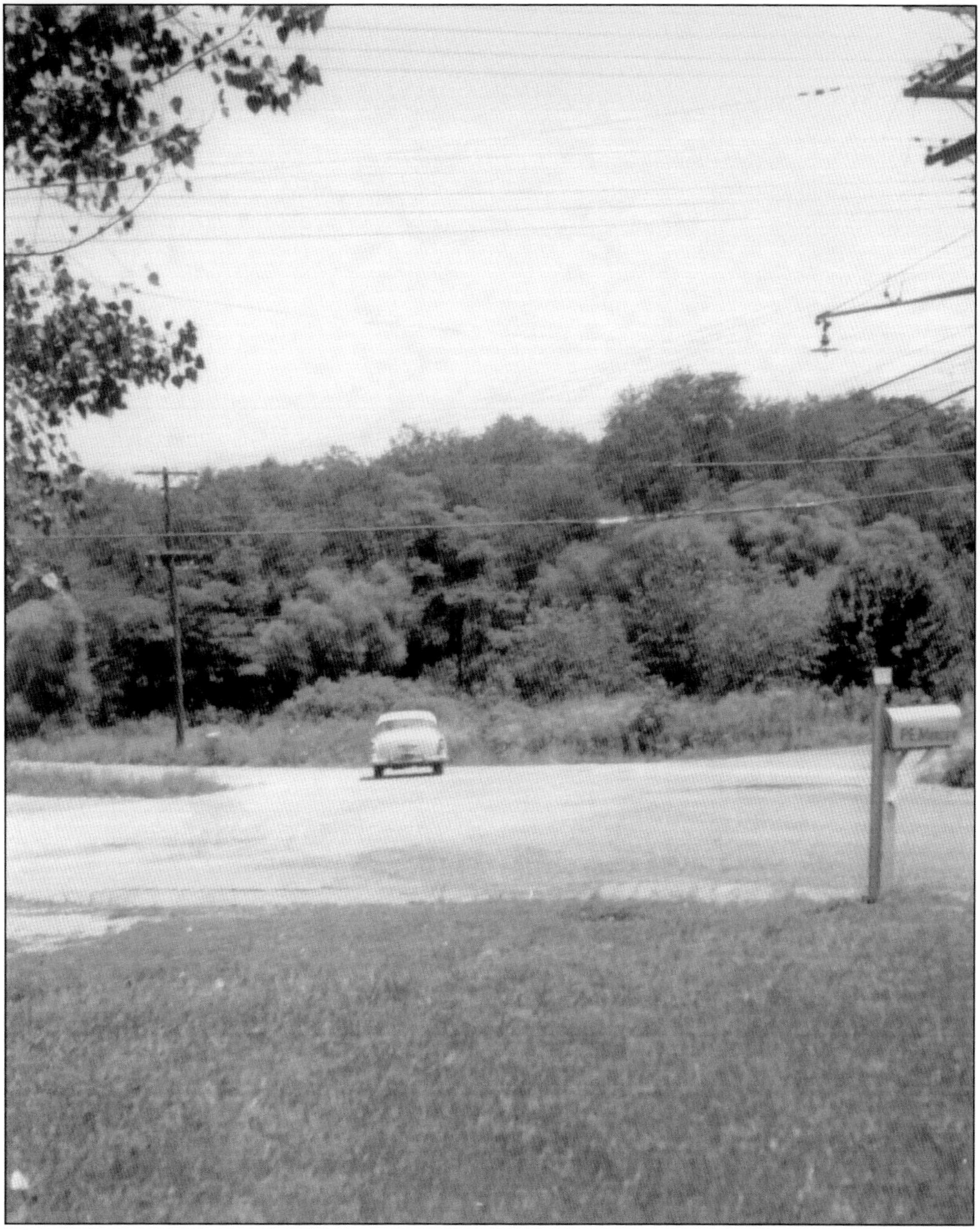

This vantage point, from the Mercer Store, faces what was once termed "boggy ground" on one map of Carnot from 1947. Today a KFC shares the site with a McDonald's, a Starbucks, and a small bank. While a lot of the development of the University Boulevard corridor in Carnot is within walking distance to many residential communities, the lack of sidewalks makes this area hostile to pedestrians. Amendments to the township planning code make sidewalks more of a priority, and future developments here will be more pedestrian friendly. (Courtesy Dr. Dale Gass.)

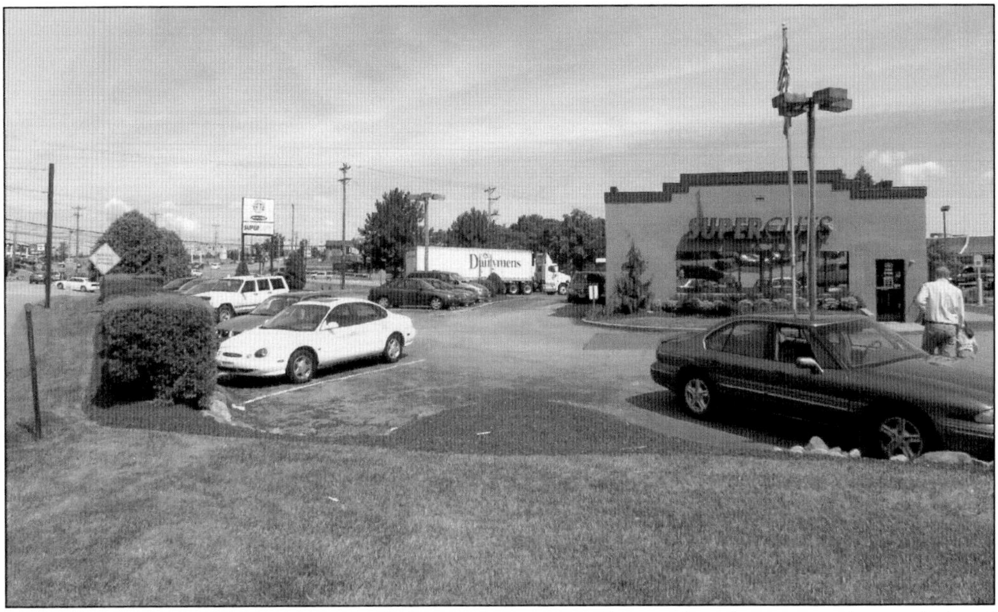

This Starbucks now sits on the site. A shopping center and several outlying parcels exist behind the Starbucks, and Robert Morris University property exists behind that. Since 1990, Moon Township officials approved more than $685 million worth of construction. In that same time period, nearly 6,000 building permits were issued.

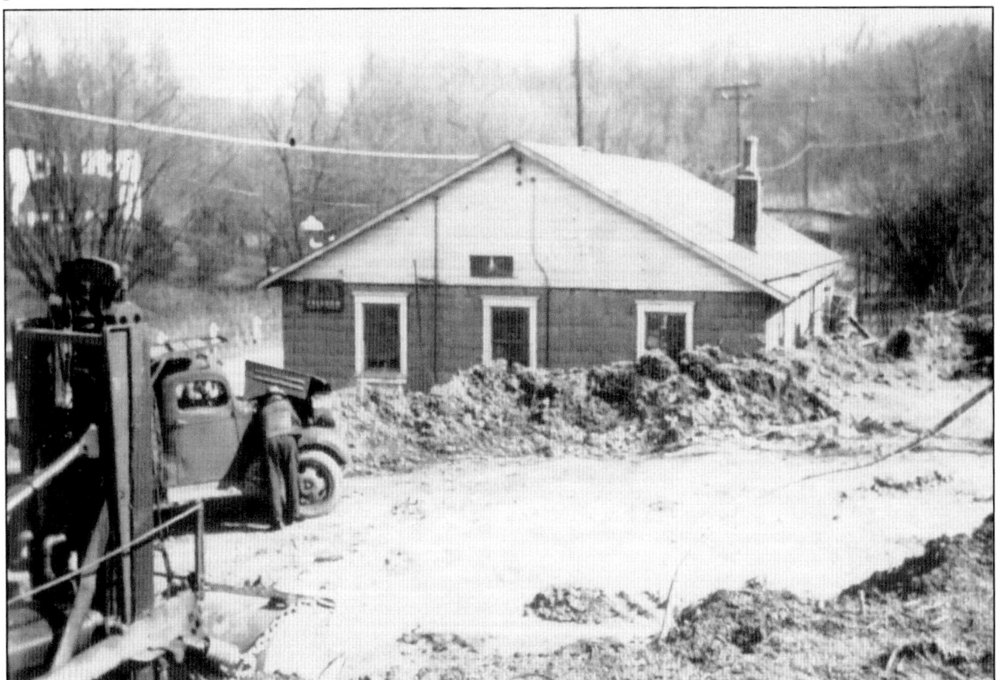

While most of Moon Township's old general stores and groceries were razed over time, one structure still stands, albeit somewhat changed from what is depicted here. A. R. Miller Hardware moved into Carnot in 1950. Prior to that, the building was a Texaco station and a blacksmith's shop prior to that. (Courtesy Dr. Dale Gass.)

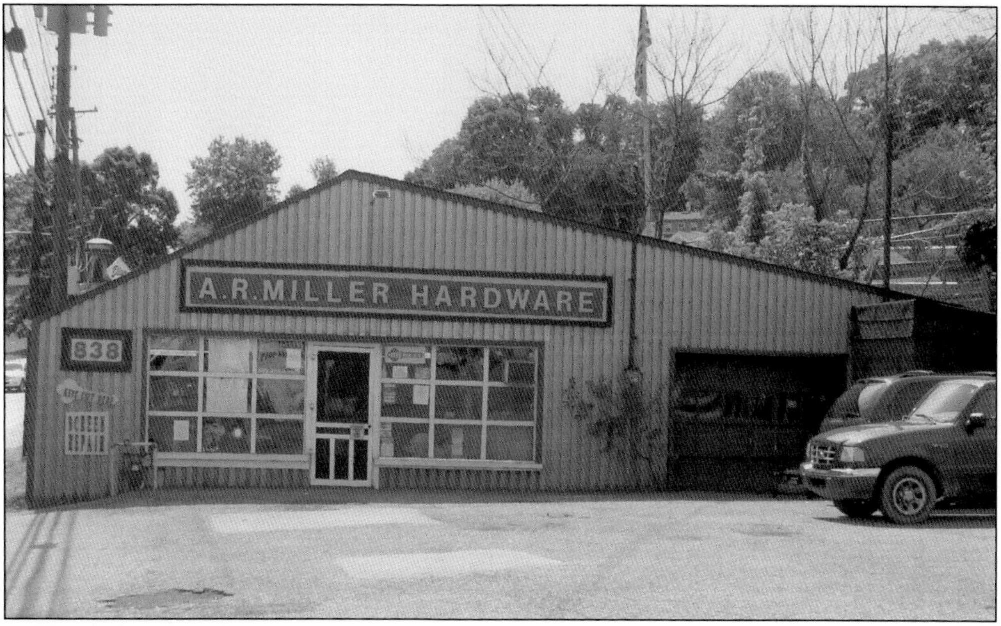

Today Miller's hardware is one of the last old-time hardware stores in the region. Moon's proximity to major highways makes it easy to visit national home improvement chains within minutes. The building was covered in aluminum siding after a 1961 tornado ripped off the roof and blew out the windows. (Photograph by Mark Berton.)

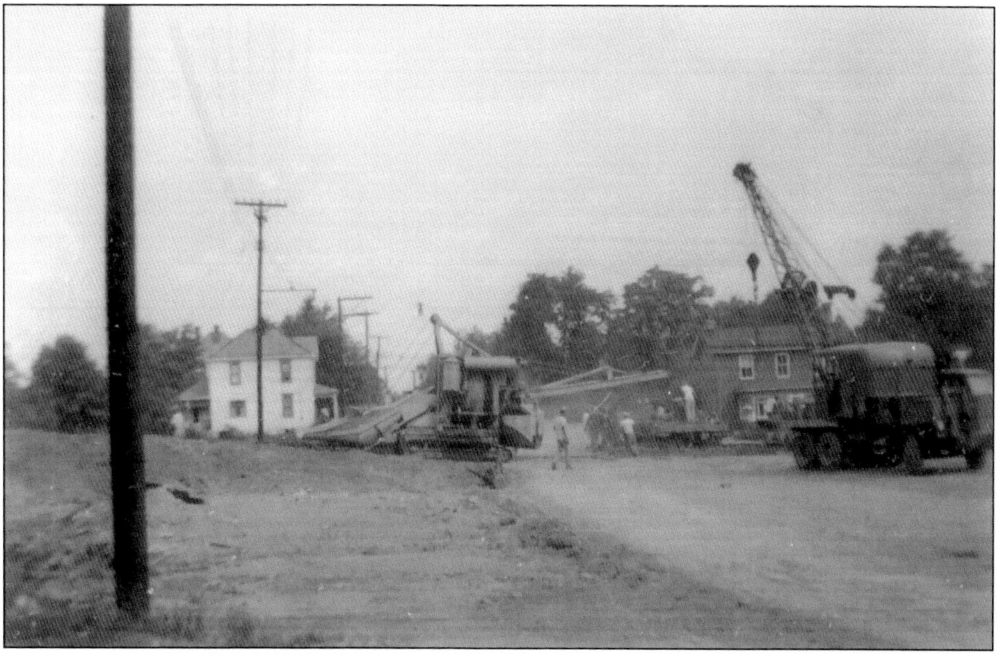

As the widening of Beers School Road commenced, the stage was set for a growth explosion in Moon. Today what was once a business district of blacksmiths and mom-and-pop stores is one of the busiest commercial districts in the county. University Boulevard not only leads to several full-scale shopping centers, it is home to several major hotel chains and a myriad of restaurants. (Courtesy Dr. Dale Gass.)

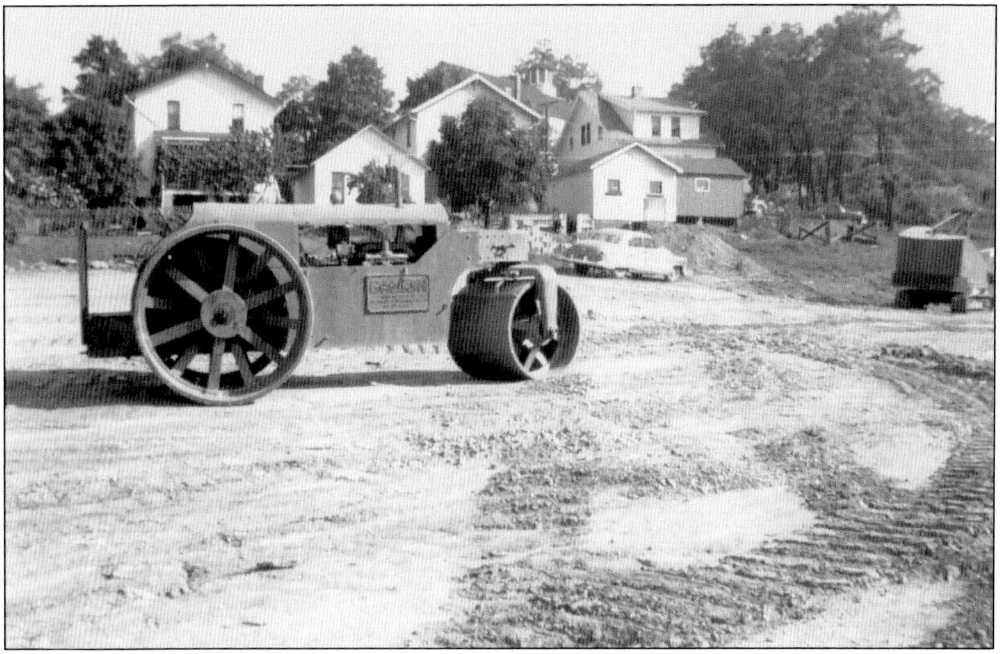

This growth, however, would not have occurred had it not been for the construction of Greater Pittsburgh International Airport. That one development spurred the unbridled growth to feed it. The roads to the old airport are peppered with hotels, motels, spas, an adult bookstore/Laundromat, and park-and-ride shuttle services. (Courtesy Dr. Dale Gass.)

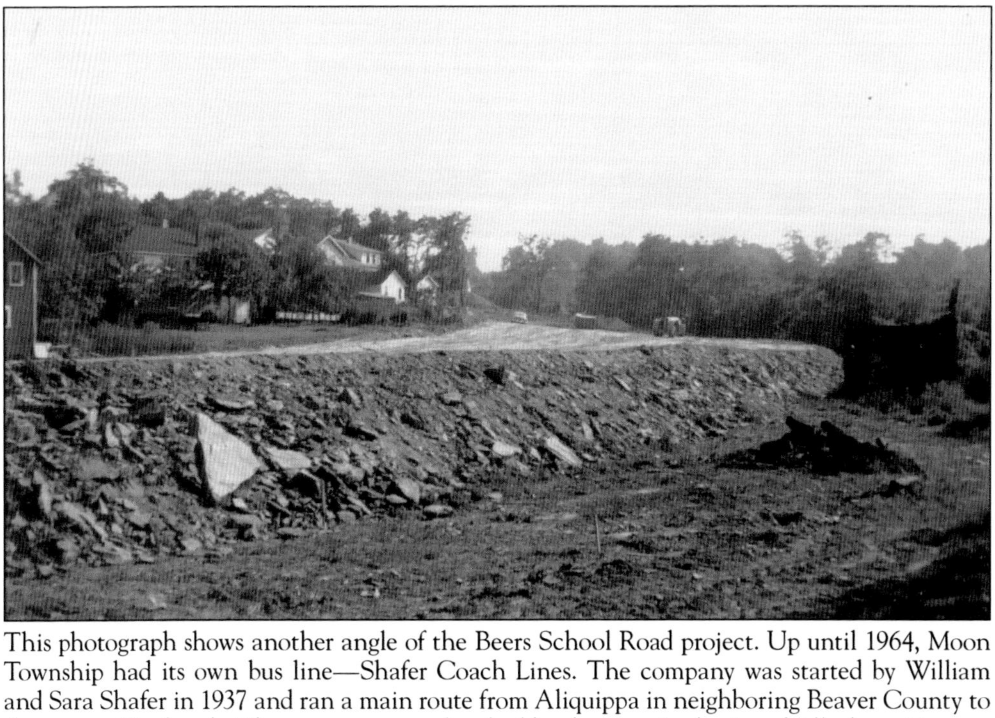

This photograph shows another angle of the Beers School Road project. Up until 1964, Moon Township had its own bus line—Shafer Coach Lines. The company was started by William and Sara Shafer in 1937 and ran a main route from Aliquippa in neighboring Beaver County to downtown Pittsburgh. The company was absorbed by the Port Authority of Allegheny County. (Courtesy Dr. Dale Gass.)

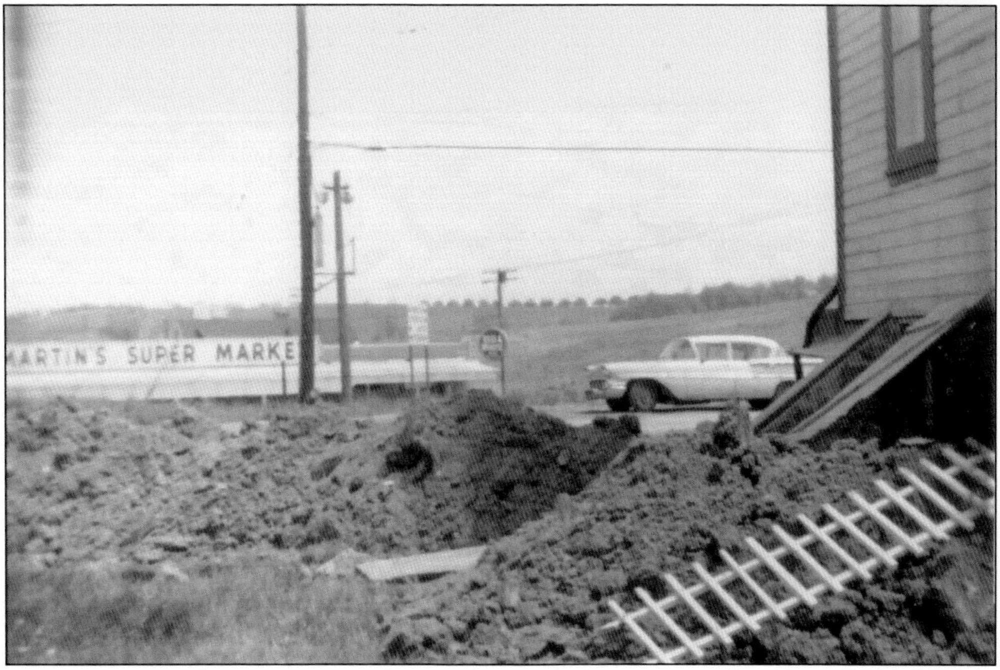

Between 1940 and 1960, the period coinciding with the conceptualization and development of the Greater Pittsburgh International Airport, the population of Moon Township grew by 65 percent from 3,733 residents to 10,608 residents. This growth highlighted the need for more efficient and modern infrastructure in the township. (Courtesy Dr. Dale Gass.)

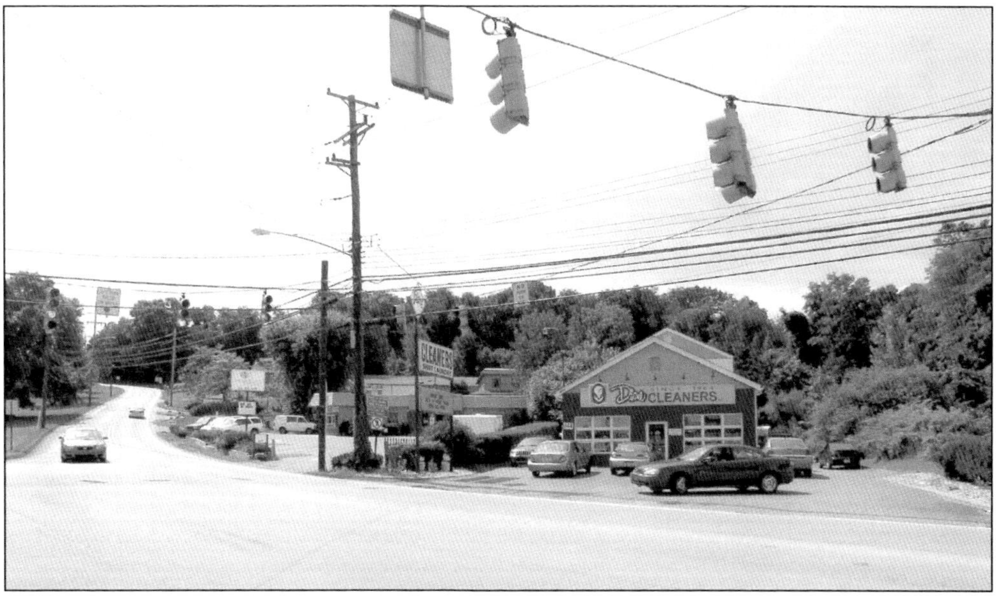

Today there are nearly 800 acres available for heavy commercial development or business park development in Moon Township. From 1996 to 2006, more than 1,200 new lots were created in the township. Nearly 4,000 building permits were issued in that same period of time, representing total construction costs of more than $487 million. (Photograph by Mark Berton.)

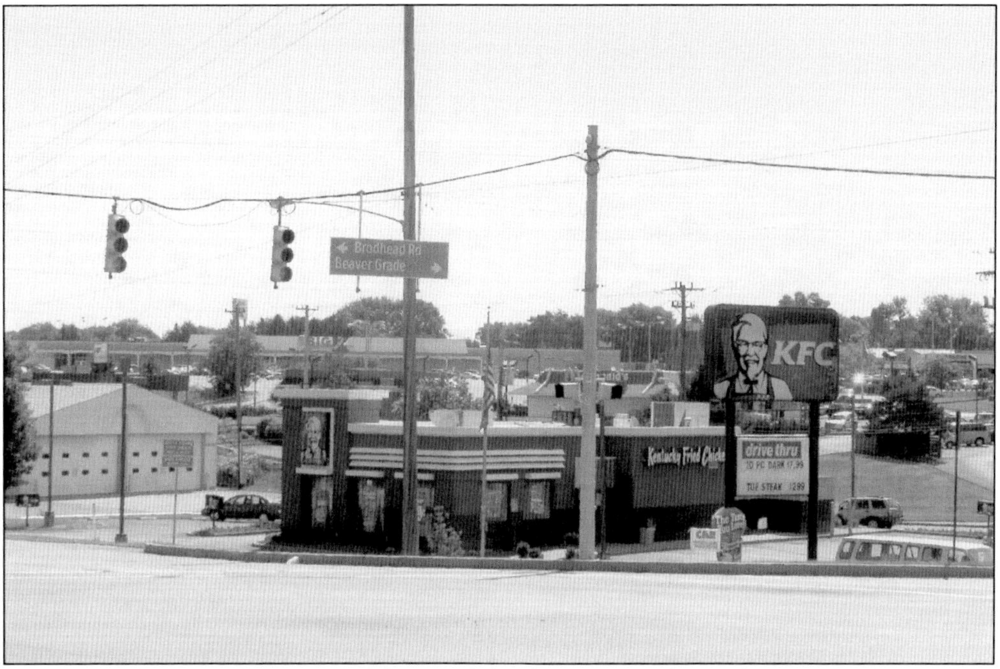

This view of Carnot shows several layers of development. Right at the corner of University Boulevard and Beaver Grade Road, a fast-food restaurant is situated where just 50 years earlier stood nothing but trees and a patch of boggy ground. Behind is the Carnot Station of the Moon Township Volunteer Fire Department and behind that a shopping center. Beyond the shopping center is the Robert Morris University property line.

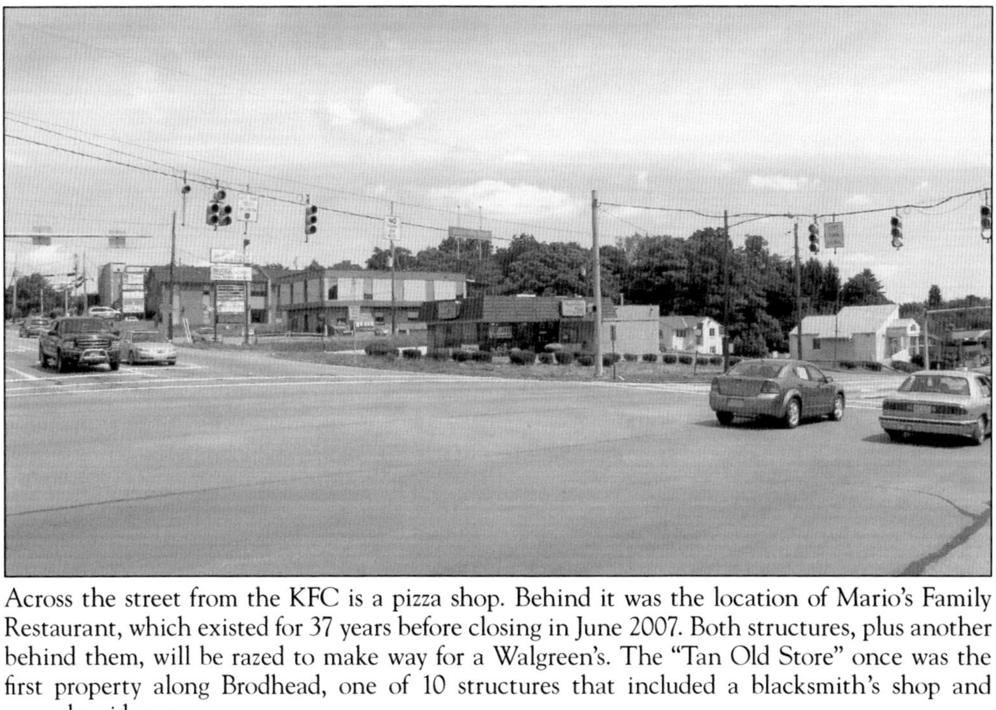

Across the street from the KFC is a pizza shop. Behind it was the location of Mario's Family Restaurant, which existed for 37 years before closing in June 2007. Both structures, plus another behind them, will be razed to make way for a Walgreen's. The "Tan Old Store" once was the first property along Brodhead, one of 10 structures that included a blacksmith's shop and several residences.

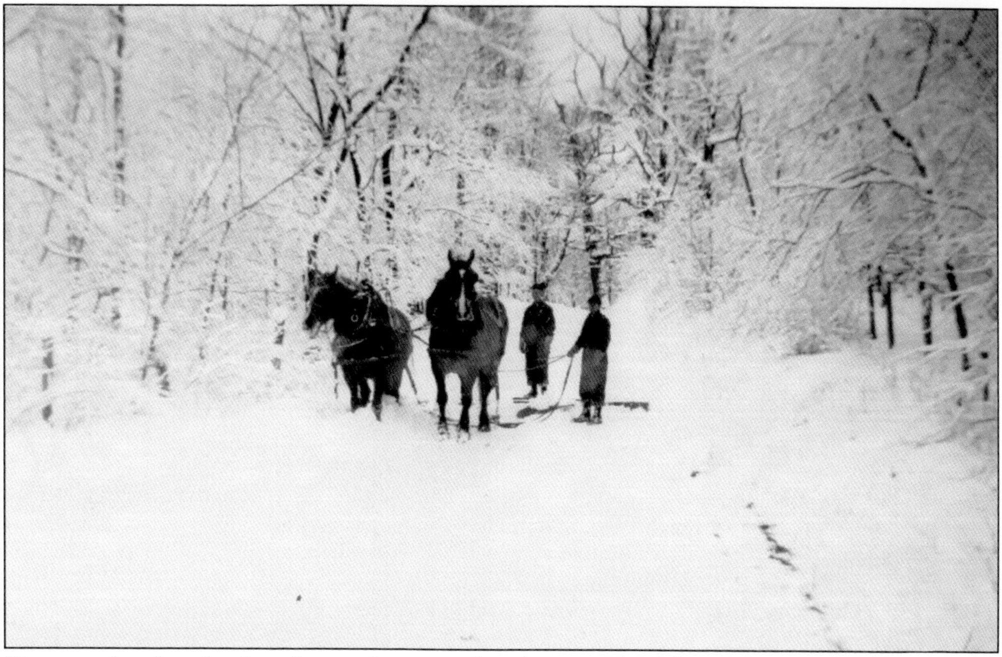

Once rural and undeveloped, as is shown in this photograph of the Meanors with a horse-drawn sled along Sharon Road, Moon quickly became a destination for post–World War II families looking for employment. The township sprung to life, doubling its population and becoming an important community in Allegheny County. (Courtesy the Meanor family.)

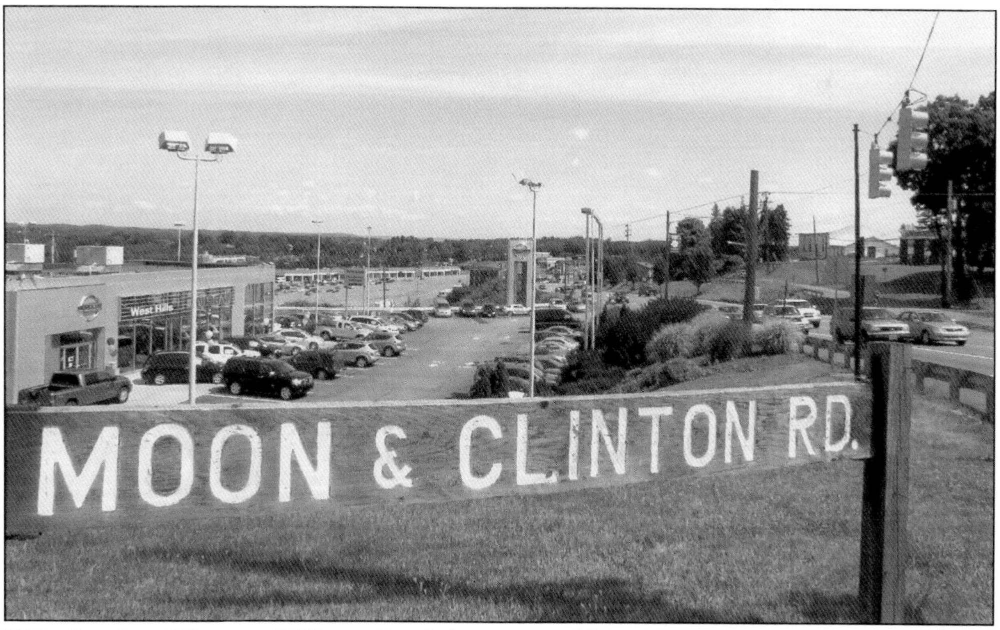

This view from Moon and Clinton Road shows several historic properties as they stand today. In the foreground, the roller rink once stood. Beyond that is West Hills Shopping Center and Brodhead Road. Across University Boulevard on a bluff is Sharon Community Presbyterian Church's original building. West Hills Shopping Center was purchased by Wal-Mart, but at the time of this writing, no official plans for development have been submitted.

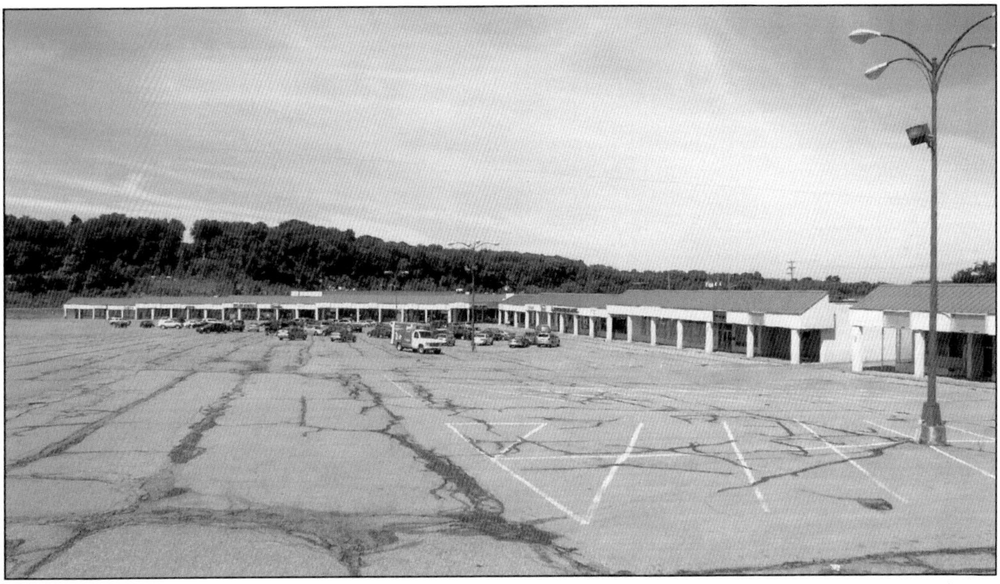

West Hills Shopping Center recently was purchased by Wal-Mart. Formal plans have not been disclosed yet, but razing the existing structures will be an unavoidable component of any plan. Early sketches show a Wal-Mart store at the rear of the basin. Behind this existing building is an off-track betting location, which will be subdivided off the property and remain after any new structures are built. (Photograph by Mark Berton.)

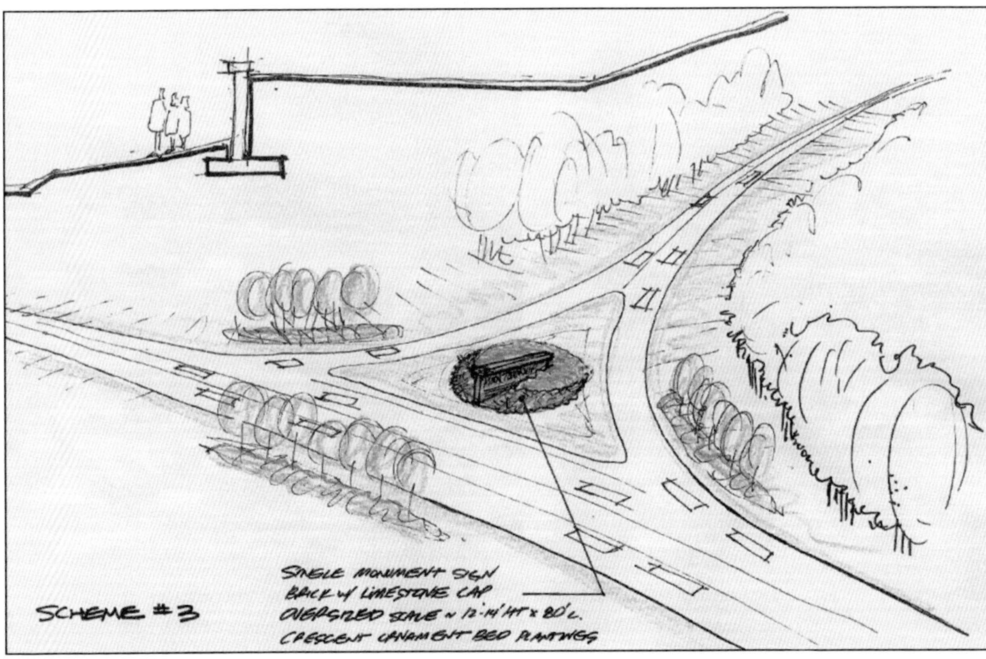

While there exist large expanses of land in Moon Township that stand to be redeveloped, Moon Township's planning department outlined some requirements to make sure future growth does not explode haphazardly. This sketch plan, for example, is a proposal for the upgrading of the University Boulevard/Stoops Ferry intersection. An emphasis of the University Boulevard corridor plan is to instill a sense of Moon's identity on all who pass through.

Two

RELIGION AND CHARITY

Moon Township is the home of many diverse people, and its proximity to the airport and a major university help to increase that diversity as time goes on. At the time of this writing, Moon Township supervisors were considering a meditation center that was proposed by developers.

While several houses of worship exist in Moon Township, the oldest by far is Sharon Presbyterian. It was founded in August 1817 under the leadership of Rev. Andrew McDonald. At that time, services were held in the homes of the congregation, and eventually in a purchased tent so long as weather permitted. There were three elders that helped McDonald in that founding year: Andrew Crooks, James McCabe, and Nathaniel Gordon.

Eventually Sharon Presbyterian Church members built a brick church, facing Beaver Grade Road. The site was later occupied by Carnot Elementary School. Shortly following its erection in 1828, Rev. S. C. Jennings became pastor of the congregation on June 24, 1829. He led the church for the next 50 years. In 1868, the old brick church was condemned and torn down. Bricks from the old church were used as part of the foundation of the new church, which was dedicated in January 1869 with a building cost of $8,000. Members of the building committee for the new church included Jeremiah Meek, William R. Newell, Dr. Breiner, Thomas Wilson, and William H. Guy.

Eventually other denominations spawned in Moon Township, increasing the amount of churches for residents to worship in. Some of these churches now reside in neighboring Crescent Township, which was created from Moon Township in 1855. Represented in Moon Township are Baptists, Catholics, Christian Alliance, Evangelical Lutherans, Methodists, and Presbyterians.

In addition to faith, Moon Township is home to many charitable organizations, including the Freemasons, Lions, and Rotary International. These organizations have grown with the community and, while their ranks are aging, still contribute to the fabric of the township. These groups can be seen proudly participating in the annual Memorial Day parade and at their various fund-raisers throughout the community.

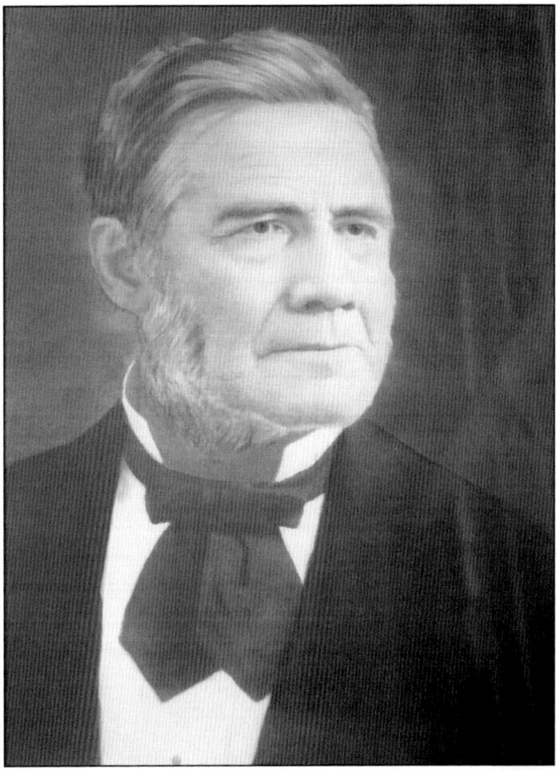

Rev. S. C. Jennings was appointed minister of Sharon Presbyterian Church in 1829 and remained there for 50 years. The year before his arrival, construction had started on a small brick church measuring just 2,000 square feet. It was finished by 1830. By 1833, Sharon Congregation had purchased land from Jeremiah Meek to build a new church.

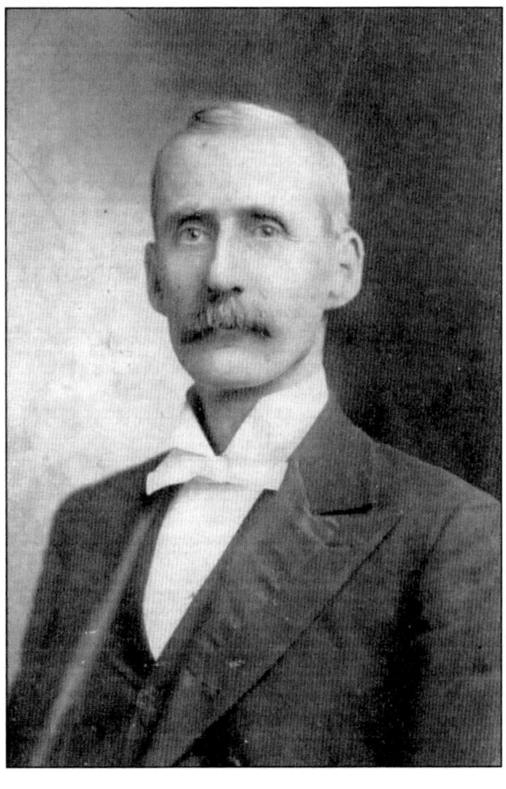

In 1884, Dr. J. M. Mercer became pastor of Sharon Presbyterian Church. He remained there for 34 years. After his 1918 resignation, Mercer became pastor emeritus of the church. The church celebrated its 75th anniversary in September 1892 with more than 1,200 people. In 1918, Rev. L. B. Wissinger took over as pastor of the Presbyterian Congregation of Sharon. (Courtesy Sharon Community Presbyterian Church.)

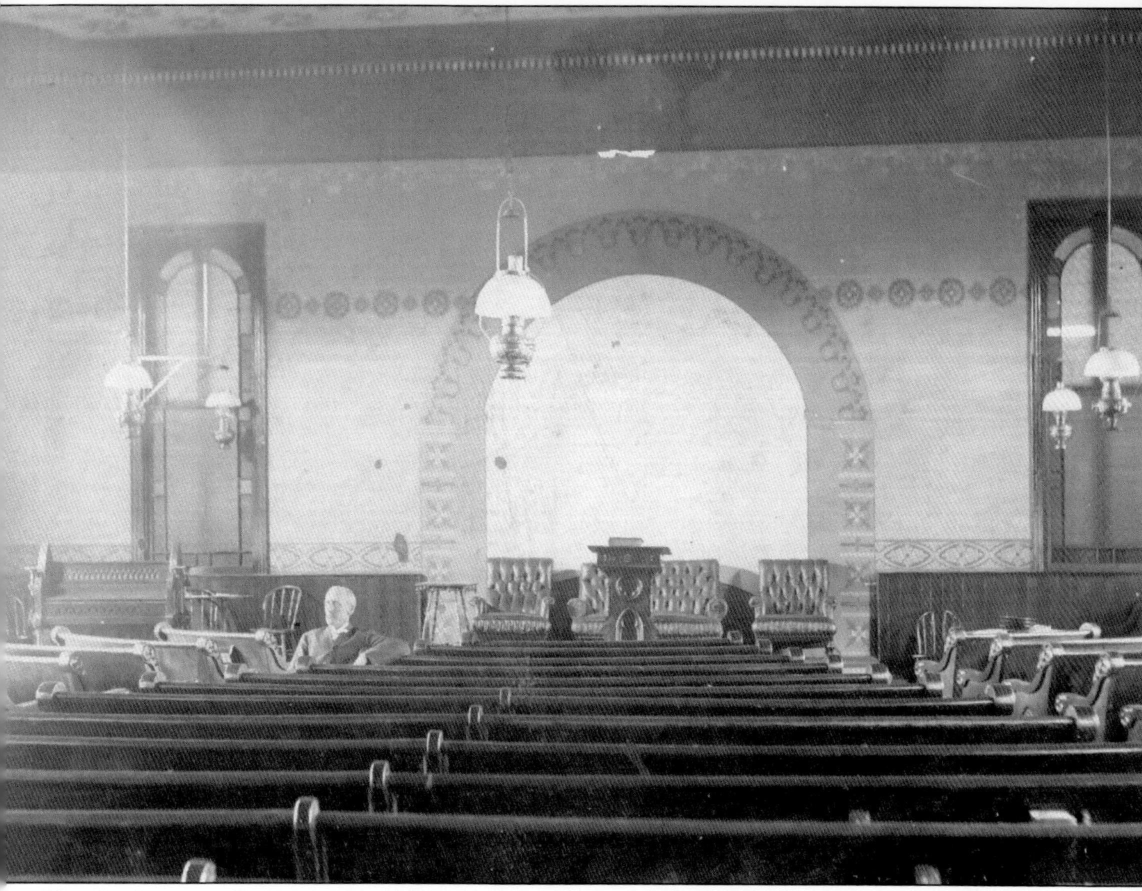

The Presbyterian Congregation of Sharon changed its name to the Sharon Presbyterian Church of Moon Township in 1956. The name changed just two years later to Sharon Community Presbyterian Church. Between the tenure of Dr. J. M. Mercer and 1958, Sharon Community Presbyterian Church saw eight pastors leading the congregation. Here Dr. J. M. Mercer can be seen sitting in the pews of Sharon Presbyterian Church. (Courtesy Sharon Community Presbyterian Church.)

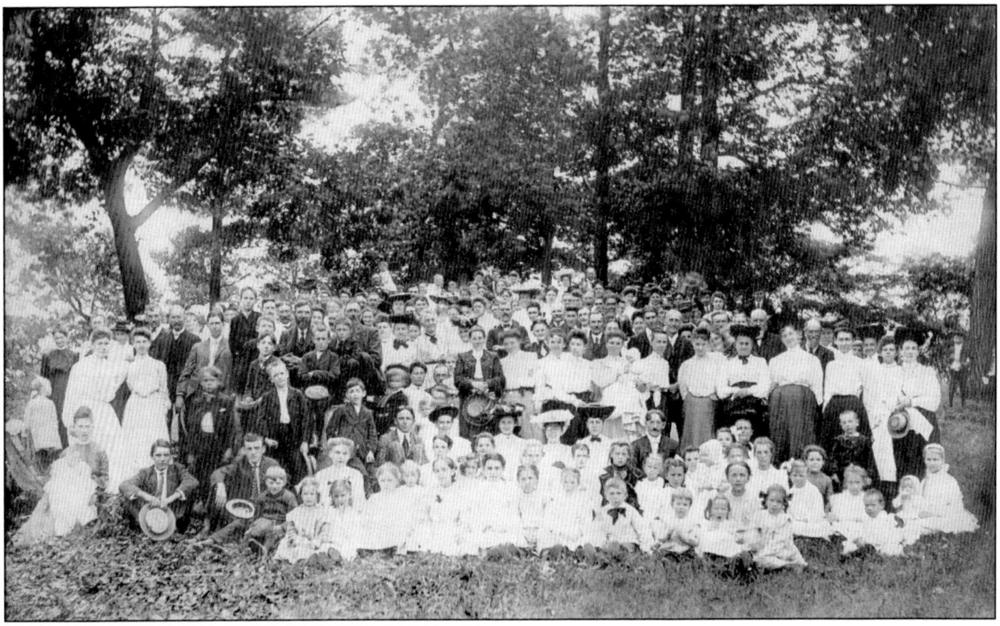

This photograph was taken August 16, 1905, and shows the full congregation of the church at that time. Church statistics show that during Mercer's tenure as pastor, the church grew by about 25 members per year on average and the congregation stood at around 200 members. When he resigned, the church's annual budget was $2,500 per year, up $1,776 from when he started more than 30 years earlier. (Courtesy Sharon Community Presbyterian Church.)

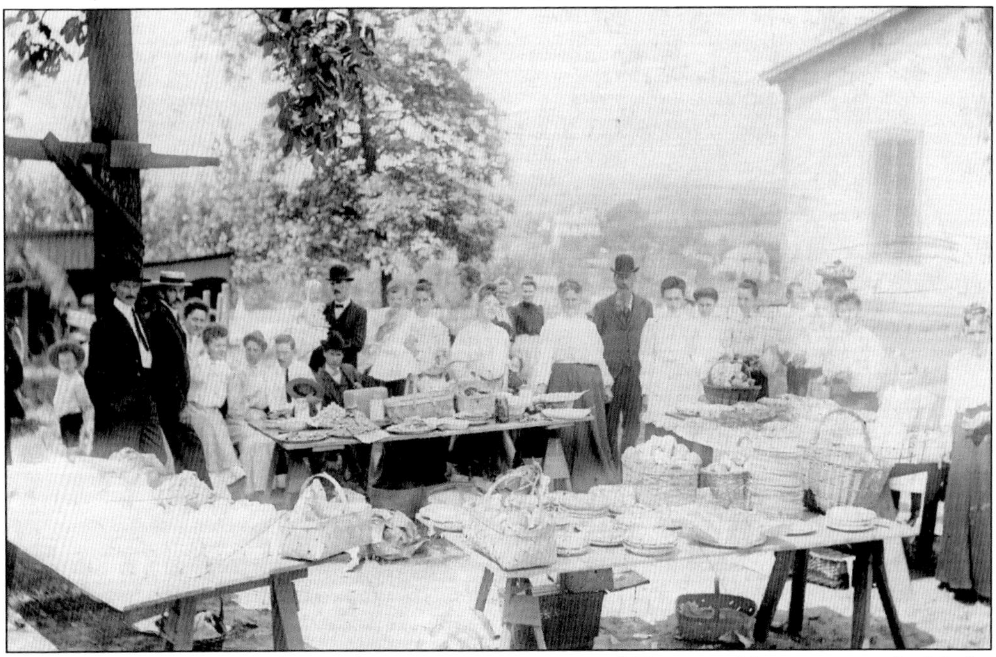

This undated shot shows the Presbyterian Congregation of Sharon celebrating outside. Under the leadership of Rev. L. B. Wissinger, who was installed in 1918, a Sabbath school was formed. The school met in the Donnan house in Flaugherty Hollow. The house was the first schoolhouse in Moon Township. (Courtesy Sharon Community Presbyterian Church.)

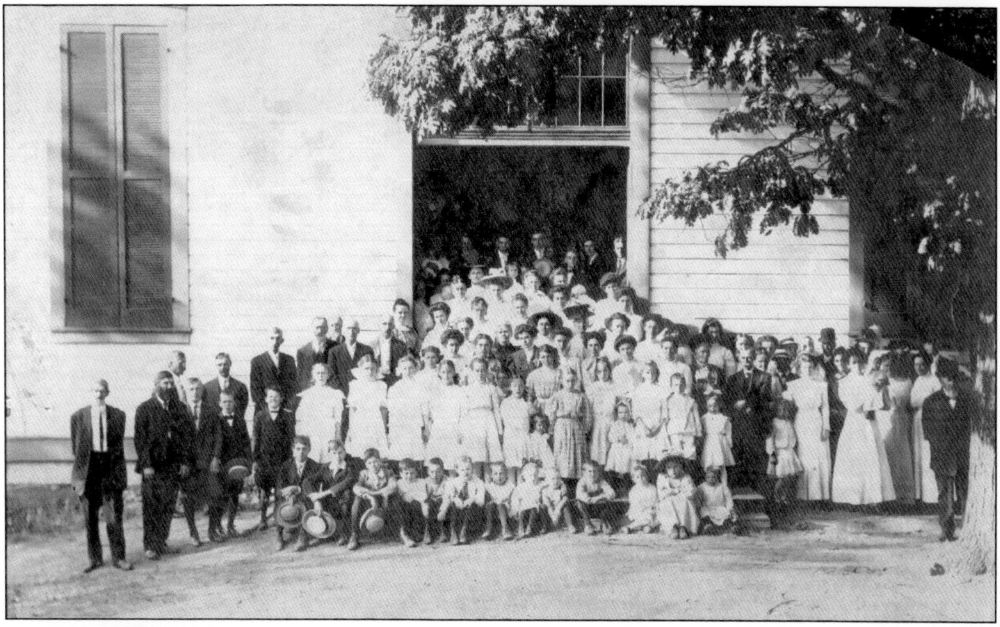

Here is another shot of the Presbyterian Congregation of Sharon at the church. The original church building closed for two months, May and June 1929, to undergo renovations. Those renovations were to be short lived as a tornado ripped through the area in July and caused major damage to the church. The project cost $2,000 and put the church into debt. (Courtesy Sharon Community Presbyterian Church.)

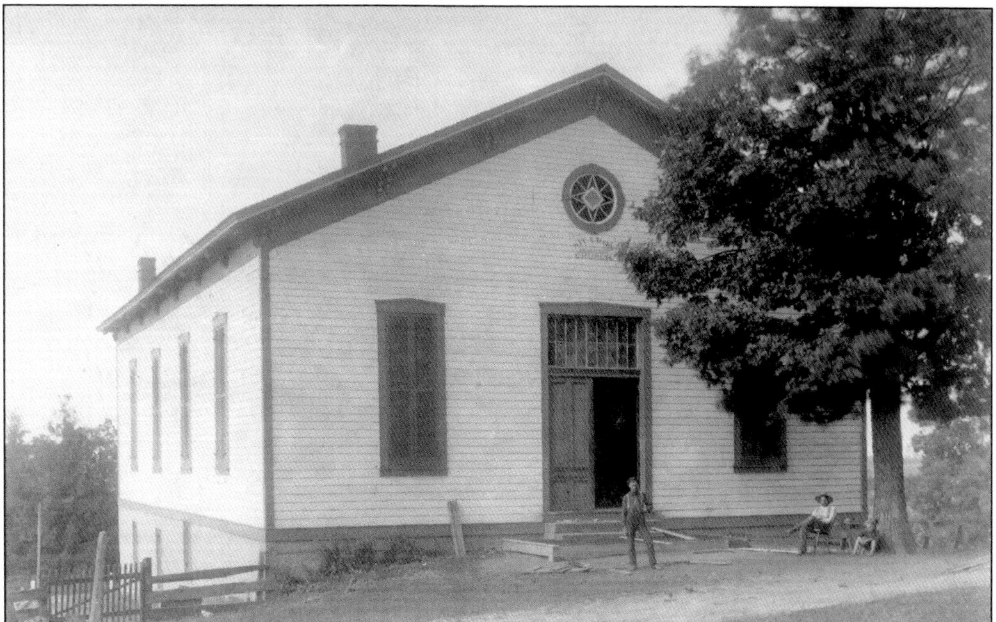

Andrew McDonald was the first pastor of Sharon Presbyterian Church, the first and oldest church in Moon Township. The church's roots can be traced back to 1817, when the Flaugherty Run Mission was first organized under McDonald. However, the church did not have a permanent home at that time, and members would meet in each other's homes for worship services.

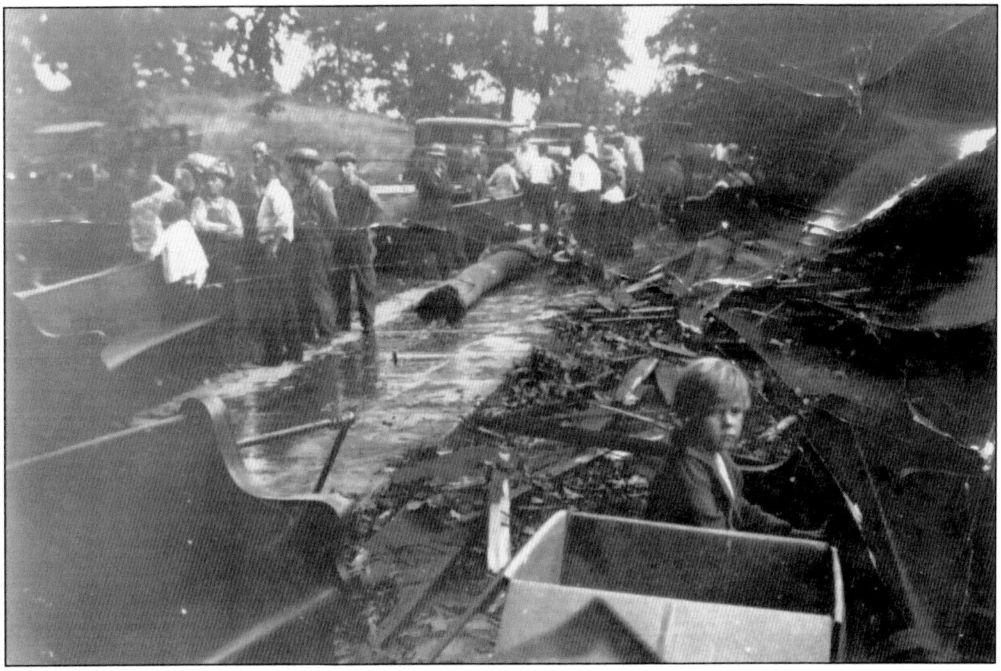

On July 12, 1929, a tornado ripped the roof off the Sharon Presbyterian Church, not even two full weeks after its June 30 centennial. The roof was thrown into the graveyard that sits beside the church. Immediately prior to the centennial, the church underwent two full months of repairs and decorating, during which $2,000 was spent. (Courtesy Nancy Mills.)

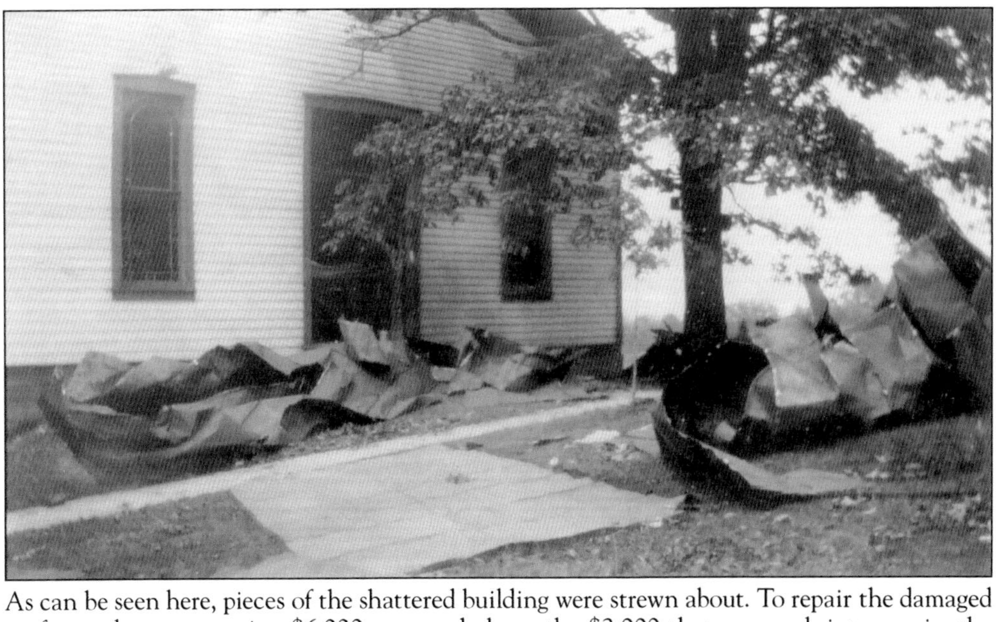

As can be seen here, pieces of the shattered building were strewn about. To repair the damaged roof cost the congregation $6,000 over and above the $2,000 that was sunk into repairs the weeks before. It reopened on Sunday, October 27, at 2:30 p.m. (Courtesy Sharon Community Presbyterian Church.)

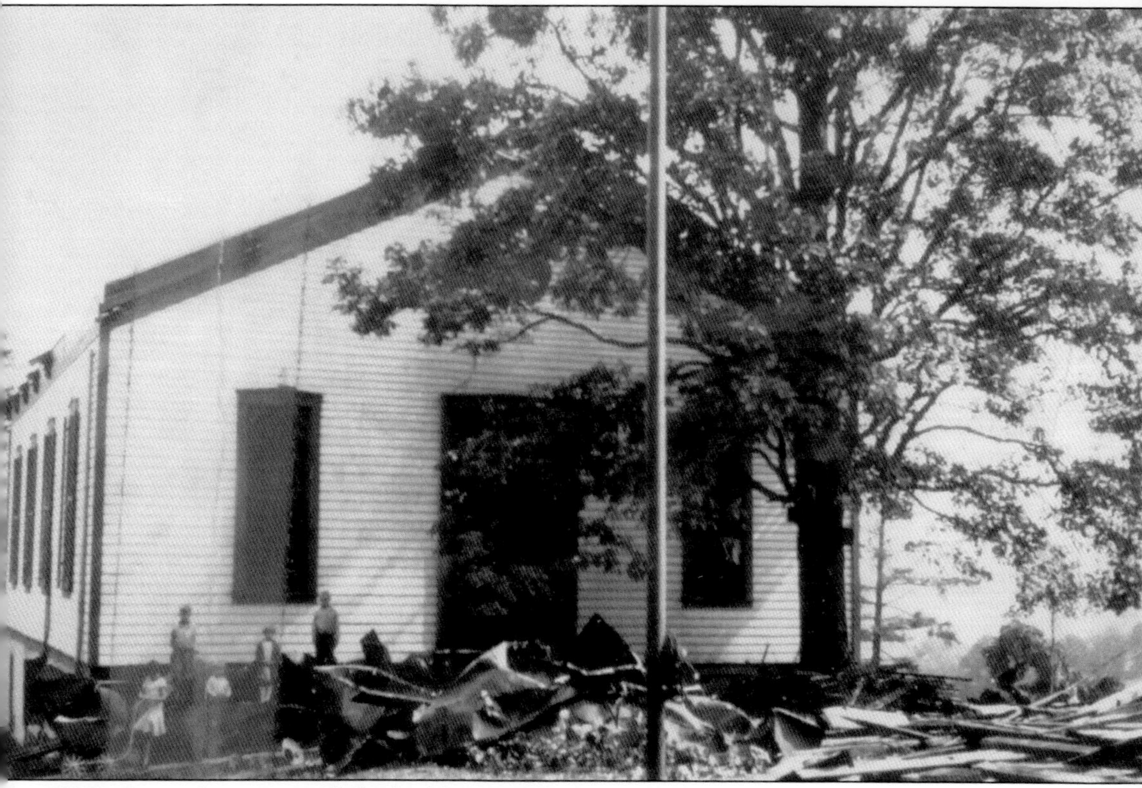

While the roof was torn off the building and the interior of the church was damaged by the torrential rains that accompanied the 1929 tornado, the remaining structure of the church was still intact and secure. Once the word got out, church historical records state that donations for rebuilding the church were abundant and came in from across the state and from neighboring states as well. (Courtesy Sharon Community Presbyterian Church.)

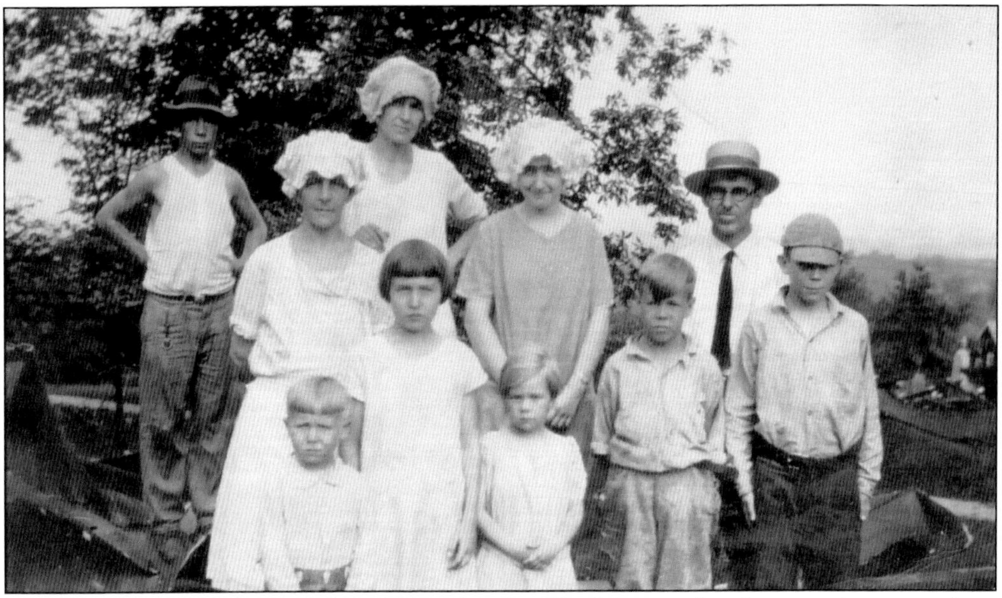

Shown here are members of the Meanor family. The Meanors lived across the street from Sharon Presbyterian Church and have been members of the congregation. This photograph was taken after the July 12, 1929, tornado that ravaged the church. The Meanors were just some of the congregants who rolled their sleeves up and helped rebuild their place of worship. (Courtesy the Meanor family.)

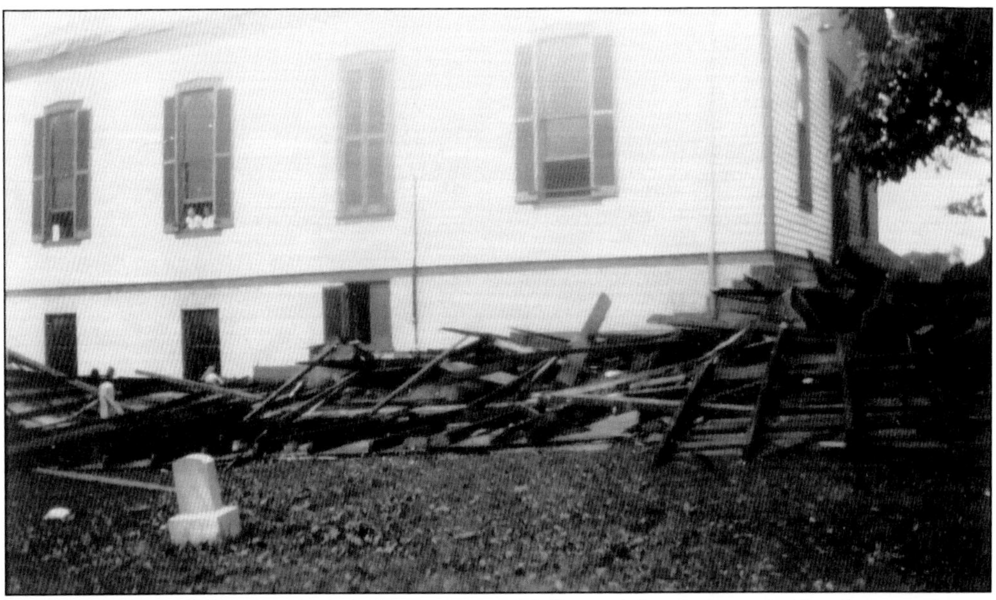

Reconstruction of the church, aided by groups of dedicated families much like the one shown here, took more than three months. A consecration and reopening ceremony took place on October 27 of that same year, and the church took on the task of moving forward once again. (Courtesy Sharon Community Presbyterian Church.)

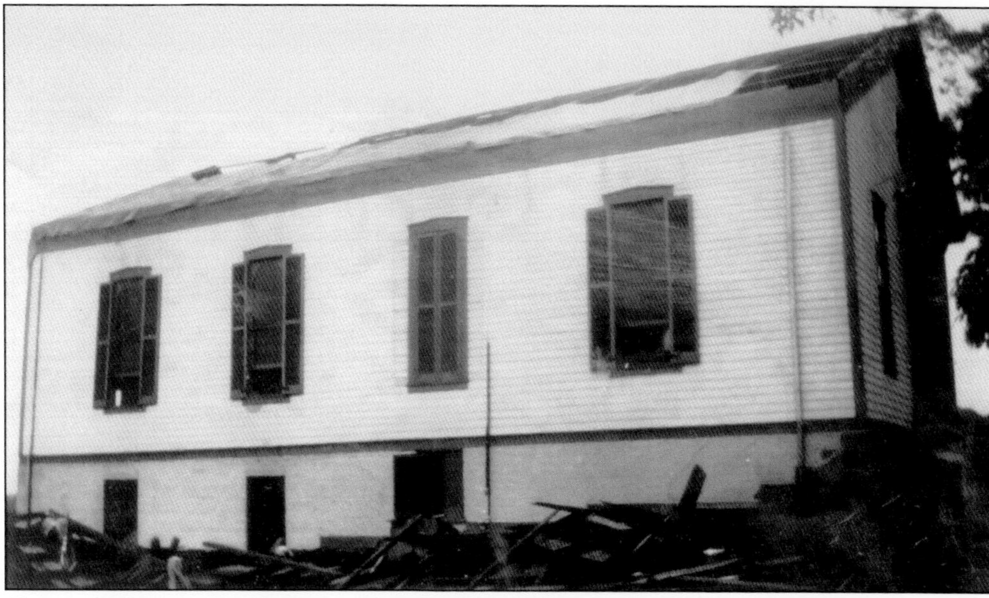

Sharon Community Presbyterian Church would remain in this renovated and restored building for nearly 30 more years, until the pace of development around them and the growth in Moon's population warranted the building of a new facility on the site. From 1920 to 1930, the township grew from 1,700 to 2,900 people. It grew by another 833 people by 1940. (Courtesy Sharon Community Presbyterian Church.)

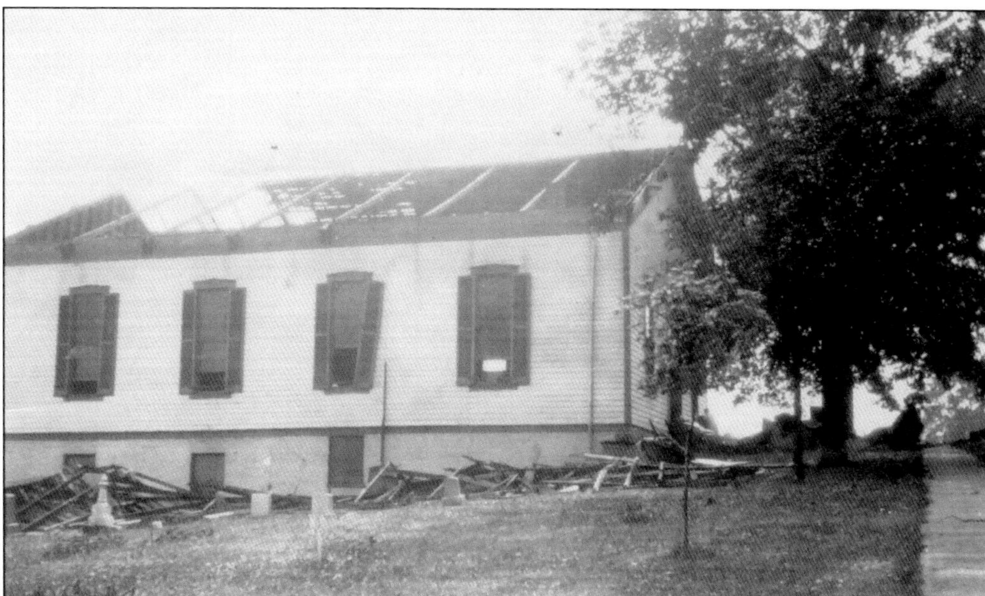

The Reverend L. O. Smith saw the church through the disastrous year of 1929 and served as pastor until 1932. After his departure, the Reverend J. M. Briceland stood at the helm of Sharon Community Presbyterian Church until 1938. Rev. Harry Preston Walrond succeeded Briceland and served the church until the end of 1942. (Courtesy Sharon Community Presbyterian Church.)

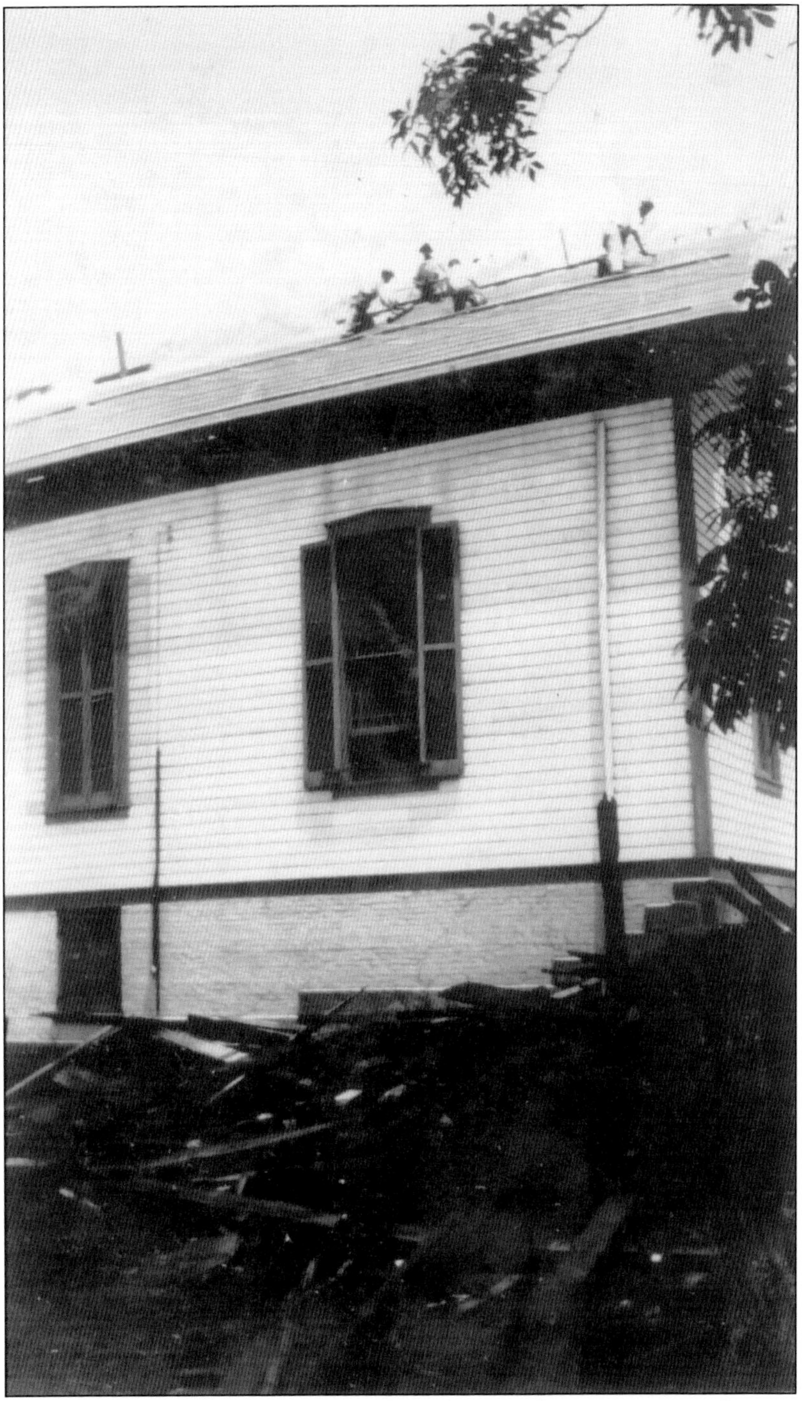

Sharon Community Presbyterian Church celebrated its 125th anniversary on June 9–14, 1942. The event was celebrated throughout the Pittsburgh Presbytery as nearby churches celebrated in the church's honor. While it was an eventful century and a quarter for the church, its growth and development really took off after World War II, when Moon's population nearly doubled. (Courtesy Sharon Community Presbyterian Church.)

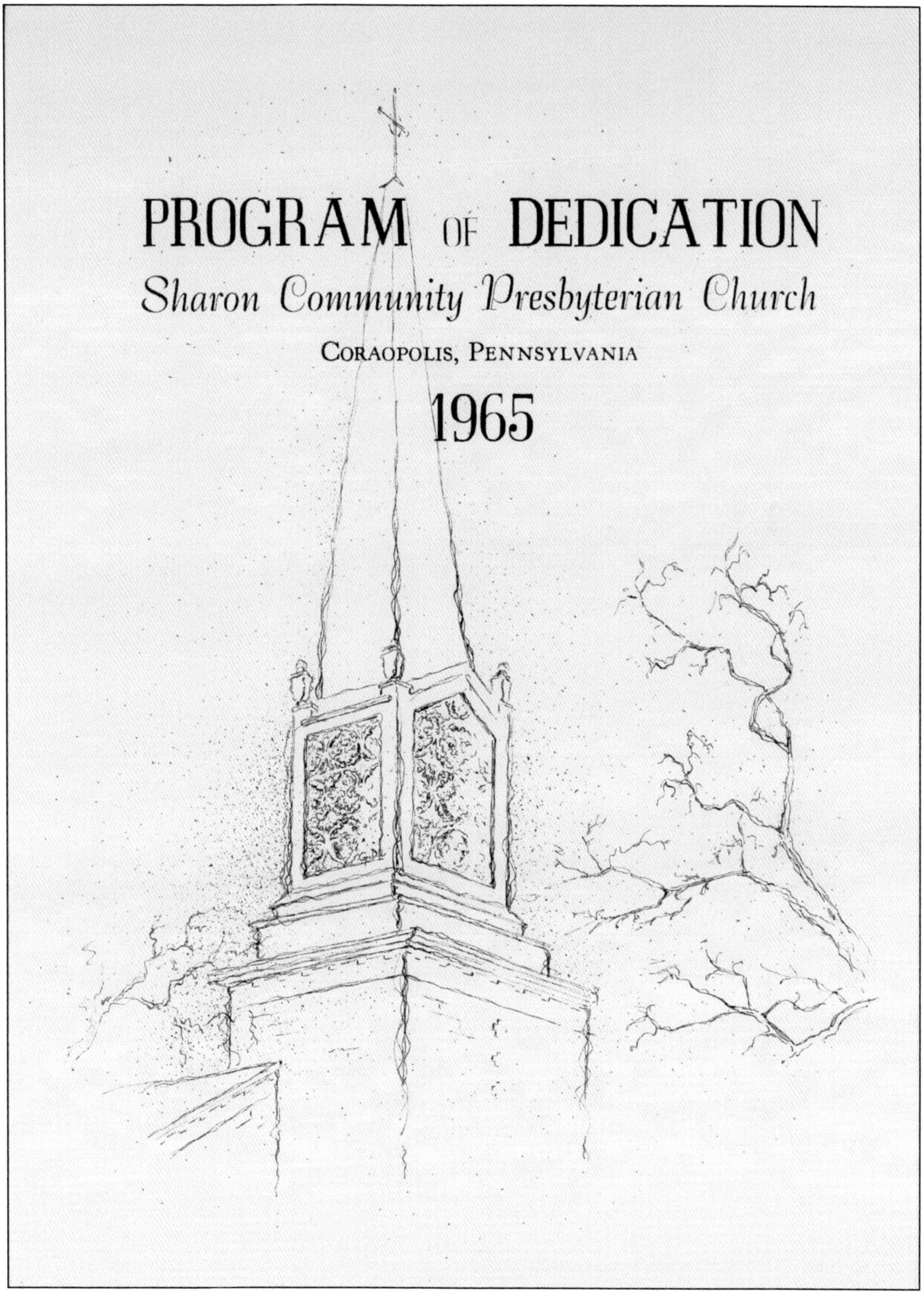

Sharon Presbyterian church borrowed $19,000 in 1950 for a repair and conversion project on the church's manse. The old manse would become a parish house and a new manse was to be constructed with the funds. By 1956, Sharon Community Presbyterian Church was bursting at the seams and the congregation began looking at plans to develop a larger church. (Courtesy Sharon Community Presbyterian Church.)

St. Philip's Episcopal Church

Moon Township, Pennsylvania

Dedication of New Church Building

November 2, 1969

4:00 P. M.

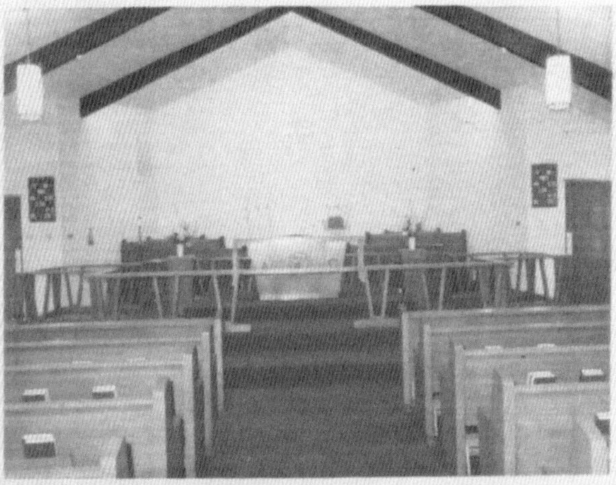

The Right Reverend Robert B. Appleyard
Bishop of Pittsburgh

The Right Reverend William S. Thomas
Suffragan Bishop of Pittsburgh

The Reverend Ewart G. Rowland Jr.
Vicar

During the 1940s, Sharon Community Presbyterian Church was the only church in Moon Township. For that reason, the church received graves from the cemetery of the Old Bell Farm Church, which was razed to make way for the Greater Pittsburgh International Airport. Churches, including St. Philip's Episcopal, did not come along until much later in Moon's history. St. Philip's was dedicated on November 2, 1969, at 4:00 p.m. with Rev. Ewart G. Rowland Jr. officiating as vicar. (Courtesy Nancy Mills.)

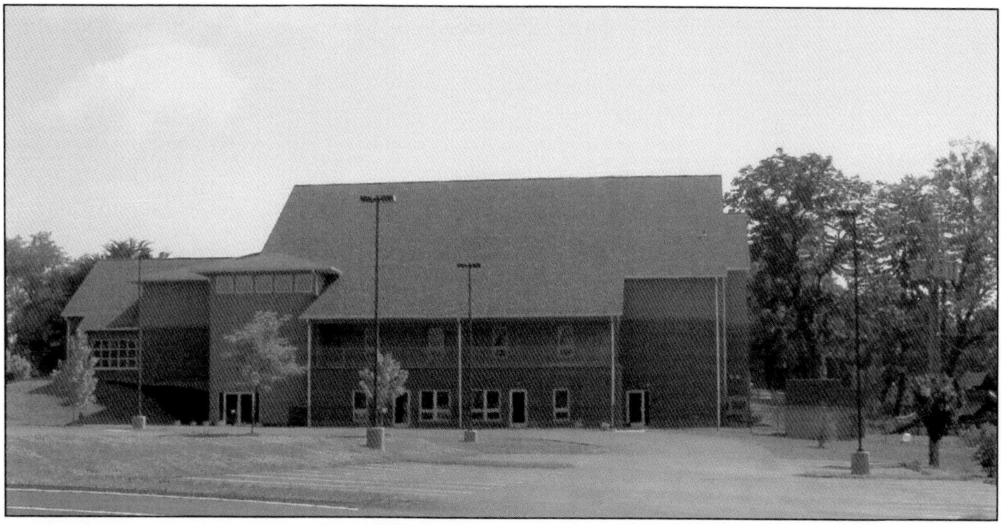

At the dedication ceremony of St. Philip's Episcopal Church, every item in the church from the alter to the pews was blessed by Right Rev. Robert B. Appleyard, bishop of Pittsburgh. St. Philip's stands along Beaver Grade Road, across the street from Cherrington Office Park. (Photograph by Mark Berton.)

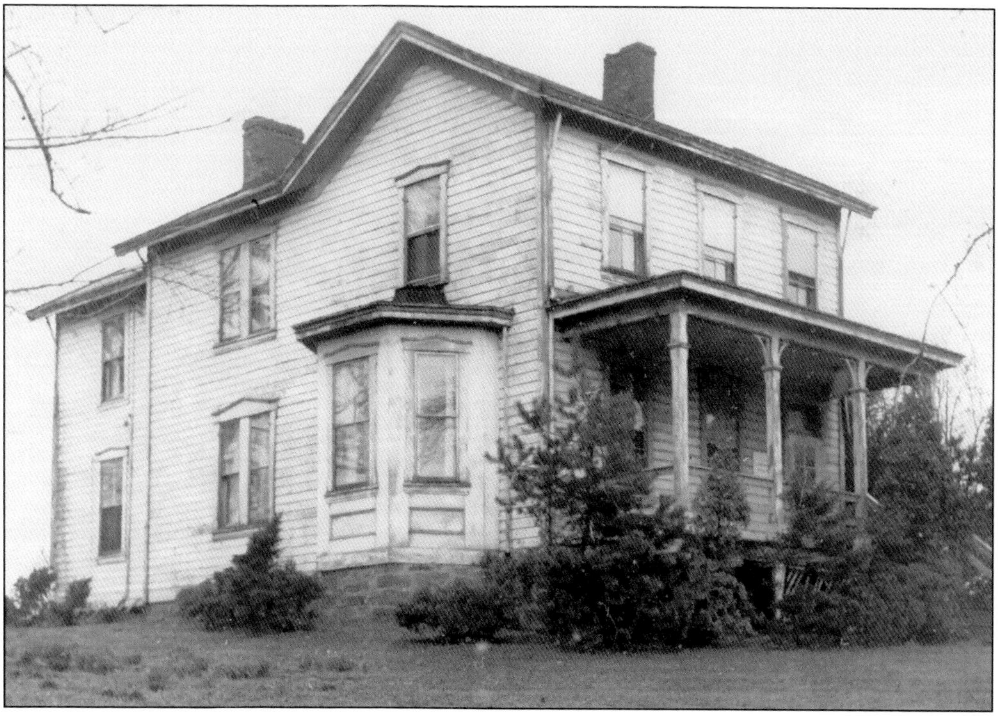

Prior to 1817, members of Sharon Presbyterian Church met in parishioners' homes before purchasing a tent for outdoor services. By 1879, Rev. S. C. Jennings, who helped the congregation ease into its new church in 1829, had more than 5,000 sermons under his belt, 321 marriages, and 769 baptisms. This was the church's parsonage during that time. (Courtesy Sharon Community Presbyterian Church.)

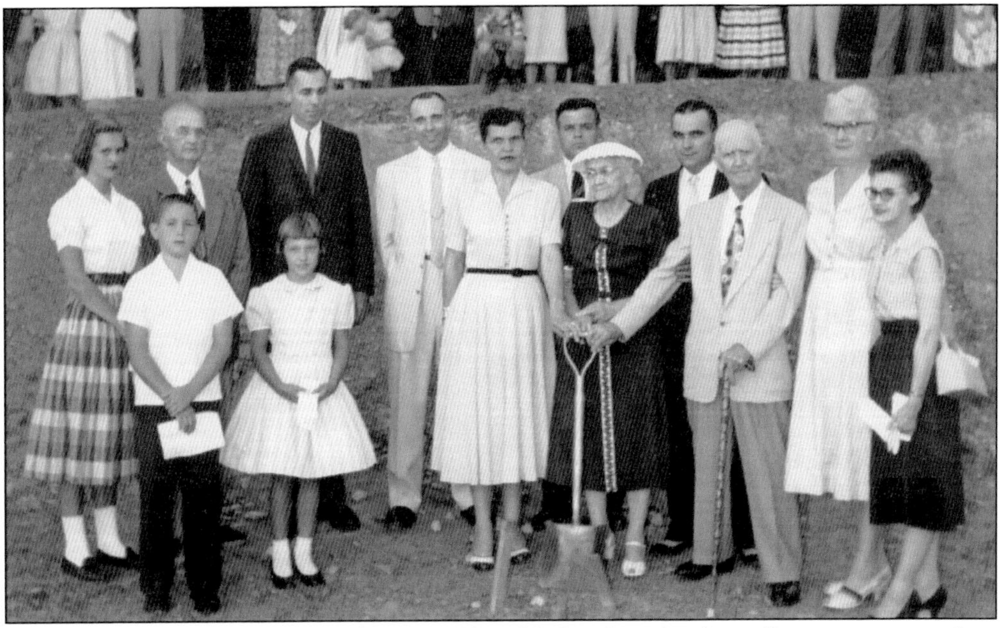

By 1957, Sharon Community Presbyterian Church's Sunday school enrollment was more than the church could handle. It was decided that the church would take on a $100,000 Christian education building project. The architect for the project was Glenn Bickerstaff. The church broke ground on August 5, 1958. At this time the entire annual church budget was just $20,000. (Courtesy Sharon Community Presbyterian Church.)

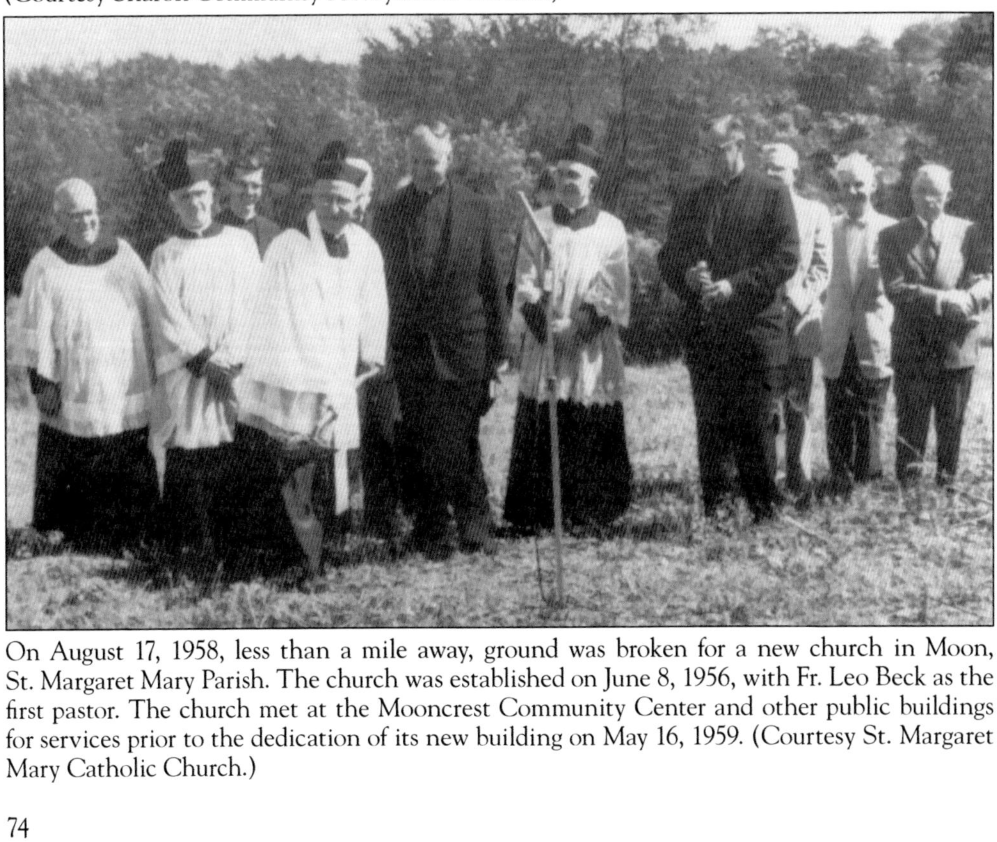

On August 17, 1958, less than a mile away, ground was broken for a new church in Moon, St. Margaret Mary Parish. The church was established on June 8, 1956, with Fr. Leo Beck as the first pastor. The church met at the Mooncrest Community Center and other public buildings for services prior to the dedication of its new building on May 16, 1959. (Courtesy St. Margaret Mary Catholic Church.)

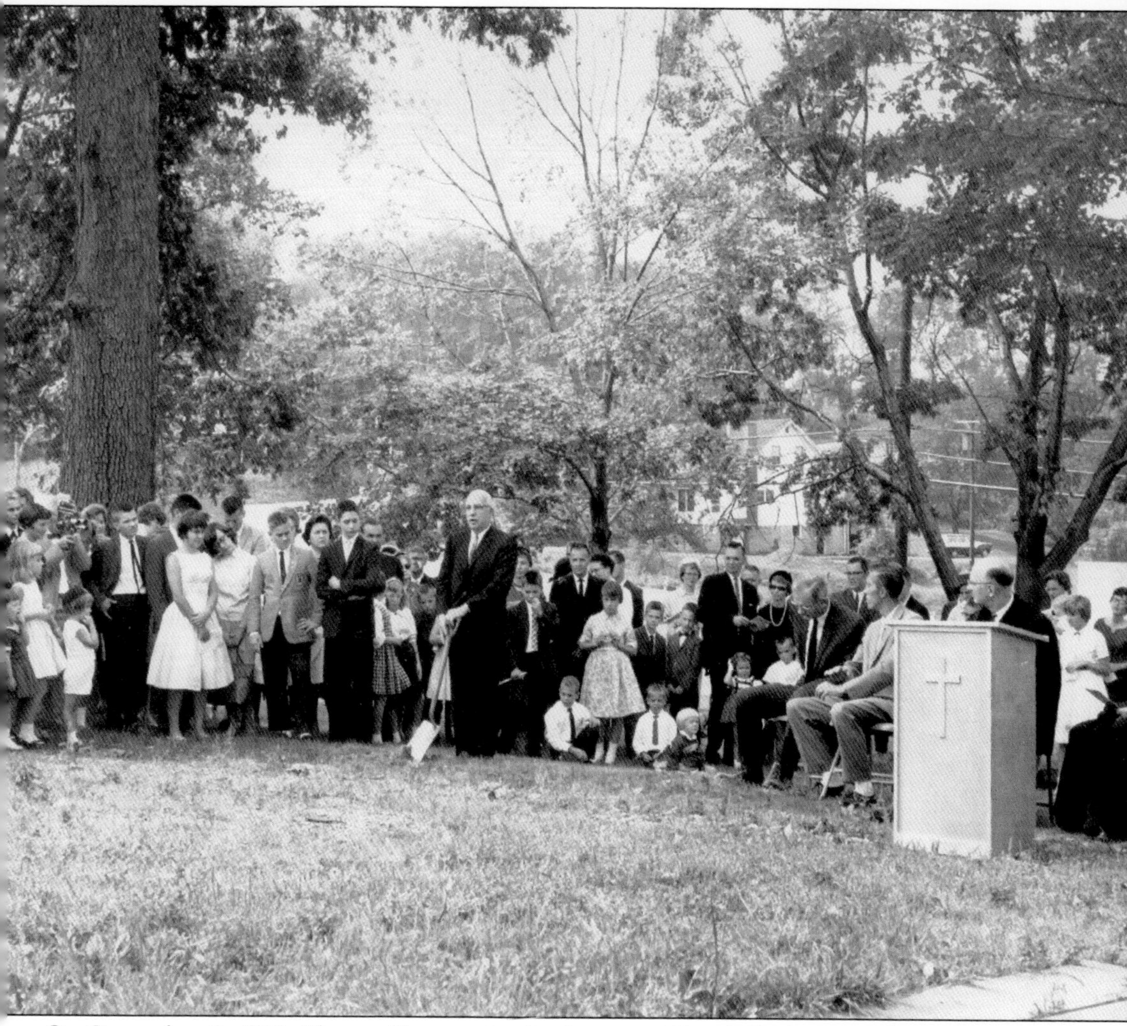

On September 8, 1963, Sharon Community Presbyterian Church broke ground again. This time, the congregation authorized the building of a new sanctuary and fellowship hall. The cornerstone was set on October 18, 1964, and the church was dedicated on April 25 and May 2, 1965. The congregation at the time was 1,226 members. (Courtesy Sharon Community Presbyterian Church.)

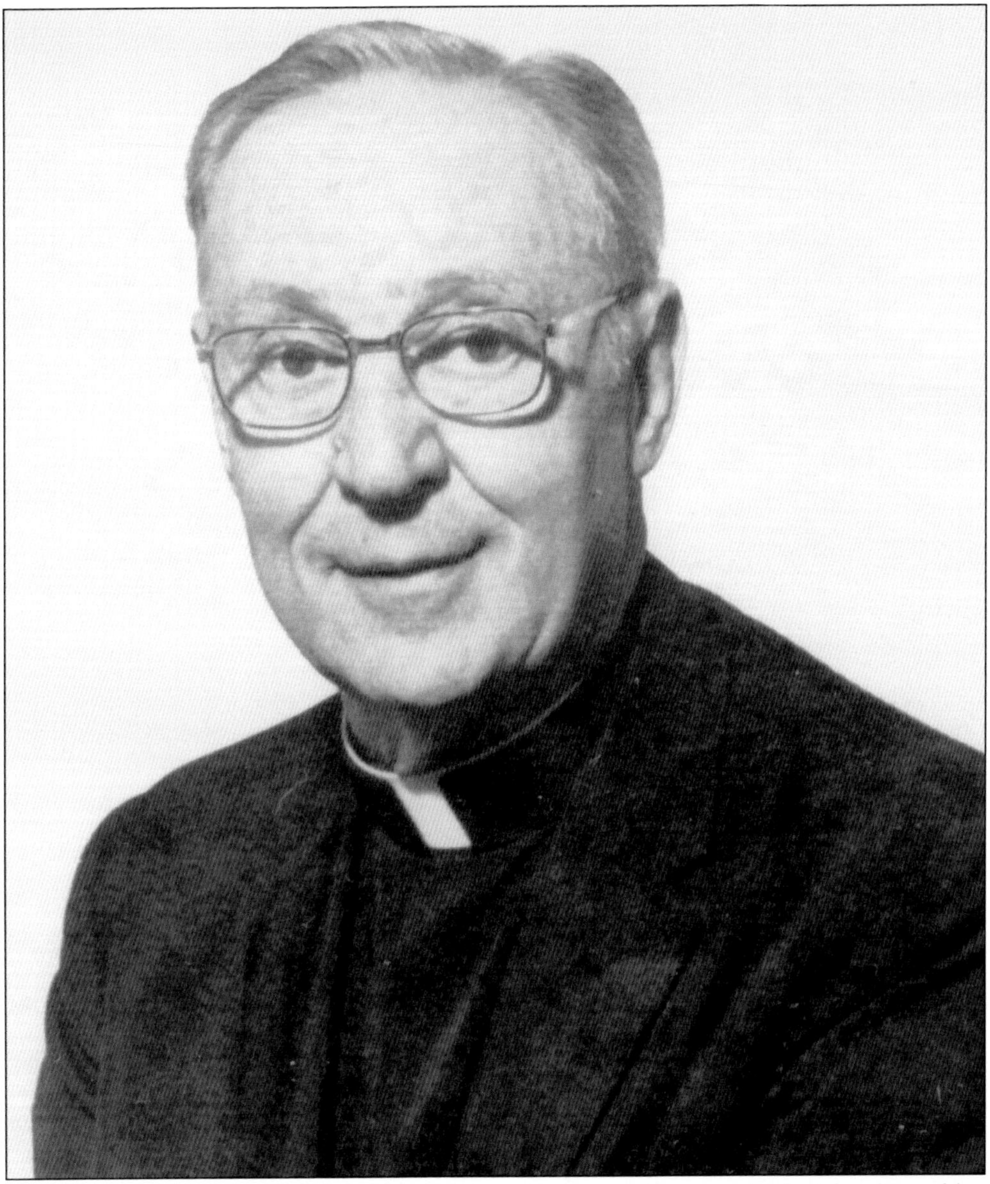

The first installed pastor of St. Margaret Mary Parish was Rev. Leo Beck. The date of his installation was June 8, 1956. However, the fledgling church did not have an official worship place, so the congregation met at the Mooncrest Administration Building for mass. The makeshift worship site was not new to the congregation, which had been meeting in a roller-skating rink while it waited for official recognition from the diocese. (Courtesy St. Margaret Mary Parish.)

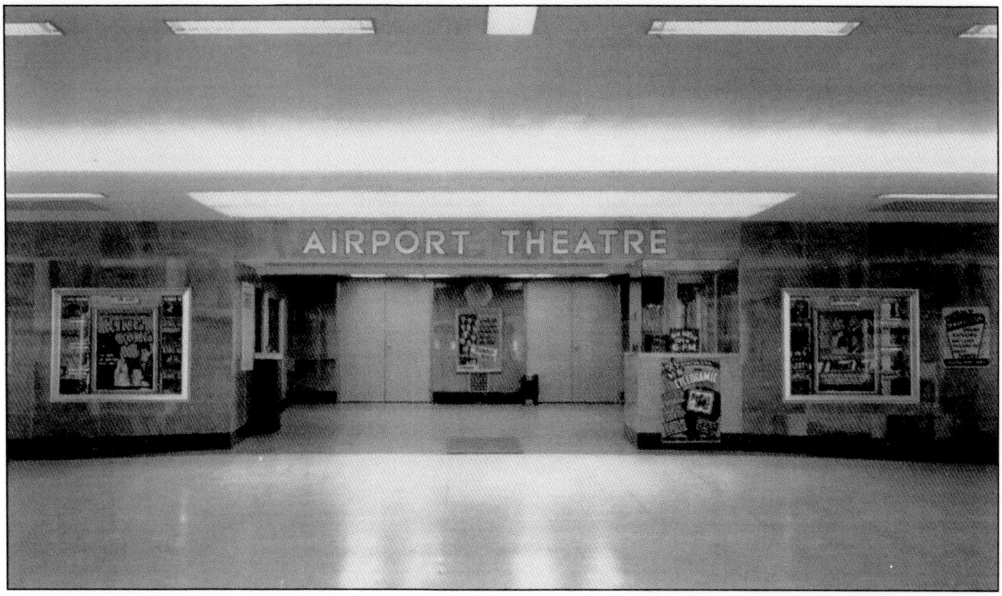

Even though the Diocese of Pittsburgh purchased the property St. Margaret Mary Parish occupies now on January 9, 1956, the groundbreaking for the new church was not until August 17, 1958. Up until the church opened its doors on May 16, 1959, parishioners met in various locations for mass, including the Greater Pittsburgh International Airport's movie theater. They also worshipped at the Mooncrest Administration Building and the Mooncrest Community Center. (Courtesy St. Margaret Mary Parish.)

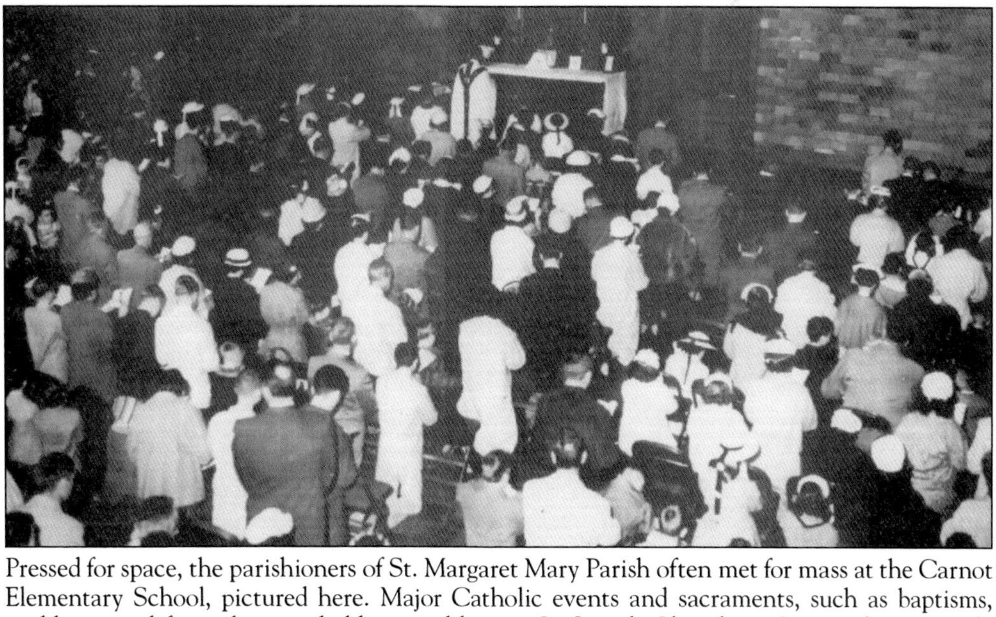

Pressed for space, the parishioners of St. Margaret Mary Parish often met for mass at the Carnot Elementary School, pictured here. Major Catholic events and sacraments, such as baptisms, weddings, and funerals, were held at neighboring St. Joseph Church in Coraopolis. An early census of Catholic families in the church's territory numbered more than 337 families. (Courtesy St. Margaret Mary Parish.)

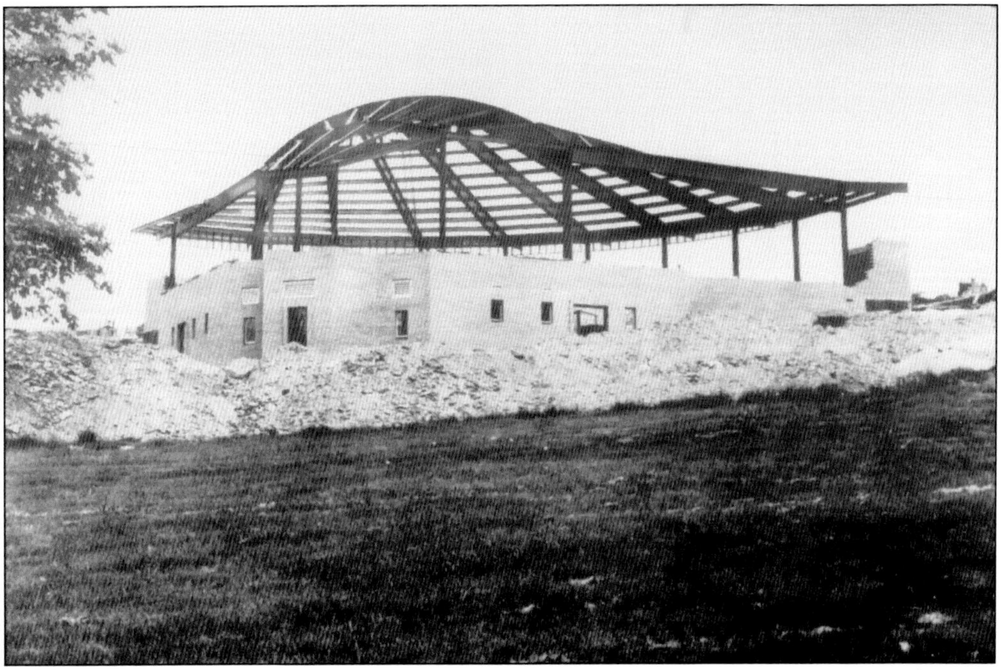

St. Margaret Mary Parish is located along Beaver Grade and Sharon Roads at the crest of a small hill. The first church built in 1959 was always referred to as the "temporary church." St. Margaret Mary's, as it is known today, was not conceived of until 1969, when architect Francis O'Connor Church designed the new church "in the round." (Courtesy St. Margaret Mary Parish.)

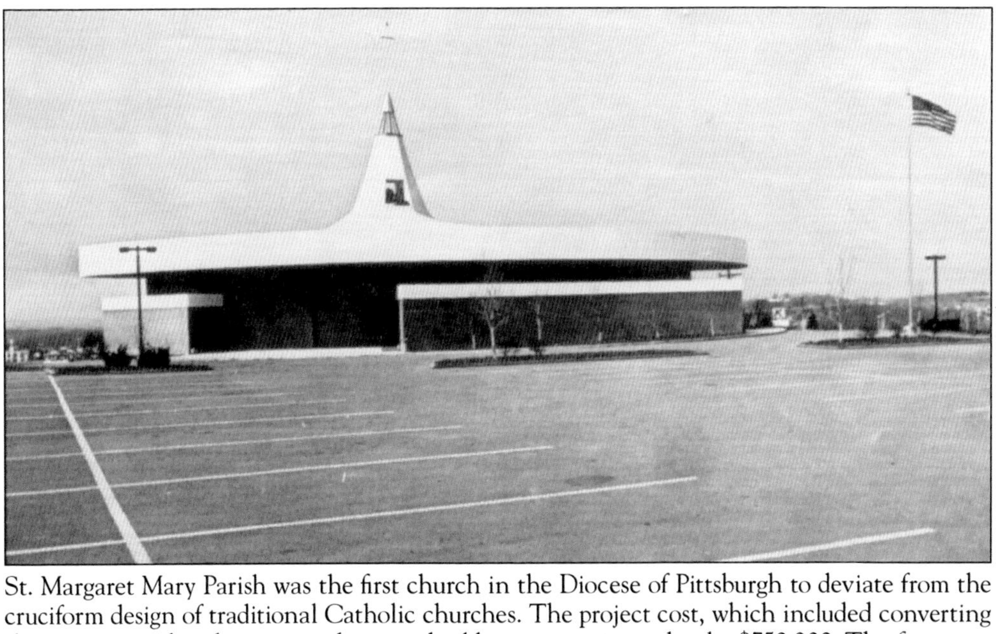

St. Margaret Mary Parish was the first church in the Diocese of Pittsburgh to deviate from the cruciform design of traditional Catholic churches. The project cost, which included converting the temporary church into an education building, was estimated to be $750,000. The first mass was held in the new building on May 1, 1972. The building was dedicated later that year on August 27 by Bishop Vincent Leonard. (Courtesy St. Margaret Mary Parish.)

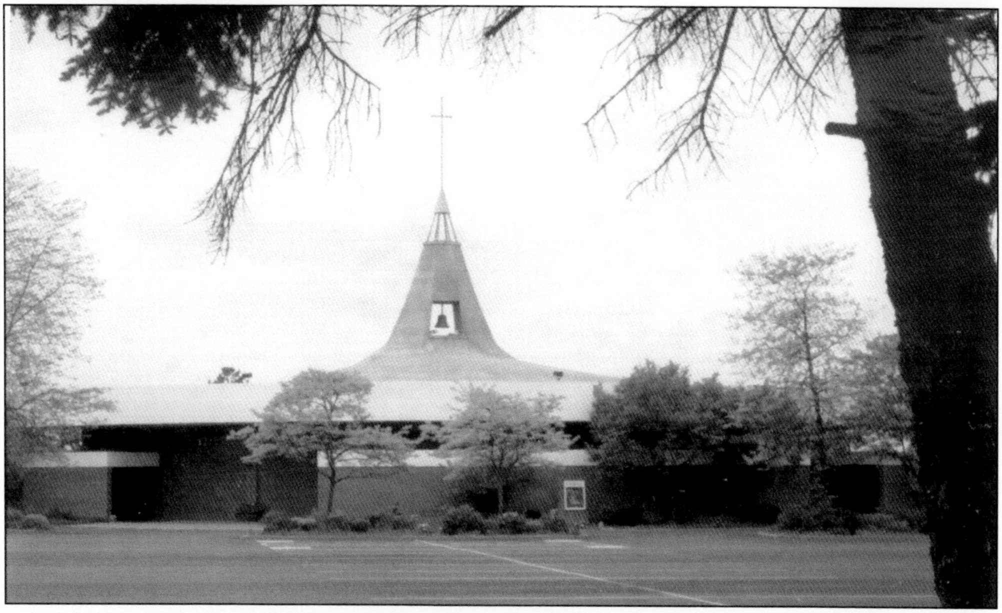

After the landscaping, St. Margaret Mary Parish blended in naturally with its surroundings. Father Beck was transferred to another parish in 1967. His replacement, Rev. John Dompka, inherited the congregation and $65,000 of church debt. Dompka mounted a campaign to eliminate that debt altogether. He succeeded in his efforts before the year's end, and on December 10, 1967, the church held a mortgage-burning ceremony. (Courtesy St. Margaret Mary Parish.)

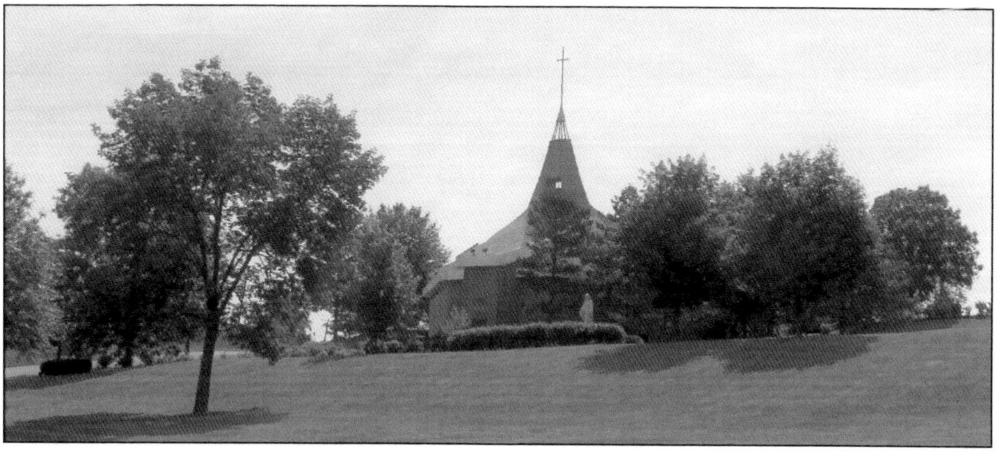

Today Rev. John Ayoob is the officiating pastor of St. Margaret Mary Parish. Ayoob was installed in 1995 by Bishop Donald Wuerl. Ayoob oversaw a church renovation project in 2004. Today St. Margaret Mary Parish serves more than 1,800 families. More than 700 students attend religious education programs at the church. (Photograph by Mark Berton.)

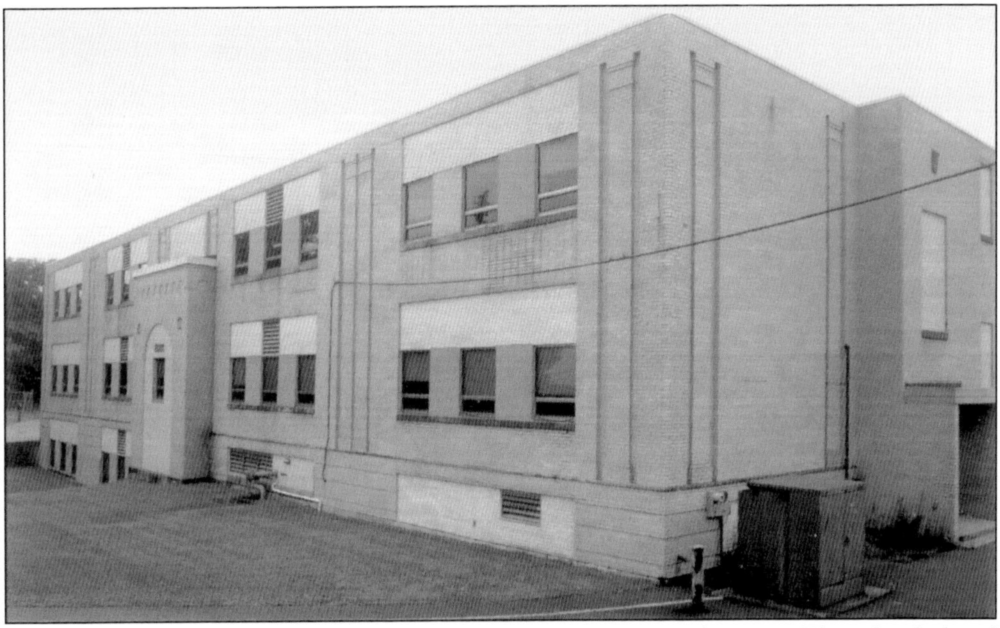

Carnot School has been host to a number of different uses over the years. The school played an integral role in the development of St. Margaret Mary Church, which used the building for weekend mass and CCD classes. More recently, the building was used as a U.S. Airways training facility. The school district closed the school while plans for a new building project are up in the air. (Courtesy St. Margaret Mary Parish.)

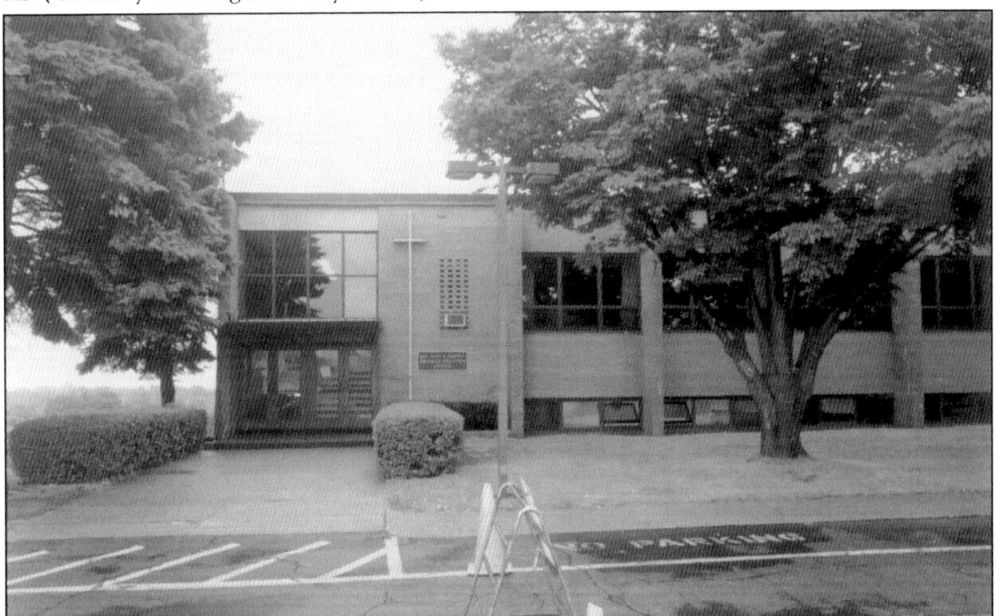

Today CCD classes and other education functions of St. Margaret Mary are held in the original "temporary church" of St. Margaret Mary Parish. This church was converted to educational use in 1972, and its official name became the Dompka Education Center after Rev. John Dompka. It houses 12 classrooms. (Courtesy St. Margaret Mary Parish.)

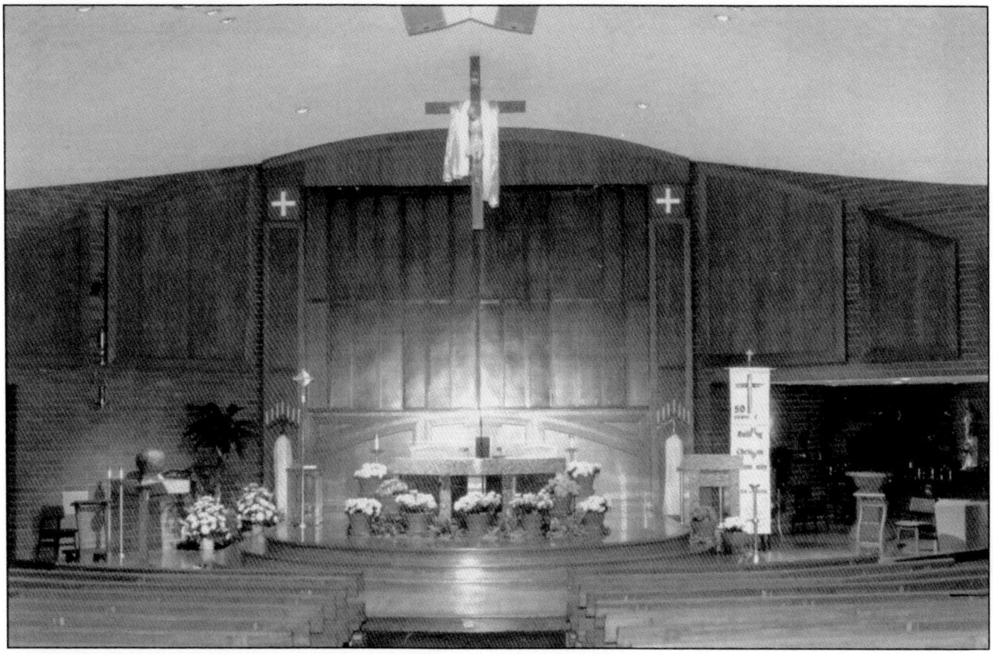

Renovations to the church in 2004–2005 completely altered the look of the church's interior. What was once a modest brick pulpit and tabernacle was replaced with granite. Hardwood floors and wall baffles were installed, as was a large, wall-size projection screen. New carpeting was laid throughout the building, and the entire internal layout of the altar was reconfigured. (Courtesy St. Margaret Mary Parish.)

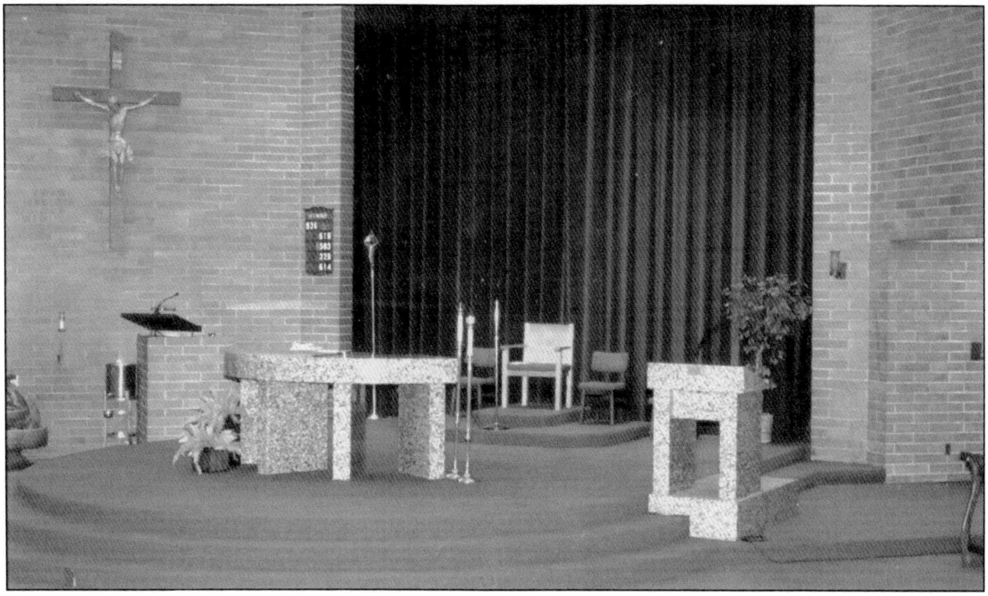

This view of the St. Margaret Mary Parish alter is what parishioners saw before the renovations. The viewing screen is concealed by the full-length red curtain. New granite pieces were installed and elevated the grandeur of the church. Today St. Margaret Mary Parish employs a finance director and a receptionist to help aid in the church's day-to-day business. (Courtesy St. Margaret Mary Parish.)

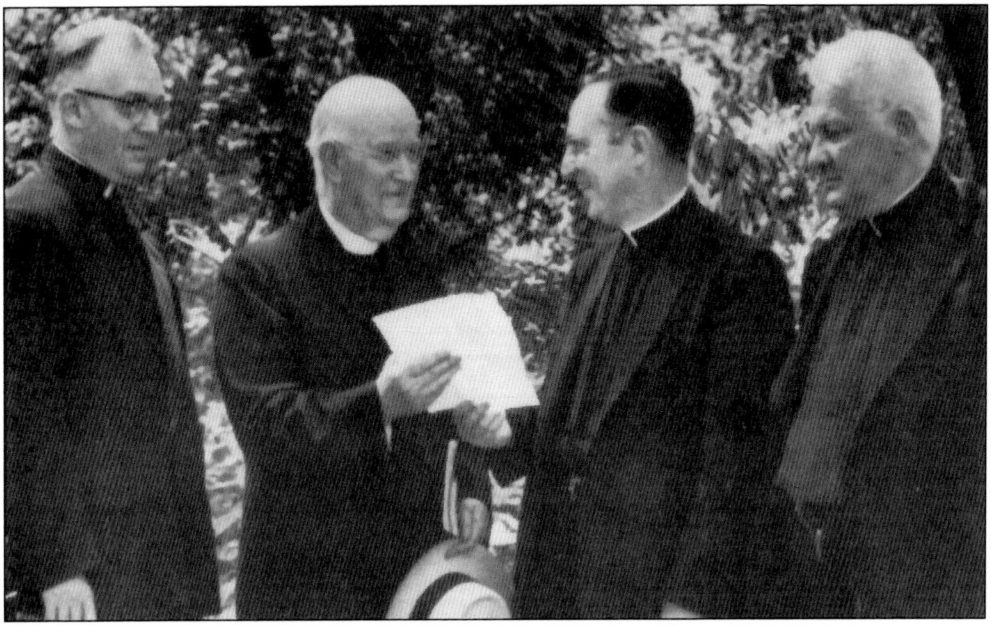

Pictured here celebrating the presentation of the canonical proclamation of St. Margaret Mary Parish, from left to right, are Rev. Robert Murphy, Rev. Philip Moore, Rev. Leo Beck, and Rev. Thomas Lappan. Murphy represented St. Joseph Parish in Coraopolis, Moore represented St. Francis Parish in McKees Rocks, and Lappan represented St. Athanasius Parish in West View. (Courtesy Nancy Mills.)

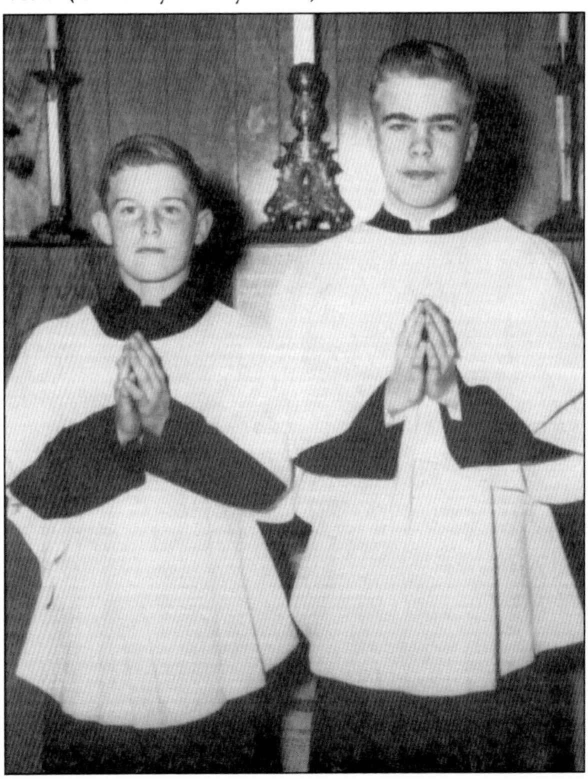

Thomas Babilon, left, and Robert Babilon, right, were the first altar boys of St. Margaret Mary Parish. Educating the youth of Moon Township has always been a focus of St. Margaret Mary Parish. Long before Moon School District had kindergarten classes, a kindergarten class was set up by Madeline Chesky and Catherine Talarico in 1962. (Courtesy Nancy Mills.)

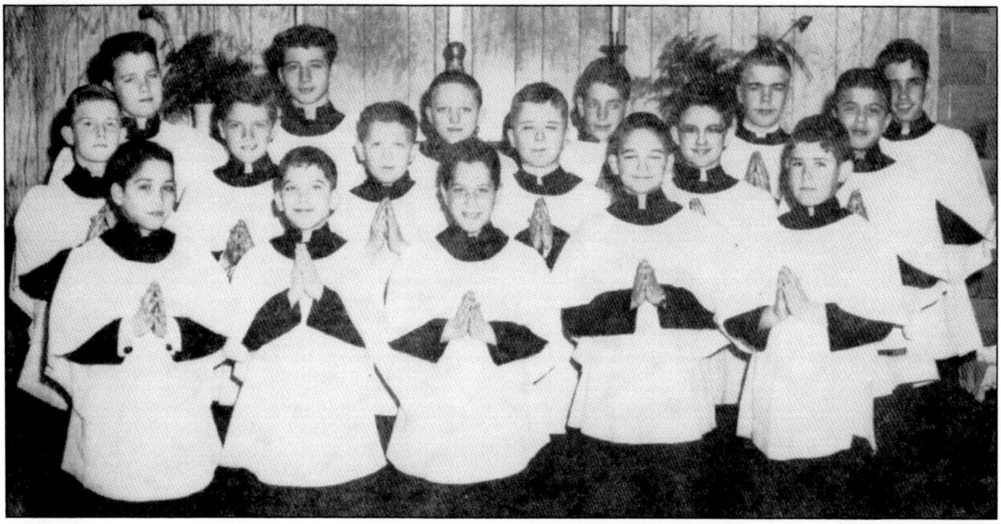

This photograph shows the altar boys of St. Margaret Mary Parish. Shown the year before his arrival are (first row) Paul Rao, Paul Talarico, Kenneth Billetdeaux, and Timothy Tomkovich; (second row) Thomas Babilon, Ronald Ladesic, Ralph Mashuda, Robert Mitsch, Brad Billetdeaux, and Richard Audia; (third row) Paul Raley, George Desko, Richard Cavallo, Robert Grice, Robert Babilon, and David Martin. (Courtesy Nancy Mills.)

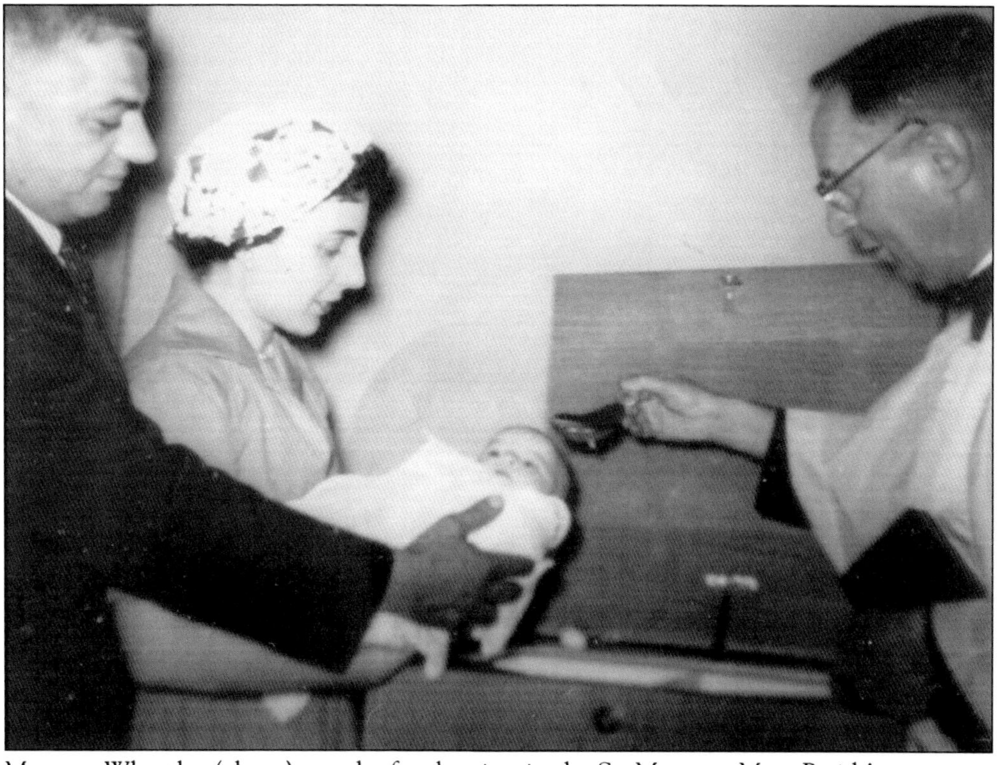

Maureen Wheatley (above) was the first baptism in the St. Margaret Mary Parish's temporary church. Her first sacrament took place on May 17, 1959, and was administered by Rev. Leo Beck. William Edward Allison was the first baptism to take place in St. Margaret Mary Parish's new building. His sacrament took place on July 8, 1956. (Courtesy St. Margaret Mary Parish.)

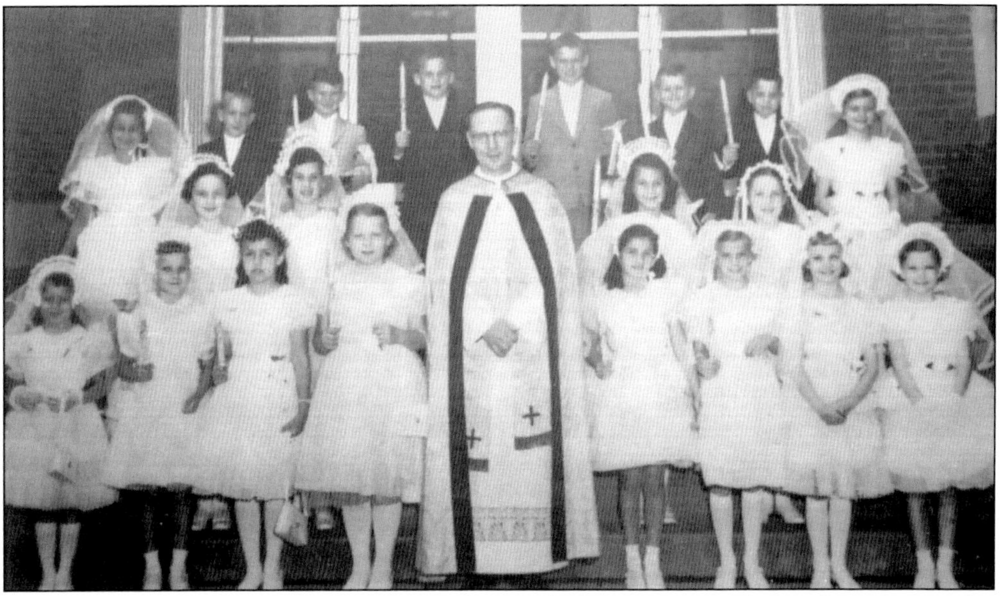

Despite the fact that this first communion class took place at St. Joseph Parish in Coraopolis, this communion class is the very first to take the sacrament for St. Margaret Mary Parish. The temporary church had not yet been completed by the time this class was ready to take its first communion. Rev. Leo Beck is pictured in the center. (Courtesy St. Margaret Mary Parish.)

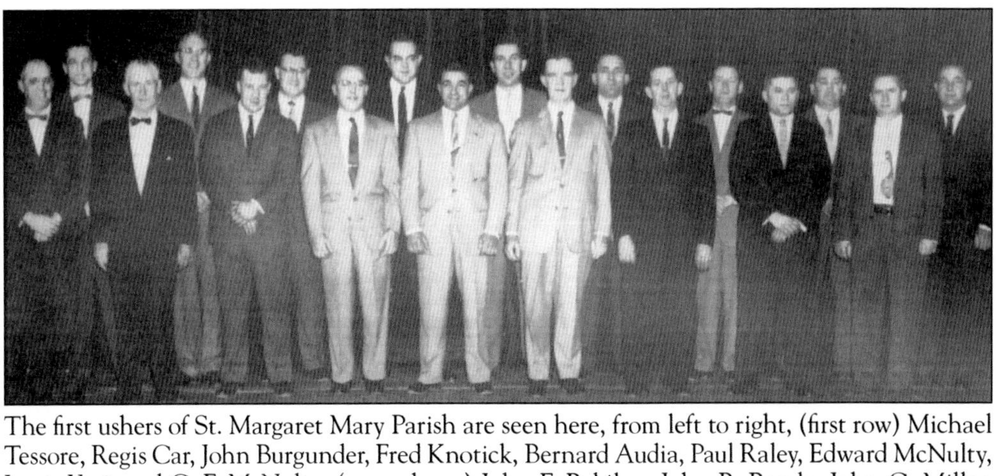

The first ushers of St. Margaret Mary Parish are seen here, from left to right, (first row) Michael Tessore, Regis Car, John Burgunder, Fred Knotick, Bernard Audia, Paul Raley, Edward McNulty, Louis Yusi, and C. F. McNulty; (second row) John F. Babilon, John B. Berola, John G. Miller, James P. Raugh, Jerry Frissora, Joseph Keppel, Stanley Kruk, George Niederriter, and James A. McArdle. (Courtesy St. Margaret Mary Parish.)

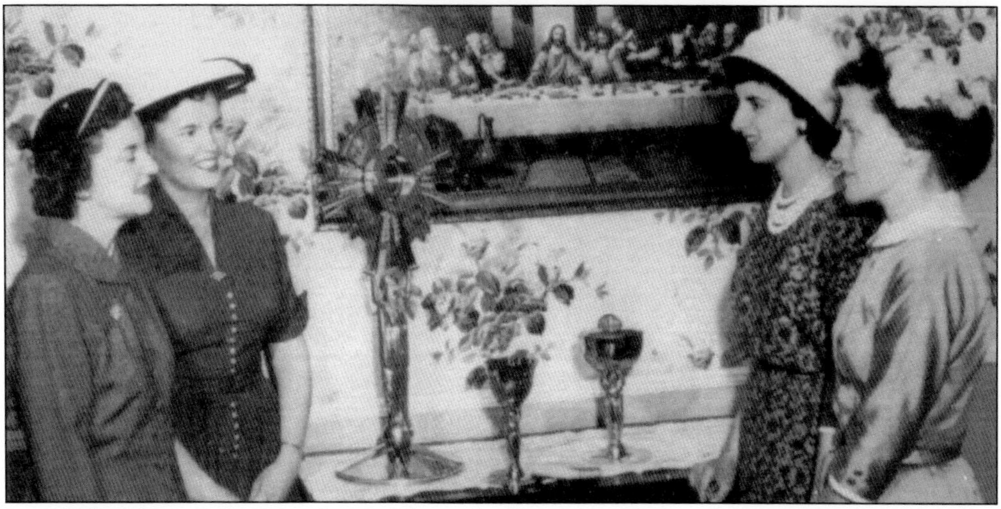

Rose Billetdeaux, Daisy Mitsch, Madeline Chesky, and Catherine Talarico (from left to right) were the officers of the Catholic Society of Moon Township, later known as the St. Margaret Mary Guild. The society tirelessly raised the funds necessary to keep the fledgling parish activities moving forward. The women also funded the cost of renting classrooms and parish Christmas parties. (Courtesy St. Margaret Mary Parish.)

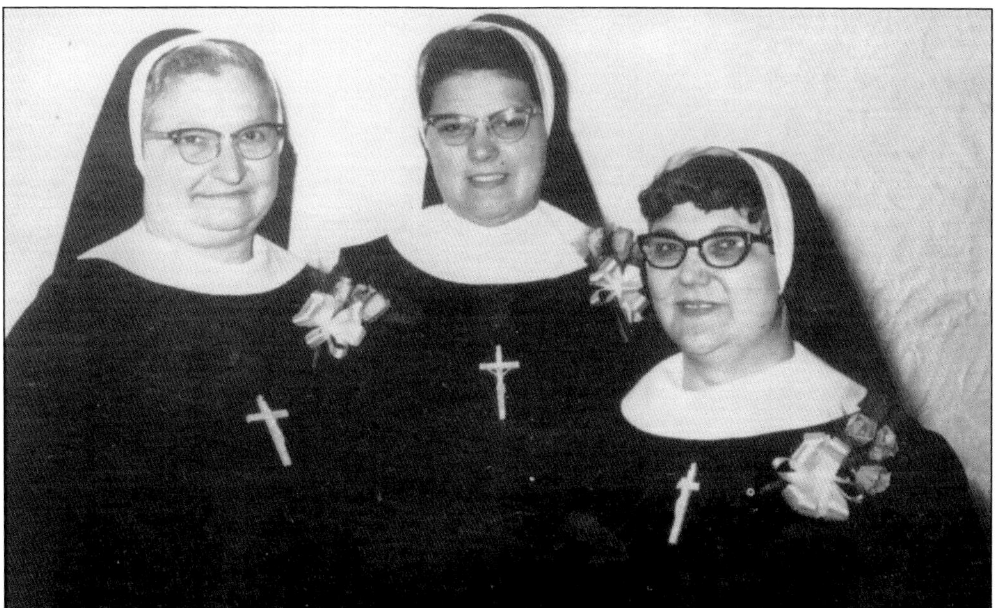

Sisters Mary Electa, Roseann, and Mary Mildred Moroz (from left to right) were Felician sisters and teachers at St. Margaret Mary Parish. The parish taught more than 1,000 students each year. The Felician sisters were based in neighboring Coraopolis. They commuted to the church in a 1968 Ford Falcon provided by St. Margaret Mary Parish. (Courtesy St. Margaret Mary Parish.)

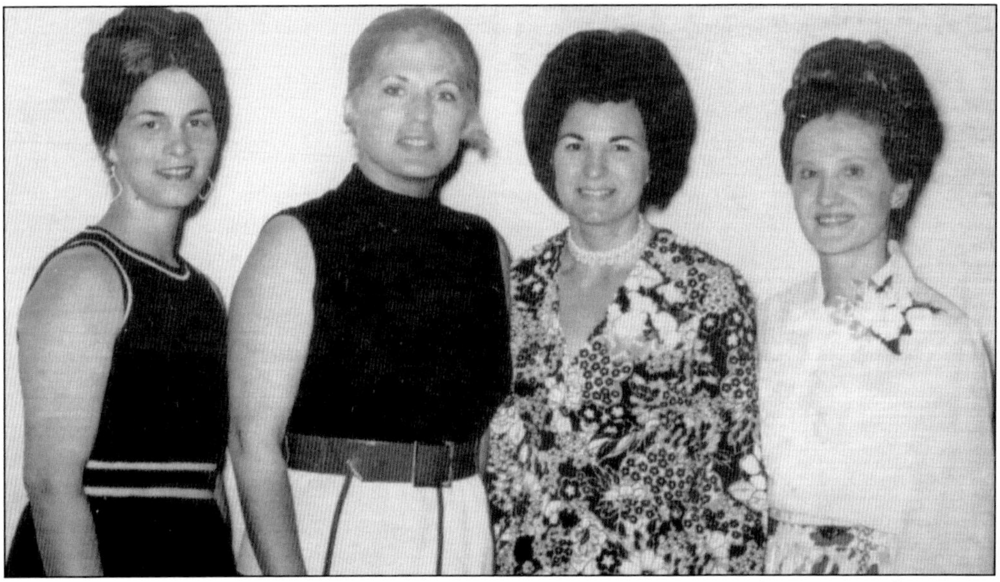

From left to right, Jackie Compston, Mitzi Downs, Marie Morgan, and Marion Nelson were officers of the Christian Mothers and Guild, formerly the Catholic Society of Moon Township. The group had more than 80 members and played an integral role in the growth of the church. These women served terms in 1972–1973 when the new St. Margaret Mary Church came on line. (Courtesy St. Margaret Mary Parish.)

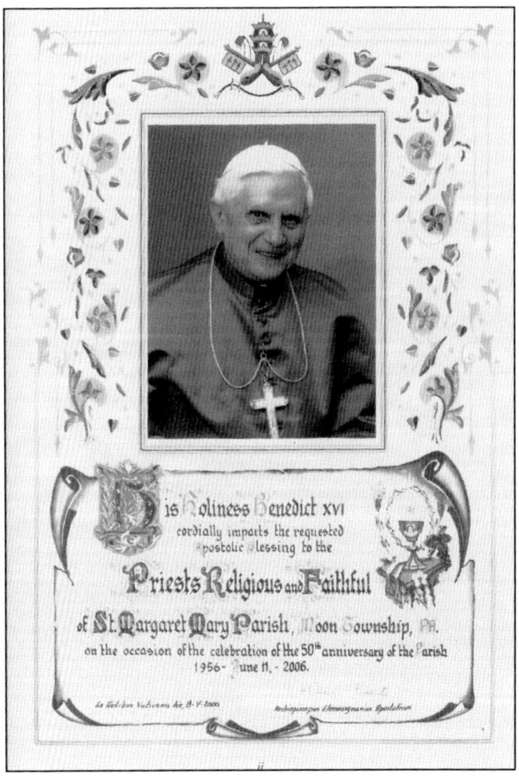

On June 11, 2006, St. Margaret Mary Parish celebrated its 50th anniversary. This official blessing from Pope Benedict XVI came from the Vatican to help St. Margaret Mary parishioners celebrate the occasion. The parish published a historical retrospective by Rev. James W. Garvey for the celebration that chronicled the church's golden anniversary. (Courtesy St. Margaret Mary Parish.)

Bishop Donald Wuerl, bishop of Pittsburgh, also sent along his thoughts and prayers to the parish on its anniversary. Wuerl wrote in this letter to the congregation, "This anniversary year witnesses the conclusion of a half-century of service provided by the parish that continues to stand in Moon Township as a witness to the enduring presence of God." (Courtesy St. Margaret Mary Parish.)

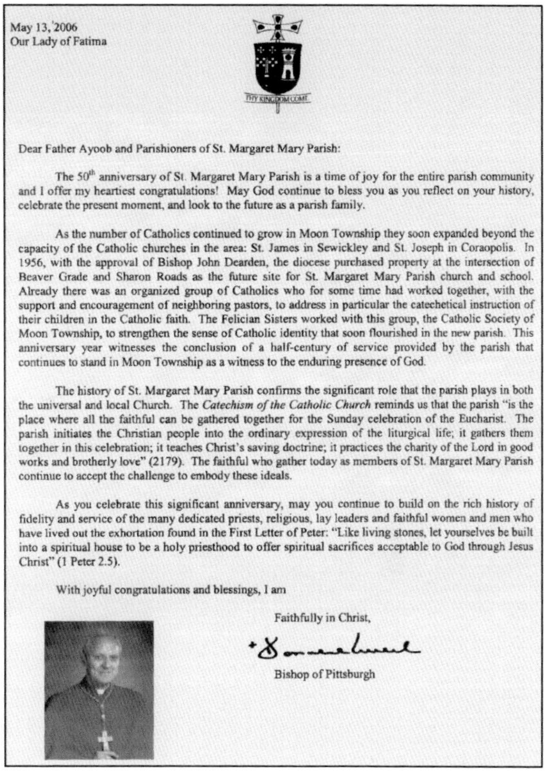

May 13, 2006
Our Lady of Fatima

THY KINGDOM COME

Dear Father Ayoob and Parishioners of St. Margaret Mary Parish:

The 50th anniversary of St. Margaret Mary Parish is a time of joy for the entire parish community and I offer my heartiest congratulations! May God continue to bless you as you reflect on your history, celebrate the present moment, and look to the future as a parish family.

As the number of Catholics continued to grow in Moon Township they soon expanded beyond the capacity of the Catholic churches in the area: St. James in Sewickley and St. Joseph in Coraopolis. In 1956, with the approval of Bishop John Dearden, the diocese purchased property at the intersection of Beaver Grade and Sharon Roads as the future site for St. Margaret Mary Parish church and school. Already there was an organized group of Catholics who for some time had worked together, with the support and encouragement of neighboring pastors, to address in particular the catechetical instruction of their children in the Catholic faith. The Felician Sisters worked with this group, the Catholic Society of Moon Township, to strengthen the sense of Catholic identity that soon flourished in the new parish. This anniversary year witnesses the conclusion of a half-century of service provided by the parish that continues to stand in Moon Township as a witness to the enduring presence of God.

The history of St. Margaret Mary Parish confirms the significant role that the parish plays in both the universal and local Church. The *Catechism of the Catholic Church* reminds us that the parish "is the place where all the faithful can be gathered together for the Sunday celebration of the Eucharist. The parish initiates the Christian people into the ordinary expression of the liturgical life; it gathers them together in this celebration; it teaches Christ's saving doctrine; it practices the charity of the Lord in good works and brotherly love" (2179). The faithful who gather today as members of St. Margaret Mary Parish continue to accept the challenge to embody these ideals.

As you celebrate this significant anniversary, may you continue to build on the rich history of fidelity and service of the many dedicated priests, religious, lay leaders and faithful women and men who have lived out the exhortation found in the First Letter of Peter: "Like living stones, let yourselves be built into a spiritual house to be a holy priesthood to offer spiritual sacrifices acceptable to God through Jesus Christ" (1 Peter 2.5).

With joyful congratulations and blessings, I am

Faithfully in Christ,

Bishop of Pittsburgh

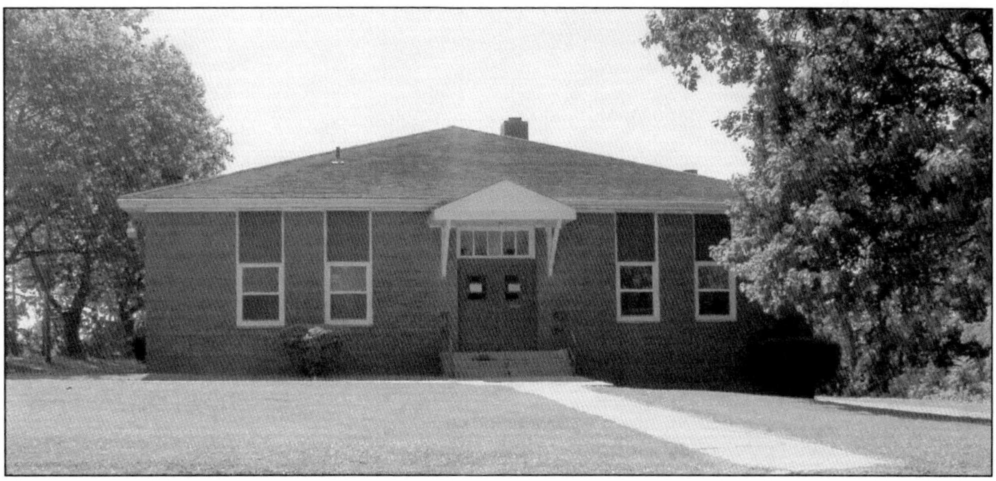

Moon also is home to several other churches from a variety of denominations. This is the Praise Center of Full Gospel Church in Moon Township's Historic Mooncrest neighborhood. Rev. Dr. Charles A. Scales Jr. is the senior pastor. Mooncrest was a World War II housing plan that fell into disrepair. Today's Mooncrest residents are mounting enormous efforts to revitalize the neighborhood through historic preservation and pursuit of grant monies to restore Mooncrest to its former stature. (Photograph by Mark Berton.)

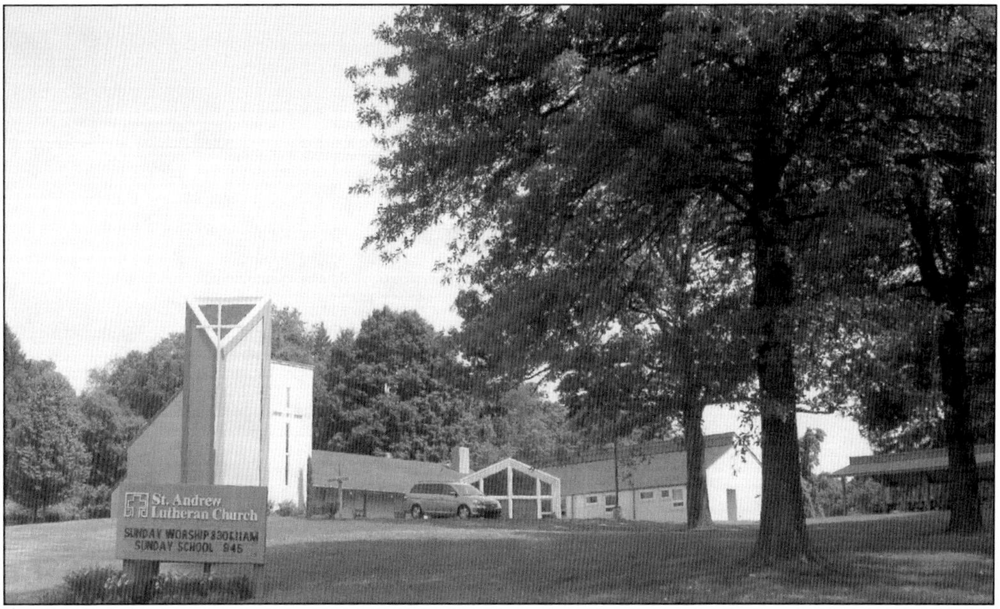

St. Andrew Lutheran Church was formed on February 24, 1963, with 60 members. Like many other churches in Moon Township, St. Andrew's first home was the Carnot Elementary School building. The current building was dedicated in 1966. It was renovated in 1995 and rededicated on January 19, 1996. The church has more than 1,000 members. (Photograph by Mark Berton.)

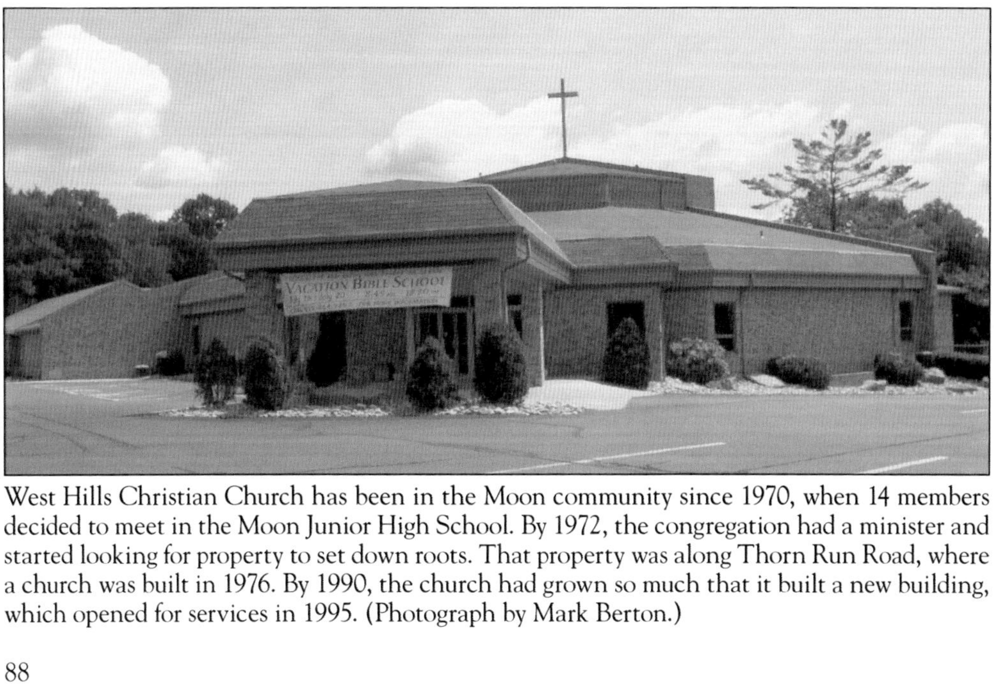

West Hills Christian Church has been in the Moon community since 1970, when 14 members decided to meet in the Moon Junior High School. By 1972, the congregation had a minister and started looking for property to set down roots. That property was along Thorn Run Road, where a church was built in 1976. By 1990, the church had grown so much that it built a new building, which opened for services in 1995. (Photograph by Mark Berton.)

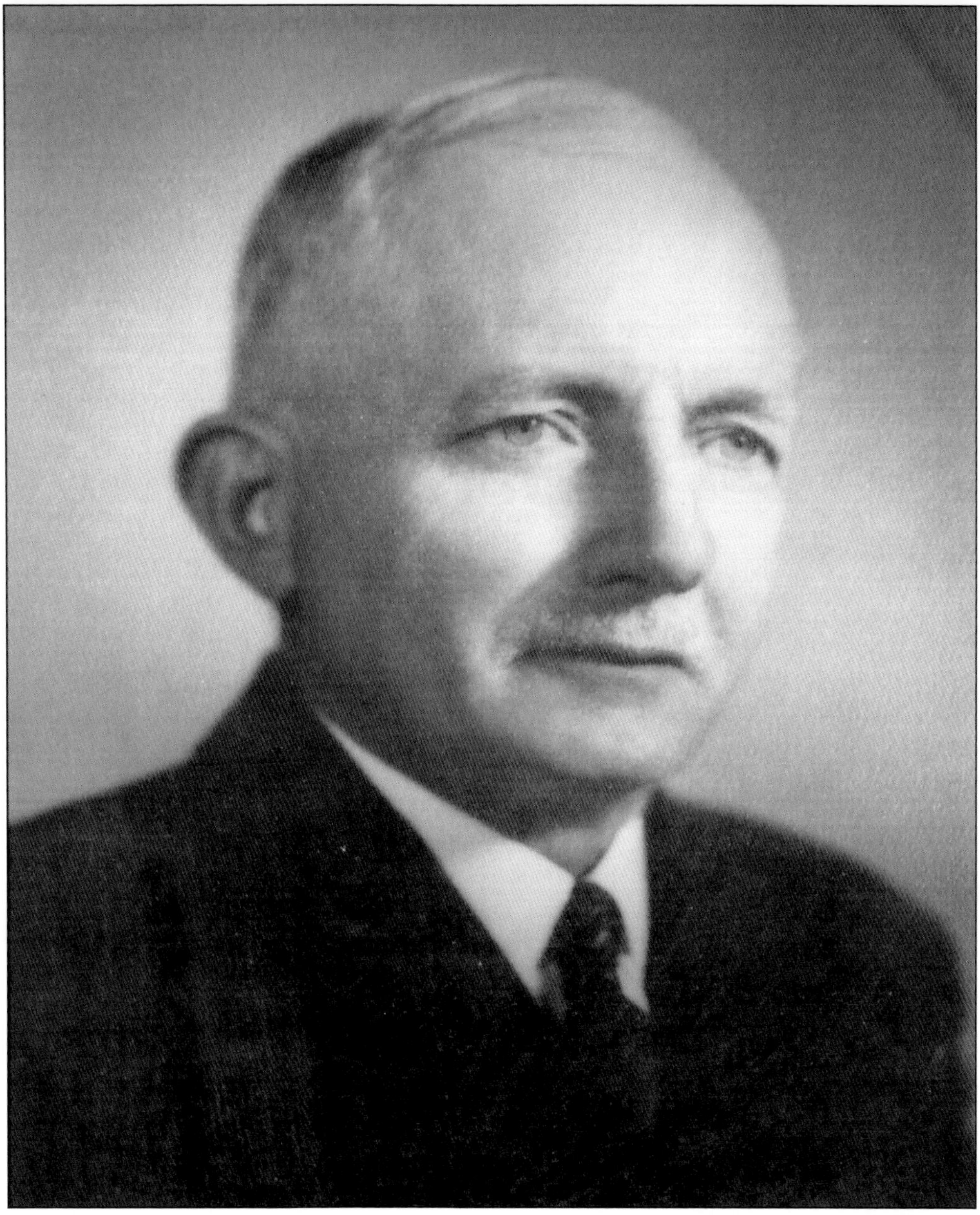

Moon Township is home to a number of charitable organizations as well as religious organizations. In addition to chapters of the Rotary International and Lions Club, Moon has a healthy Masonic presence. Wilson C. Dickson, pictured here, was the first worshipful master of Coraopolis-Moon Masonic Lodge 674. The portrait was presented in 1947 by the Coraopolis Chapter No. 300 Royal Arch Masons. (Courtesy Coraopolis-Moon Masonic Lodge 674.)

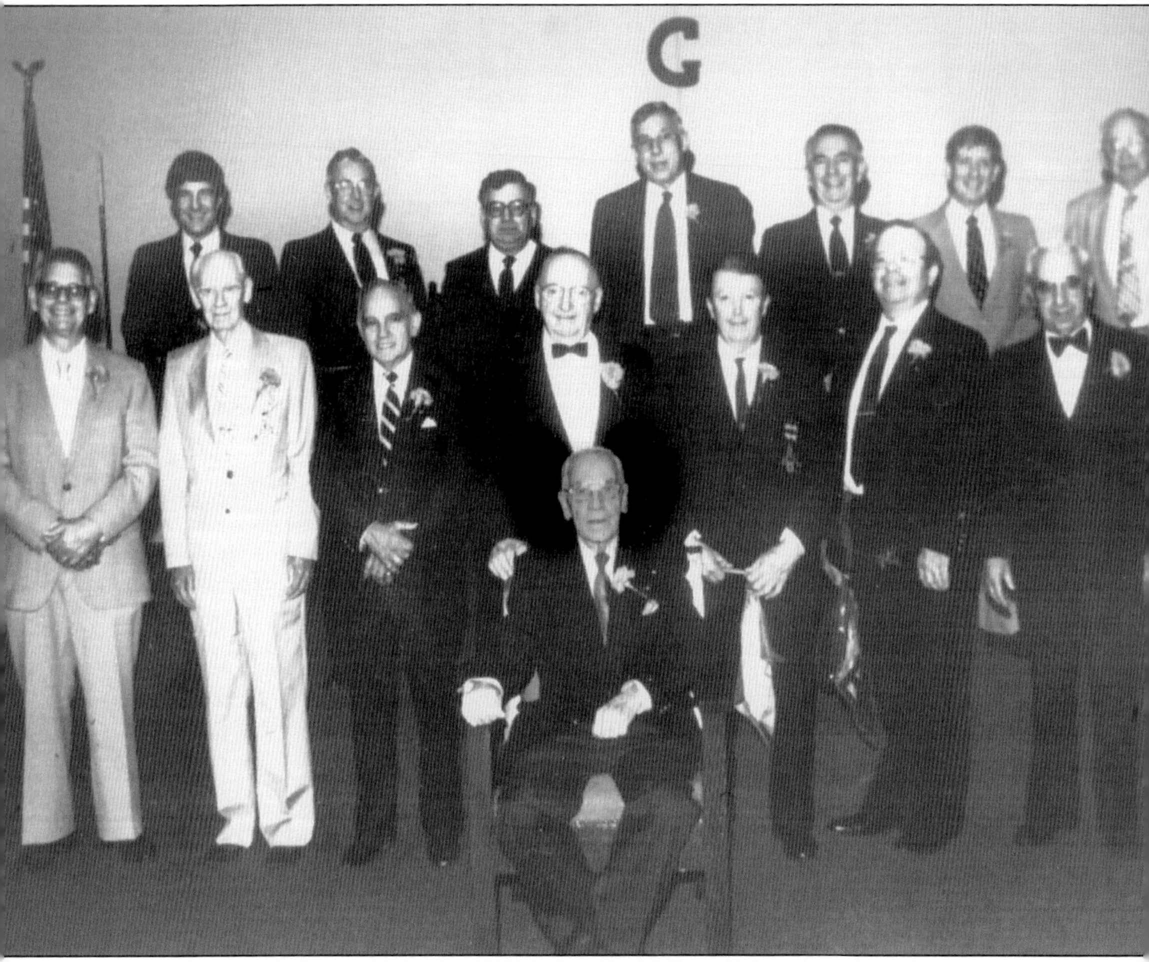

Coraopolis-Moon Masonic Lodge 674 was constituted on June 26, 1913. The lodge's current meeting place broke ground on September 28, 1969. On September 14, 1970, the lodge held its first meeting. The lodge has more than 250 active members and stands to support community programs such as the DARE programs for both the Moon and the Coraopolis police departments. Lodge members also raise money for scholarships to deserving students. (Courtesy Coraopolis-Moon Masonic Lodge 674.)

Three

TAKING FLIGHT

Without a doubt, the most influential force guiding the future of Moon Township today is the Pittsburgh International Airport, which straddles several municipal boundaries. Pittsburgh International Airport is the latest incarnation of several airports serving the region, dating back to Bettis Field, which was little more than a manicured cow pasture with the formal name of Pittsburgh-McKeesport Airdrome.

In 1928, growing demand for air traffic warranted a $1.5 million bond issue to erect a county airport. Allegheny County Airport opened on September 11, 1931, and served the public until 1952 when Greater Pittsburgh International Airport opened for business in Moon Township. This facility was in service twice as long as the old Allegheny County Airport, but was criticized as being a "Taj Mahal" facility when it was first constructed. Despite its success, this facility was eventually deemed too small to handle the air traffic of the Pittsburgh Metropolitan Region.

For this reason, and the fact that Allegheny County officials courted U.S. Airways as a staple tenant, another groundbreaking took place in 1987 on Pittsburgh International Airport. Work continued until 1992, when the $837 million project was finally completed. A fall ribbon-cutting celebration included then governor Bob Casey and Sen. Arlen Specter. Today Pittsburgh International drives much of the business in the region and Moon Township in particular. A good portion of Moon Township is owned by the airport authority and is being developed by the authority for its purposes.

In addition to Pittsburgh International Airport, Moon is home to the 911th Airlift Wing and the 171st Air Refueling Wing. These facets of the airport alone account for several hundred civilian jobs in and near Moon Township. It also accounts for one of the region's biggest-draw activities—the Wings over Pittsburgh Air Show, which is now in its eighth year. The Wings over Pittsburgh Air Show draws well over 100,000 people during the annual two-day event and even shuts down parts of Route 60 for some of the aerial acrobatic demonstrations.

Because of its proximity to Pittsburgh International Airport, Moon Township is often the first location in western Pennsylvania that visitors and dignitaries see.

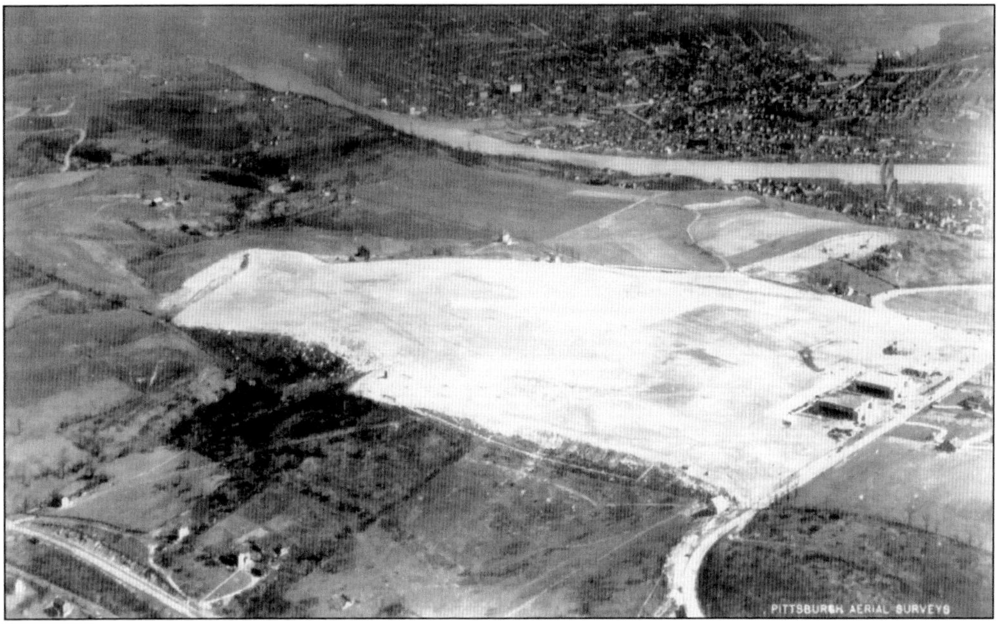

Bettis Airfield, originally named the Pittsburgh-McKeesport Airdrome, was the first substantial airport in the Pittsburgh region. Two smaller fields preceded it, Mayer and Rogers Fields. This 1935 photograph shows the field from the air. The airfield was renamed Bettis Airfield in honor of Lt. Cyrus Bettis, a 1925 Pulitzer Air Speed Trophy holder who died in a plane crash. (Courtesy Carnegie Library of Pittsburgh.)

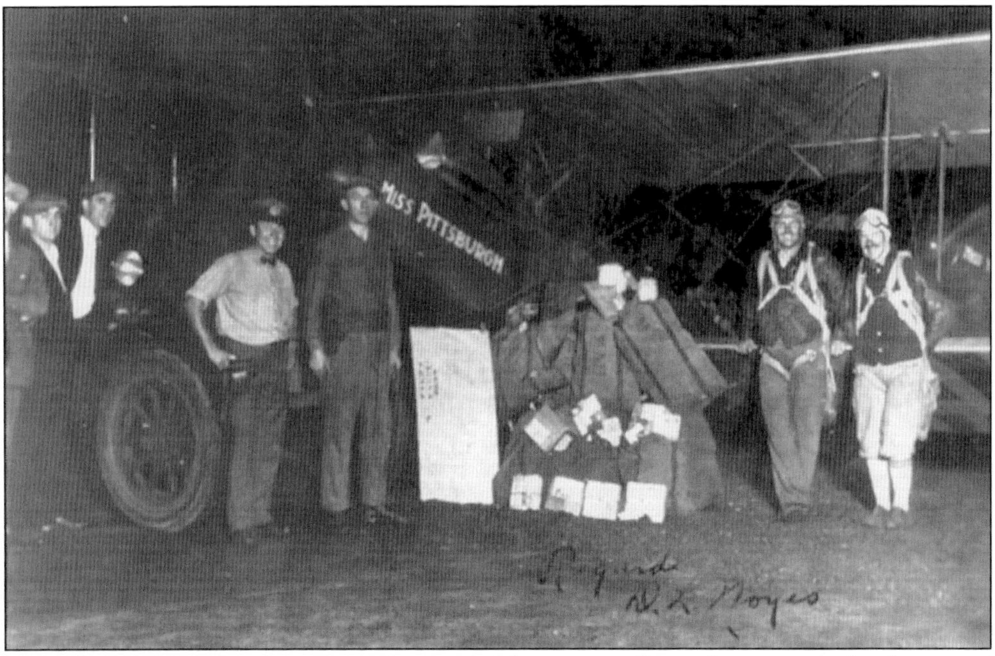

Airmail quickly became the primary function of the airport. Shown here is an undated postcard of airmail pilots and their cargo. The plane is the *Miss Pittsburgh*. Airmail first arrived at Bettis Airfield from Cleveland, Ohio, on April 21, 1927. Clifford Ball, Inc., was the sole airmail operator flying into and out of Bettis Airfield. (Courtesy Carnegie Library of Pittsburgh.)

This aerogram bears the postmark of the first airmail flight between Cleveland and Pittsburgh. The plane arrived around 2:30 in the afternoon to a reported crowd of 2,000 automobiles and about 7,000 people. Clifford Ball, Inc., flew the mail into and out of Pittsburgh. The company later grew into Capital Air Lines, which was eventually acquired by United Airlines. (Courtesy Carnegie Library of Pittsburgh.)

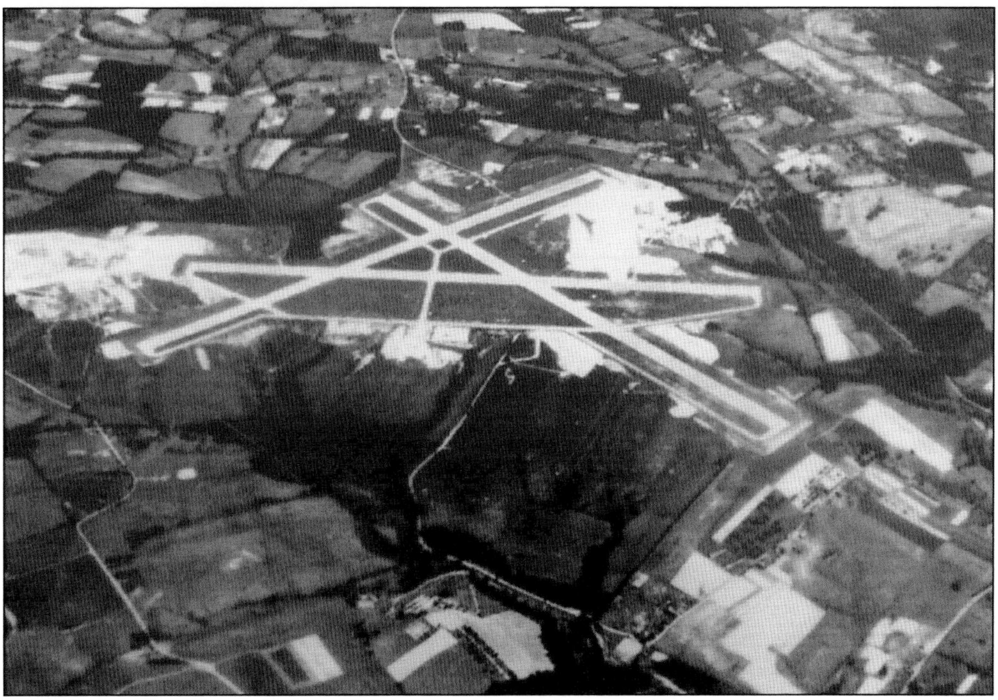

By 1928, air traffic at Bettis Airfield grew so quickly that Allegheny County issued $3 million in bonds to build a full-scale airport. The Allegheny County Airport opened for business in 1931 and remained in service until 1952 when the business of the air landed in Moon Township. (Courtesy Carnegie Library of Pittsburgh.)

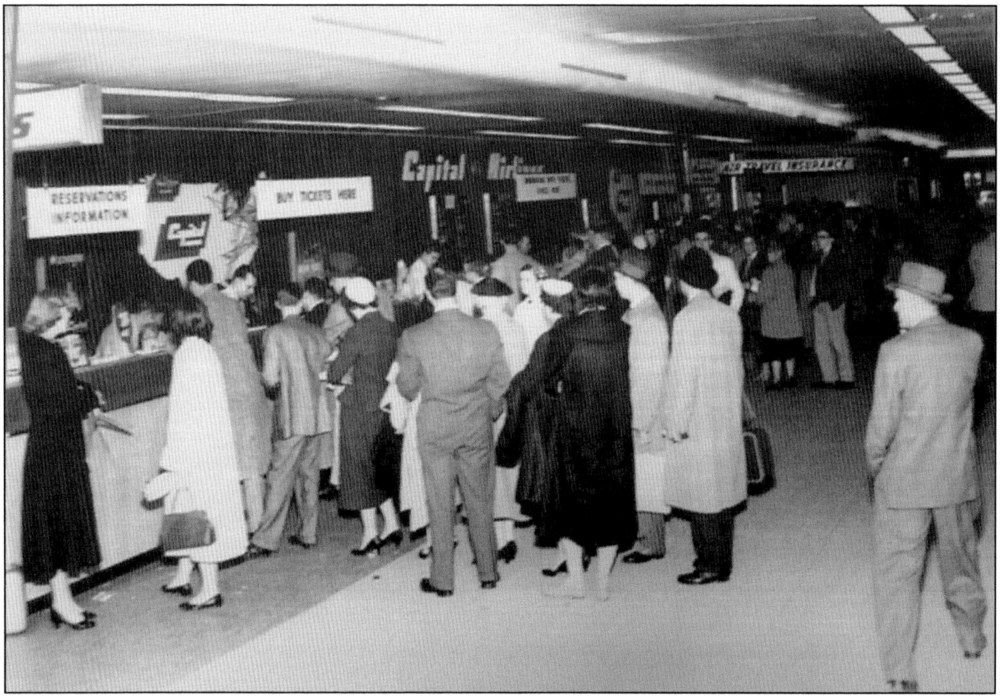

The counter of the old Allegheny County Airport bustled continuously with customers. The airport also featured amenities such as a hospital, pilots' quarters, weather station, and pressroom. While its art deco style was a sign of high culture in the 1930s, it could not come close to what architects had in mind for the next generation of Pittsburgh's airports—Greater Pittsburgh International. (Courtesy Carnegie Library of Pittsburgh.)

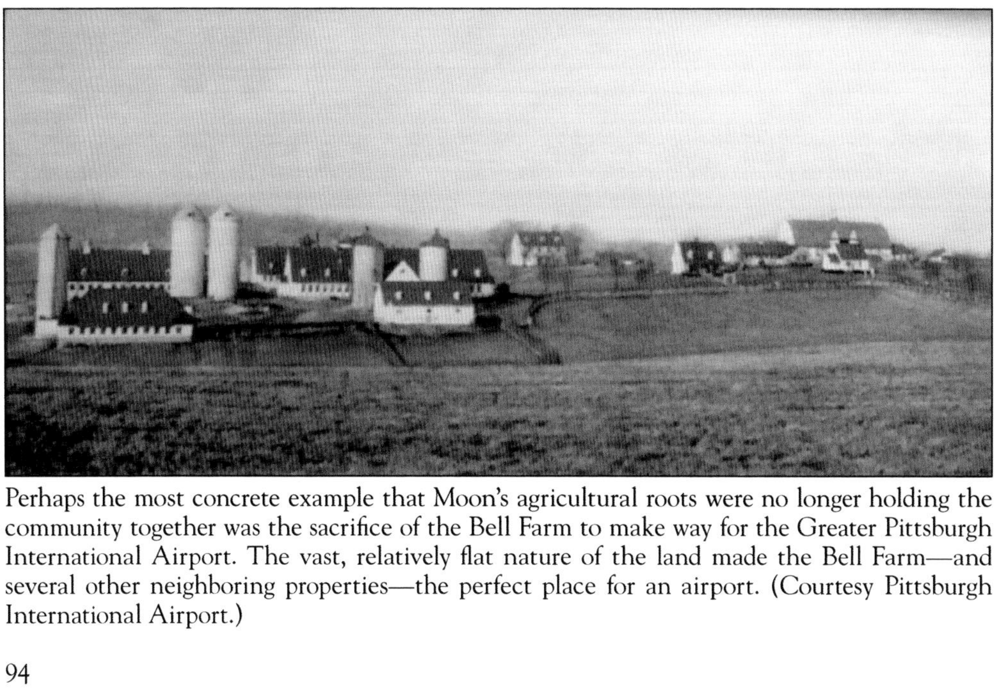

Perhaps the most concrete example that Moon's agricultural roots were no longer holding the community together was the sacrifice of the Bell Farm to make way for the Greater Pittsburgh International Airport. The vast, relatively flat nature of the land made the Bell Farm—and several other neighboring properties—the perfect place for an airport. (Courtesy Pittsburgh International Airport.)

The official groundbreaking ceremony for Greater Pittsburgh International Airport took place on July 18, 1946. John Sweeney was the first director of the Allegheny County Department of Aviation. Initially there was little public support for the $33 million project. Those voices silenced over the subsequent years as their complaints that the facility was too big and too expensive were disproved. (Courtesy Pittsburgh International Airport.)

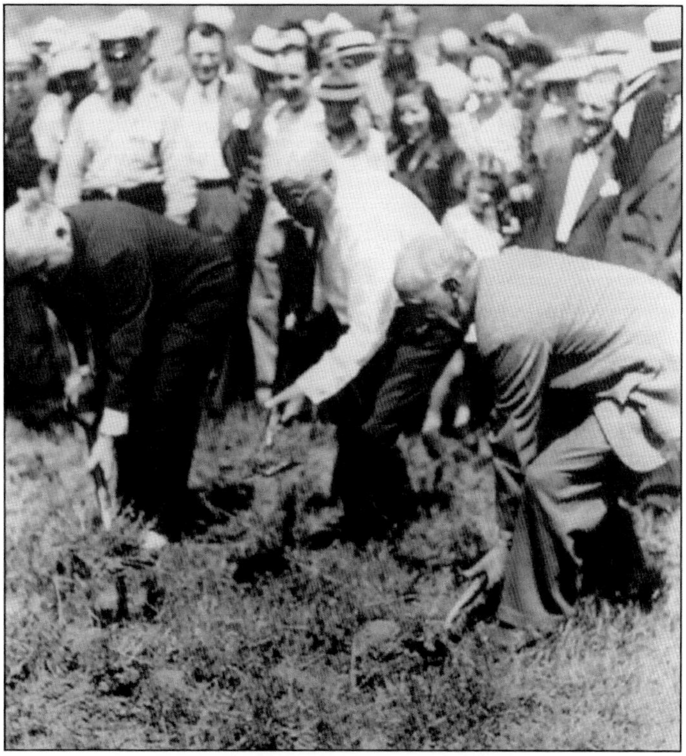

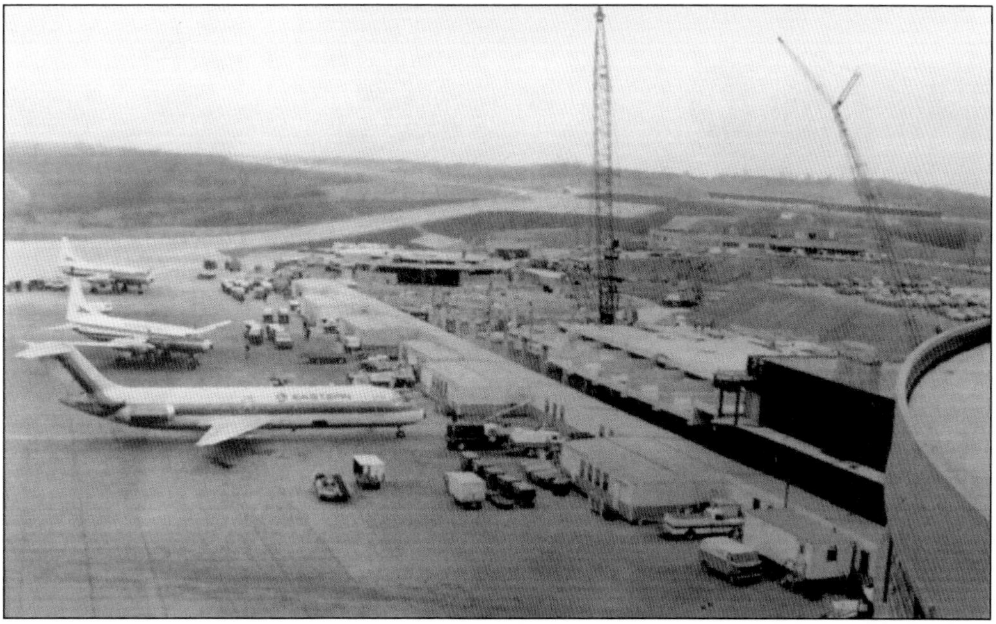

In 1959, the first jetliner landed in Pittsburgh. Flying for TWA, flight 29 flew out of Pittsburgh, stopped in Chicago, and flew on to Los Angeles. TWA was also the first airline to have an accident at the new airport. In 1952, just six months after the airport's dedication, a twin-engine plane made a belly landing after its landing gear failed. There were no reported injuries. (Courtesy Carnegie Library of Pittsburgh.)

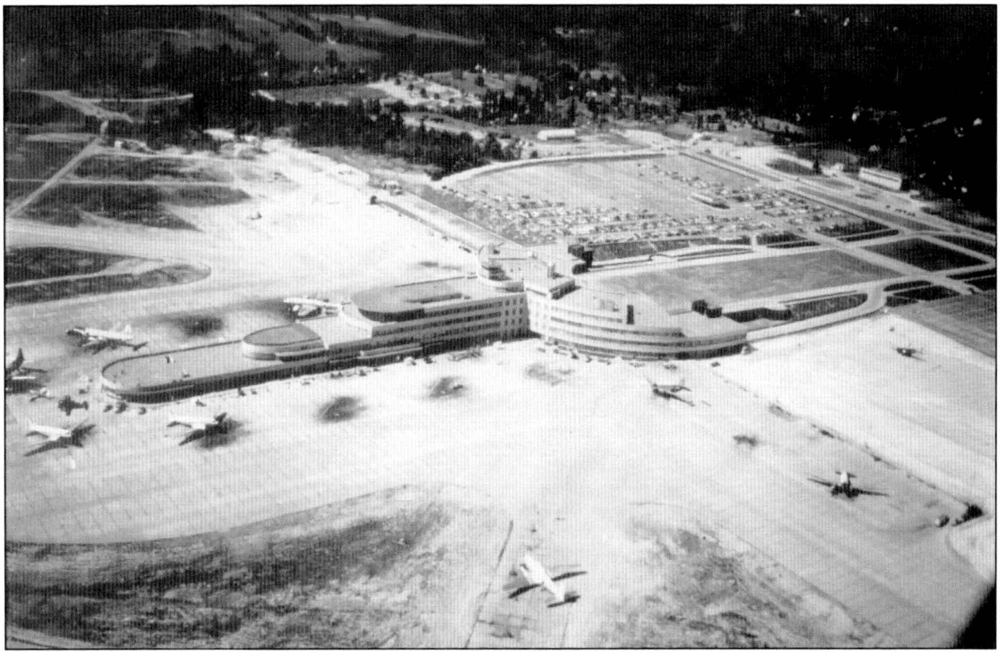

More than 100,000 people came to the May 31, 1952, dedication of Greater Pittsburgh International Airport. The airport was served by All American, Capital, Eastern, Northwest, and Trans World airlines. The terminal had 10 gates. In addition, the airport housed a movie theater and nightclub. (Courtesy Carnegie Library of Pittsburgh.)

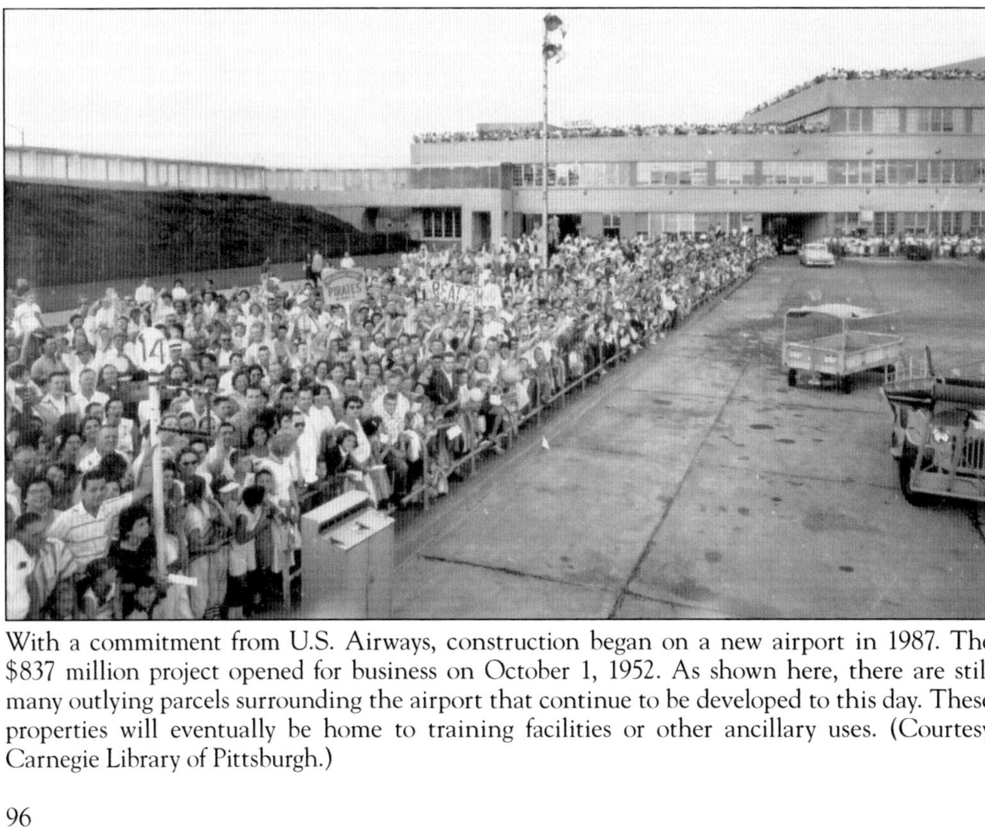

With a commitment from U.S. Airways, construction began on a new airport in 1987. The $837 million project opened for business on October 1, 1952. As shown here, there are still many outlying parcels surrounding the airport that continue to be developed to this day. These properties will eventually be home to training facilities or other ancillary uses. (Courtesy Carnegie Library of Pittsburgh.)

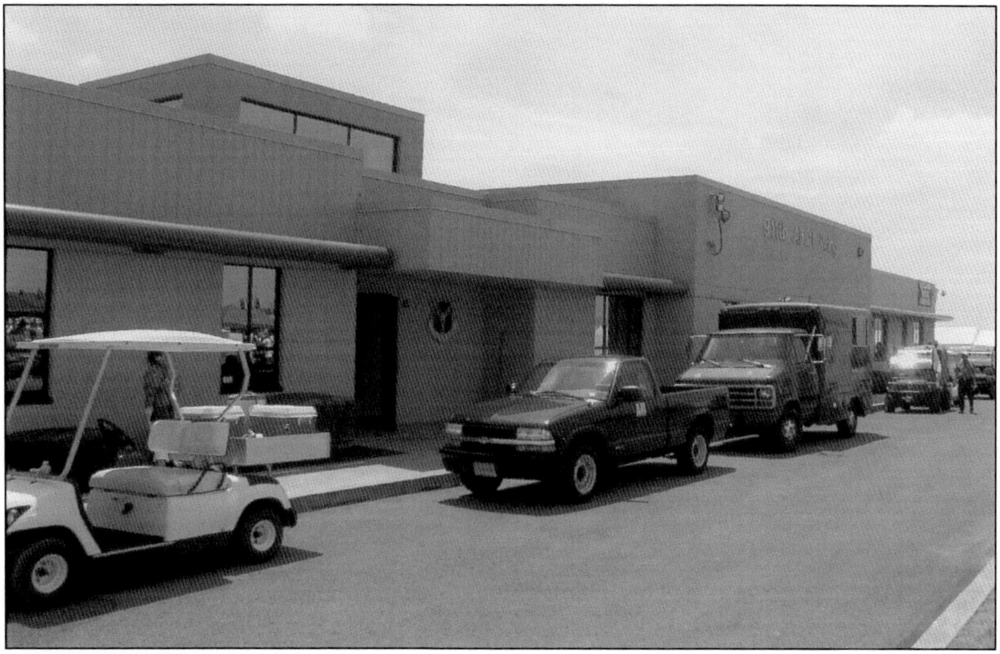

Part of the airport's history is the fact that Pittsburgh is home to the 911th Airlift Wing, which originated as a defense base on the Bell Farm several years before Greater Pittsburgh International Airport broke ground. The official designation of the 911th Airlift Wing did not take effect until 1963. (Photograph by Mark Berton.)

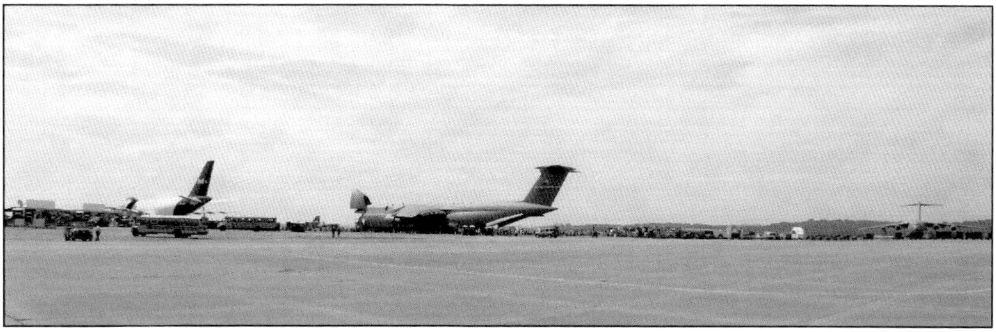

In 1945, the 911th Airlift Wing base was a fuel depot for military aircraft traveling cross-country. After World War II, the base became a reserve training center. It later became an aerospace defense command center. That designation was discontinued in 1958. Reservists from the base participated in Operations Desert Shield, Desert Storm, and Southern Watch. Reservists from the 911th also aided in the Bosnian conflict. The base lends itself to humanitarian services for domestic causes as well.

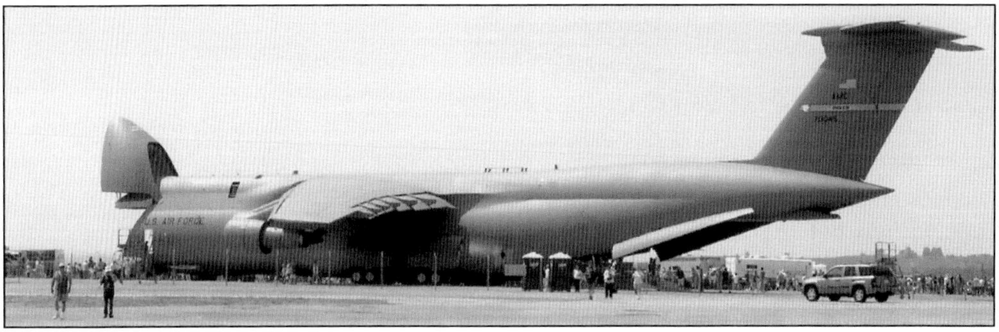

On several occasions, the base has been threatened with closure. These efforts were met with an enormous public outcry in favor of keeping the base open, especially from political representatives of Moon Township. Not only does the base provide hundreds of jobs in Moon, it holds an annual air show that attracts hundreds of thousands of visitors to the township each year. (Photograph by Mark Berton.)

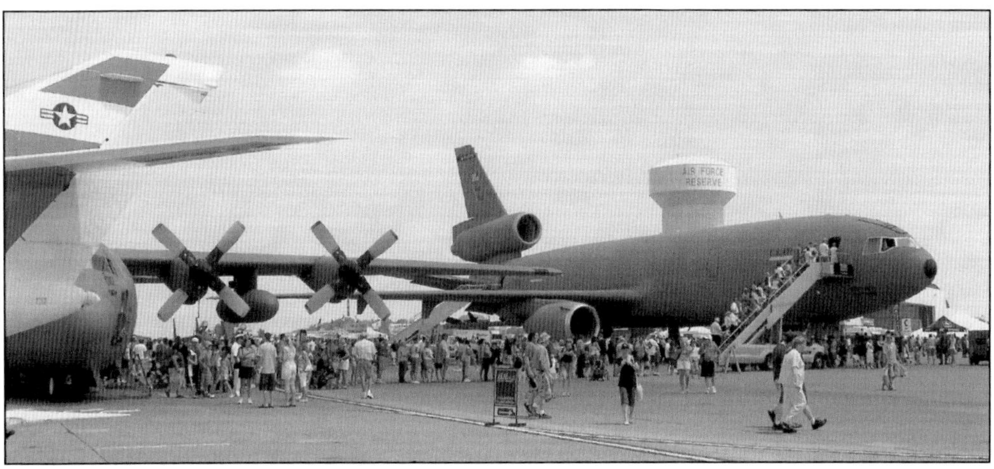

Wings over Pittsburgh, an annual air show in Moon Township, is an enormous celebration of the history of flight. The event is free and open to the public and includes aerial acrobatics by the U.S. Air Force Thunderbirds, U.S. Army Sky Soldiers, U.S. Air Force Drill Team, and more. The two-day air show gives people the ability to get up close to the aircraft, and the aerial acrobatics can be seen miles away in neighboring communities.

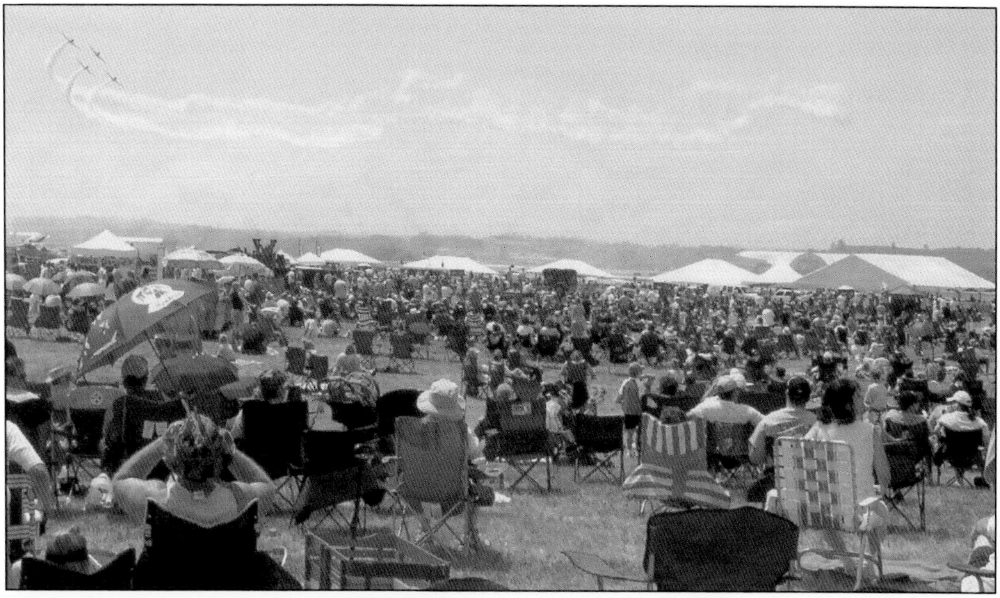

While the fun and excitement of the Wings over Pittsburgh air show provide an entertaining view of the 911th Airlift Wing, serious work is performed there every day. The base currently has a presence in Asia for Operation Enduring Freedom and has been an asset in Kosovo, Kuwait, Bosnia, and Panama. (Photograph by Mark Berton.)

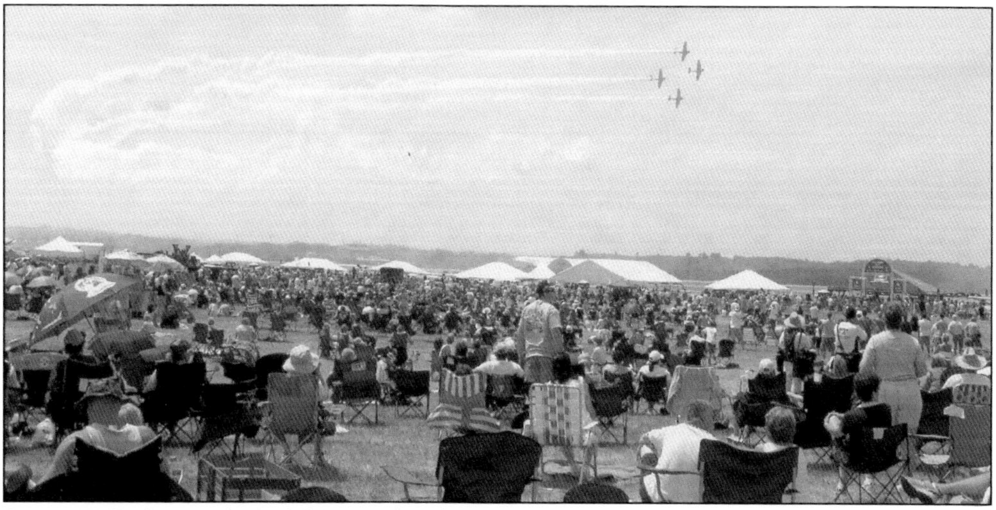

Since 1997, the 911th Airlift Wing has been under the jurisdiction of the 22nd Air Force, operating out of Dobbins Air Reserve Base in Georgia. The primary plane of the 911th is the C-130 series. Prior to the C-130s, the 911th flew C-124 Globemasters and C-123K Providers. The unit switched over to C-130s in 1980. (Photograph by Mark Berton.)

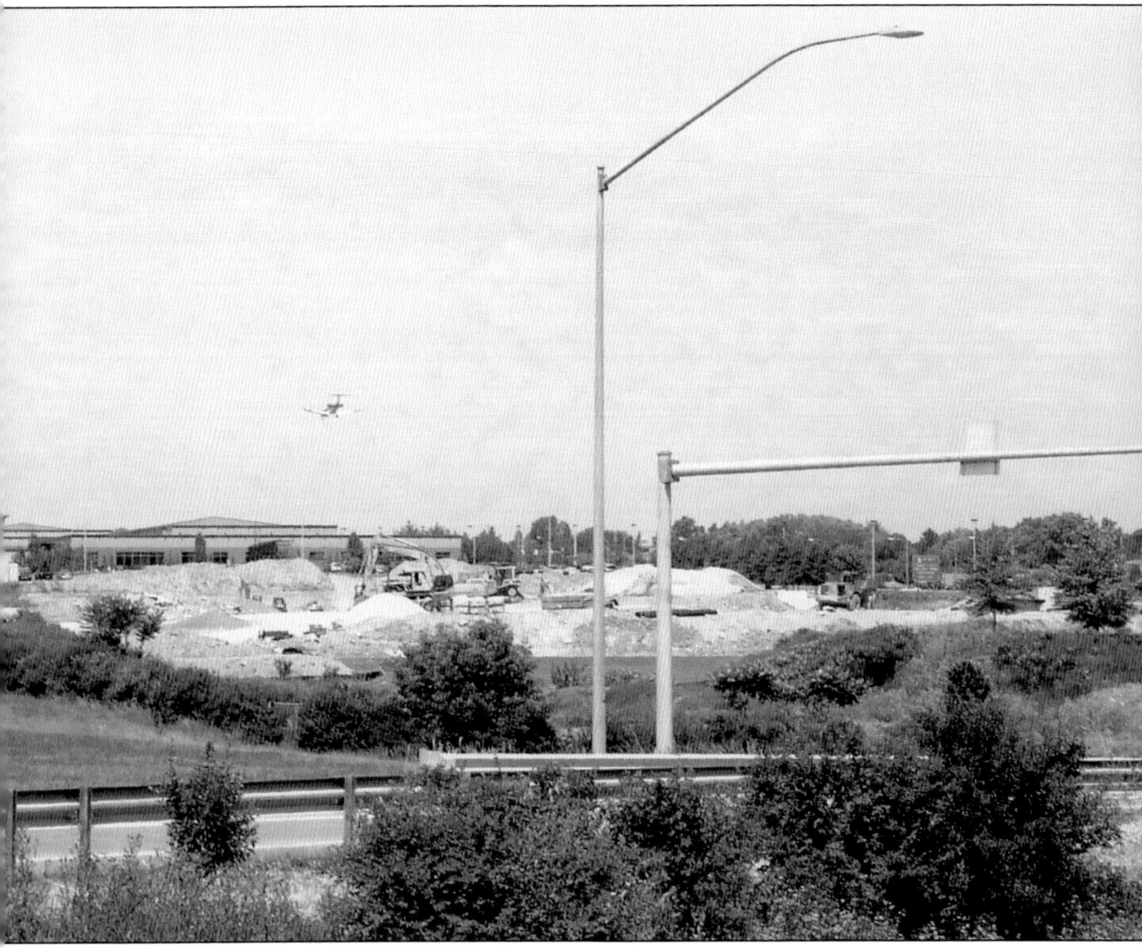

Today the Pittsburgh International Airport continues to grow and developments, such as the Airside Business Park, grow just alongside of it. The business park is situated on the site of the former Greater Pittsburgh International Airport. The park is comprised of several identical three-story buildings with their own amenities such as delis and fountains. This photograph shows just one of the many sites around the airport that are currently under development. (Photograph by Mark Berton.)

Four

EDUCATION, COMMUNITY, AND PLACE

Moon Township is not only the home to the Moon Area School District, which is comprised of both Moon and Crescent Townships, but of Robert Morris University as well. This distinction has had a unique influence on the community. Firstly, just 1,200 of Robert Morris University's 5,100 students live on campus, but many live in the surrounding condominium and apartment communities, such as Fox Hollow and Colony West. This constant replenishing of young people in the community, coupled with the traffic from Pittsburgh International Airport, means a constantly changing commercial landscape in Moon Township. Trendy restaurants such as Primanti's thrive in Moon, as do pizza shops and breakfast anytime–style restaurants such as Eat'n Park.

Built on more than 230 acres in the township, Robert Morris University has been a good neighbor to Moon Township since 1962. At that time, Robert Morris University was known as Robert Morris Junior College, upgrading its moniker from Robert Morris School. Prior to that, Robert Morris School was the Pittsburgh School of Accountancy. Today Robert Morris University's 30 undergraduate and nearly 20 master's/doctoral programs are a draw to students from all over the country. For those who are not ready for college, Moon Area School District has six public schools: Moon Area High School, Moon Area Middle School, J. A. Allard Elementary, Bon Meade Elementary, J. H. Brooks Elementary, and R. Hyde Elementary. Another school, McCormick, currently is under renovation. The district's original school, Carnot Elementary, closed for education. However, it later reinvented itself as a training building for U.S. Airways. That designation was short-lived, and the school closed after an airline reorganization and downsizing. The school remains closed today.

From a single schoolhouse, the district has grown tremendously with the times to a student population approaching 4,000. According to Standard and Poor's, that enrollment has a minority makeup of less than nine percent. One-quarter of Allegheny County's 43 school districts rank higher in reading proficiency, and greater than one third lead Moon area in math proficiency, according to the Standard and Poor's 2005 numbers. Moon Area School District is in the top 10 of the least economically disadvantaged students in the county.

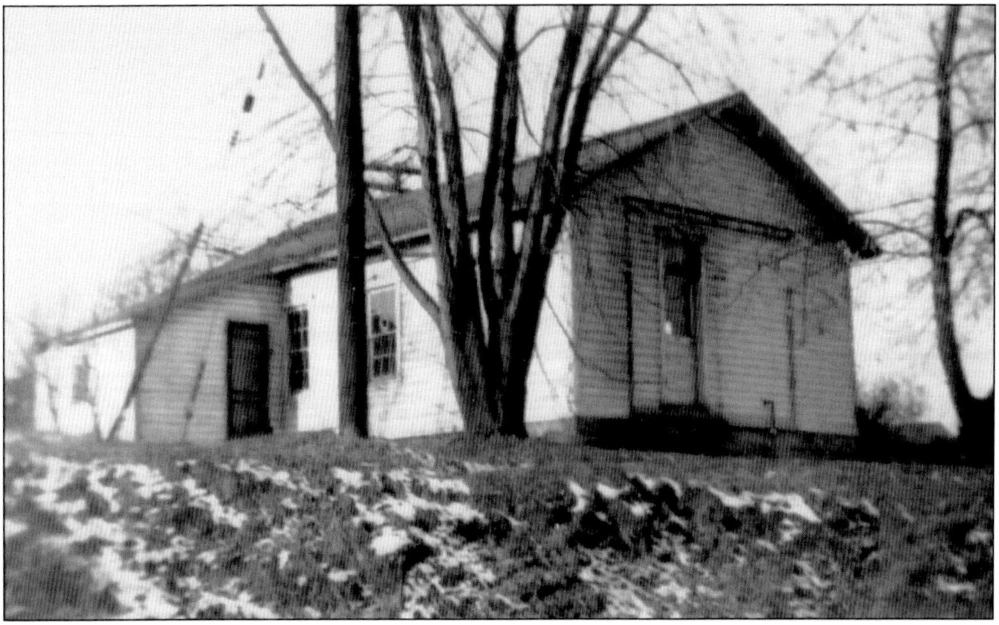

Before the multimillion-dollar school district that is now Moon Area School District was formed, a smattering of one-room schoolhouses peppered the rugged landscape of Moon. Shown here is the Donnan House, arguably the first of these schoolhouses. Classes typically had fewer than 30 students. (Courtesy Sharon Community Presbyterian Church.)

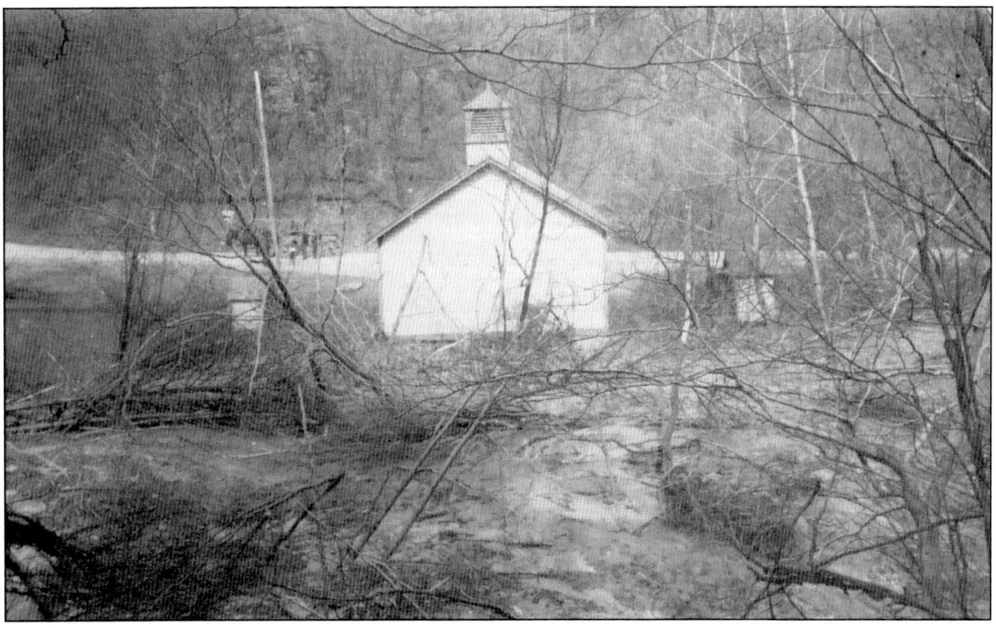

Schoolhouses such as the Stoops Ferry School were responsible for graduating the youth of Moon. It was not until 1917 that the first serious talks of consolidating the schools in Moon took place. By 1928, J. Arnold Allard became supervising principal over these schools. Over time, several of these wooden buildings burned to the ground. Others were converted into residential homes. (Courtesy Eliot and Marjorie Johnson and the Crescent-Shousetown Area Historic Association.)

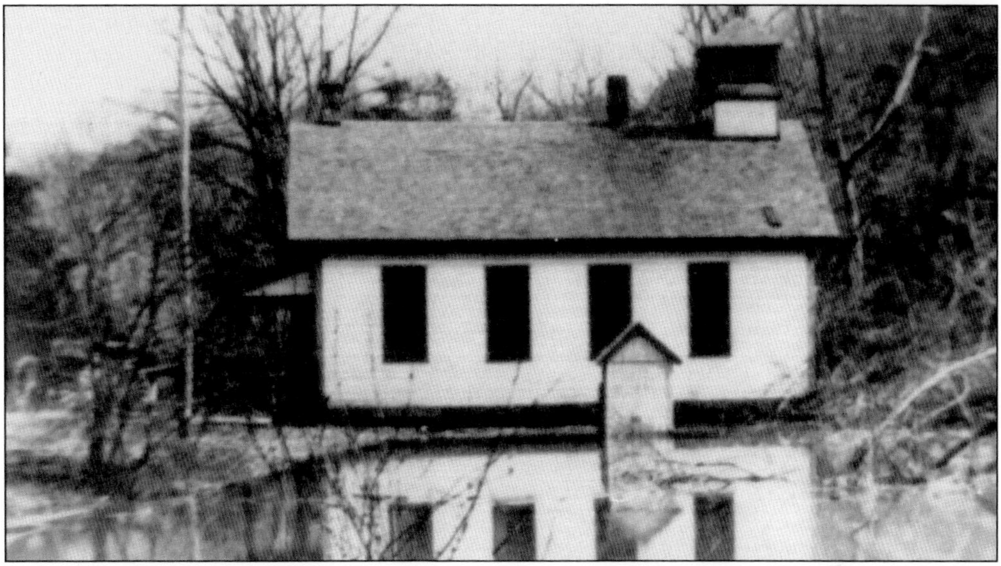

This view of the Stoops Ferry School shows more of the debris that surrounded it following an undated landslide. The valley along University Boulevard in the Stoops Ferry area still is prone to slides. One such slide closed down the roadway following the aftermath of Hurricane Ivan in 2002. Despite the potential for danger, a few brave souls chose to build homes on these slopes, which affords them gorgeous views of the Ohio River and the village of Sewickley across the river. (Courtesy Eliot and Marjorie Johnson and the Crescent-Shousetown Area Historic Association.)

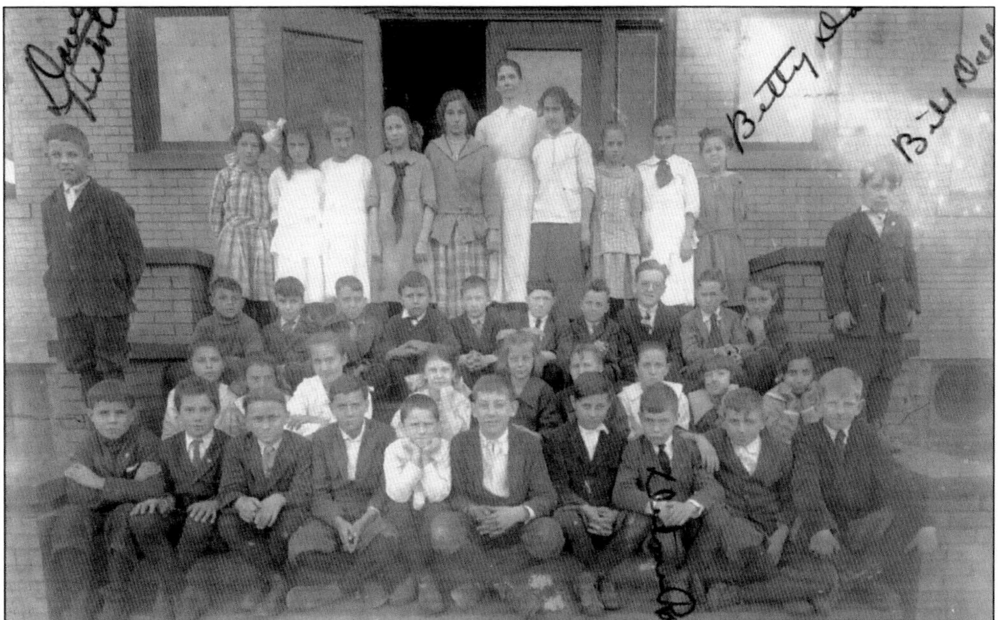

This undated class picture shows students from Carnot Elementary School. The original school was located on the property of Sharon Community Presbyterian Church. It was a wooden structure that was later replaced in 1914. The new Carnot Elementary School had four rooms rather than two and stood until 1948. (Courtesy the Meanor family.)

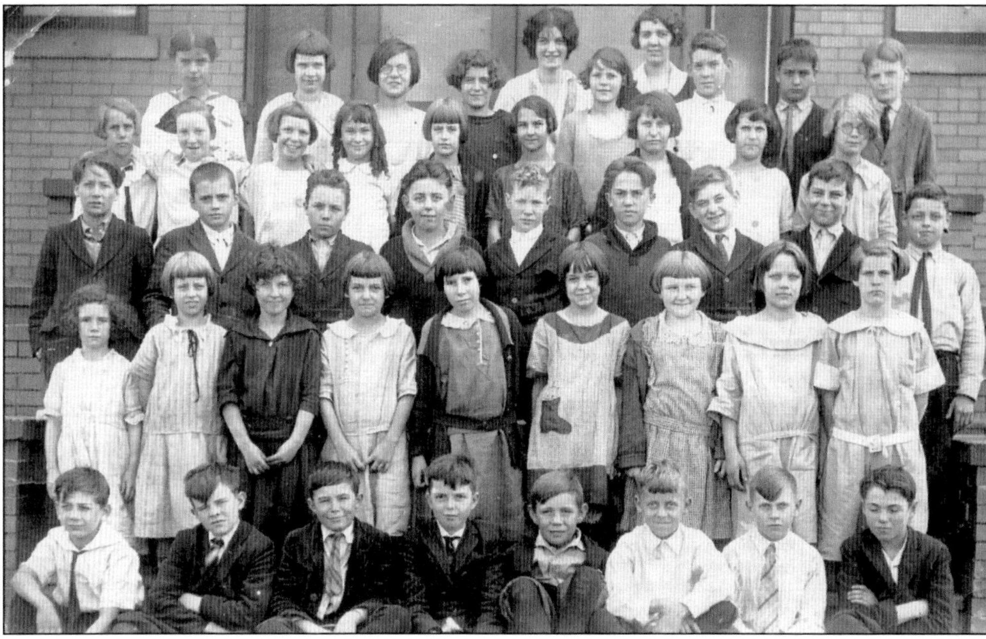

Many students passed through Carnot Elementary School, which was rebuilt yet again in 1931. The following year, the school district converted the new Carnot Elementary School into the district high school. The old Carnot Elementary School was put back to its original use. The first class to graduate high school in Moon Township did so in 1936. (Courtesy Nancy Mills.)

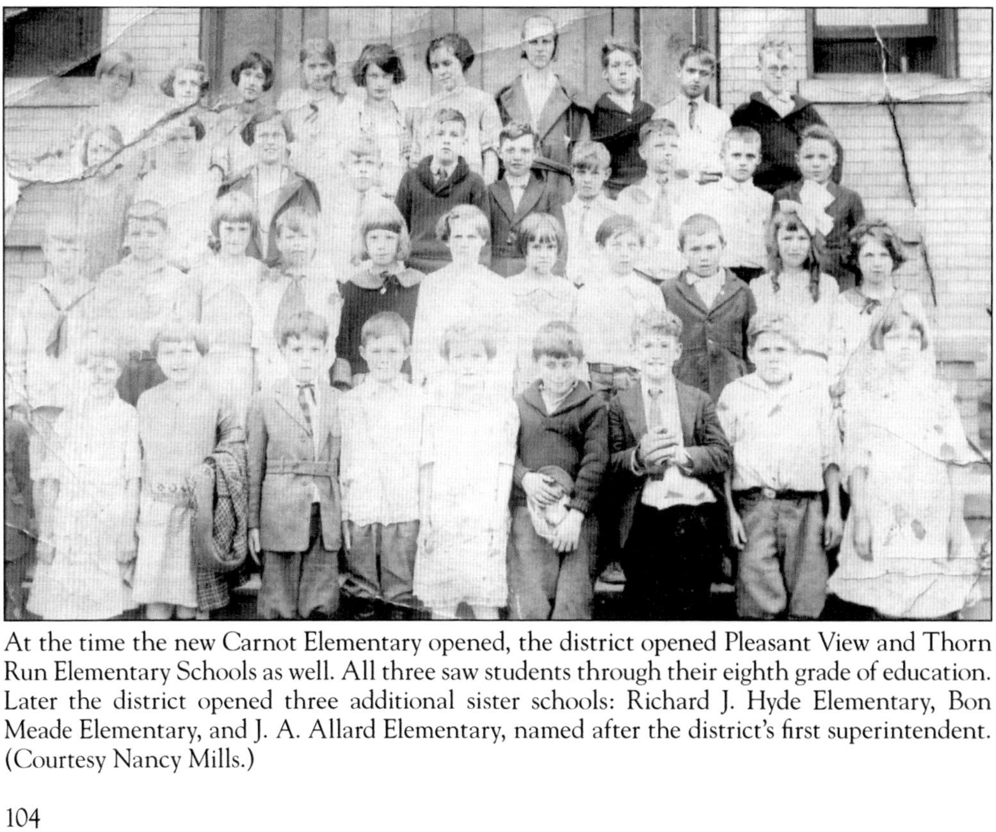

At the time the new Carnot Elementary opened, the district opened Pleasant View and Thorn Run Elementary Schools as well. All three saw students through their eighth grade of education. Later the district opened three additional sister schools: Richard J. Hyde Elementary, Bon Meade Elementary, and J. A. Allard Elementary, named after the district's first superintendent. (Courtesy Nancy Mills.)

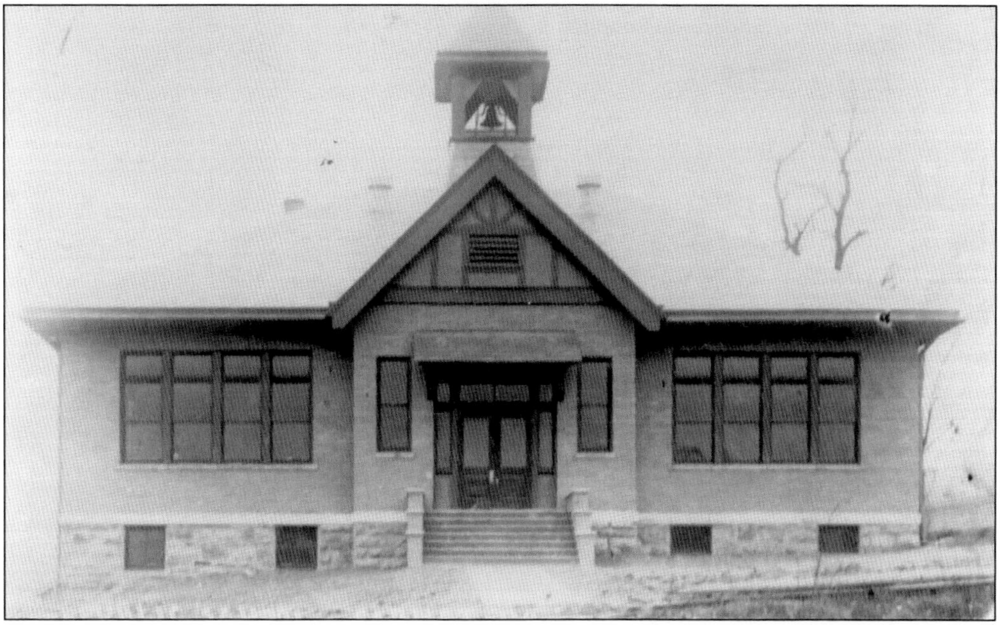

This front-on shot shows the symmetry and simplicity of Carnot Elementary School. The yellow-brick structure stood for less than 35 years. During the Great Depression, teachers in the district were forced to work with half of their lights on and cut their heating bills by 50 percent. During this time, the teachers also took home half their pay, an arrangement that continued until the summer of 1933. (Courtesy Dr. Dale Gass.)

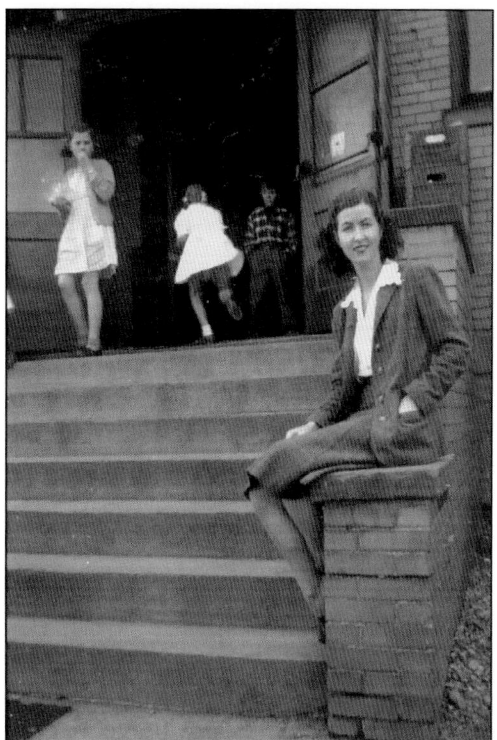

Teaching the students of Moon was Eleanor Springer-Perrott. The Springer family was well known in Moon Township, having been a residing family since 1856. The family had a large farm that was divided up among family members over time. A portion of the Albert Springer Farm was taken by eminent domain to make way for the Greater Pittsburgh International Airport. (Courtesy Nancy Mills.)

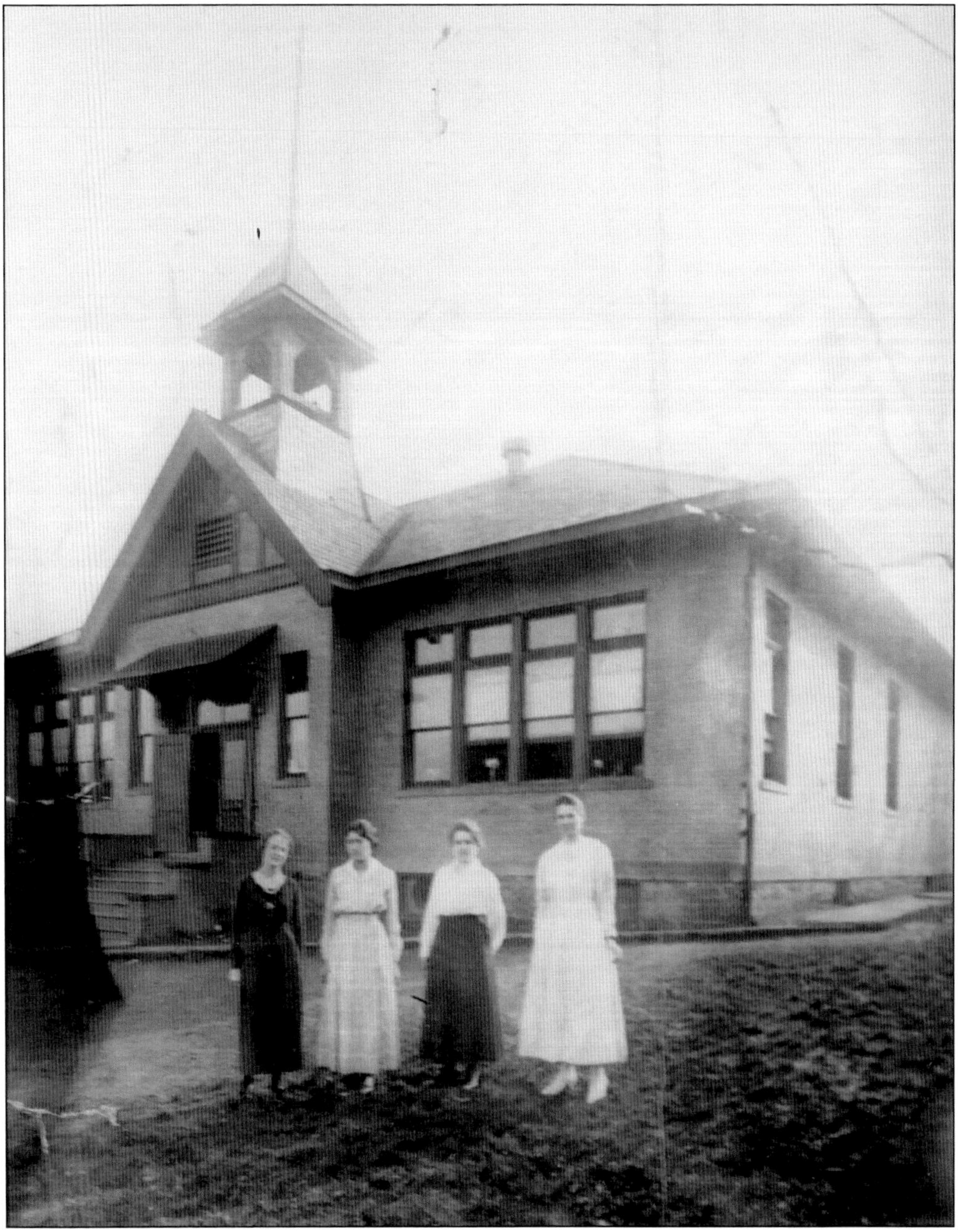

This undated photograph shows four women, presumably teachers in the four-room Carnot Elementary School behind them. At the time of this writing, Moon Area School District is embroiled in a highly political debate over whether to build additional school buildings in the district. The approval of several hundred new housing starts in 2006 will mean potentially as many new students for the growing district as new families move in. (Courtesy Nancy Mills.)

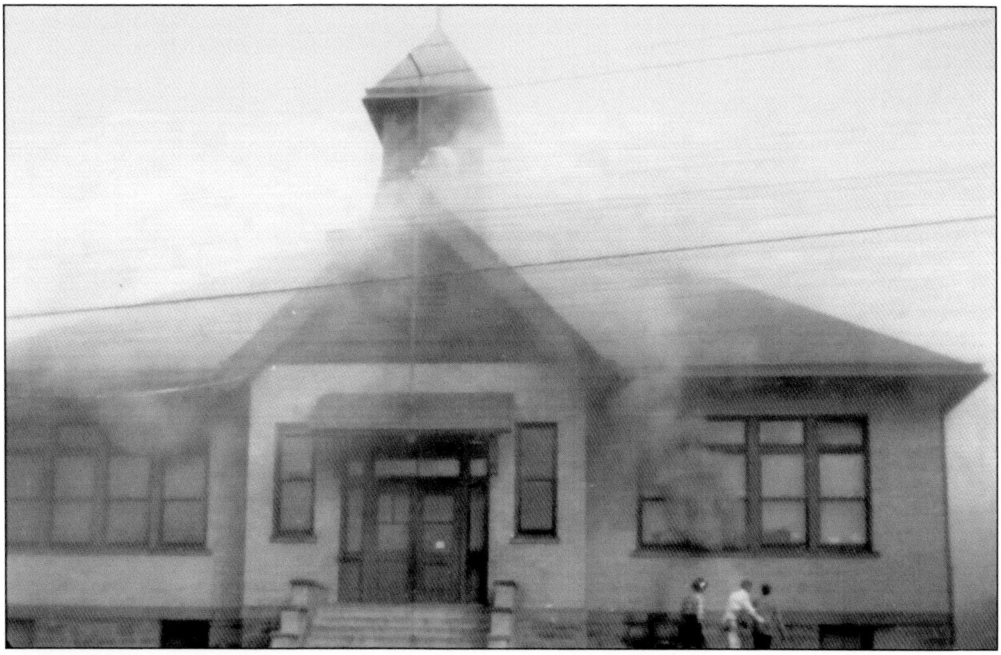

Fire struck the Carnot Elementary School in April 1948. This photograph shows that fire in progress. The school's janitor, Milton Hissam, perished in the blaze. No other injuries were reported from the event, but despite the integrity of the yellow-brick structure, the damage was enough to shut the school down for good. (Courtesy Dr. Dale Gass.)

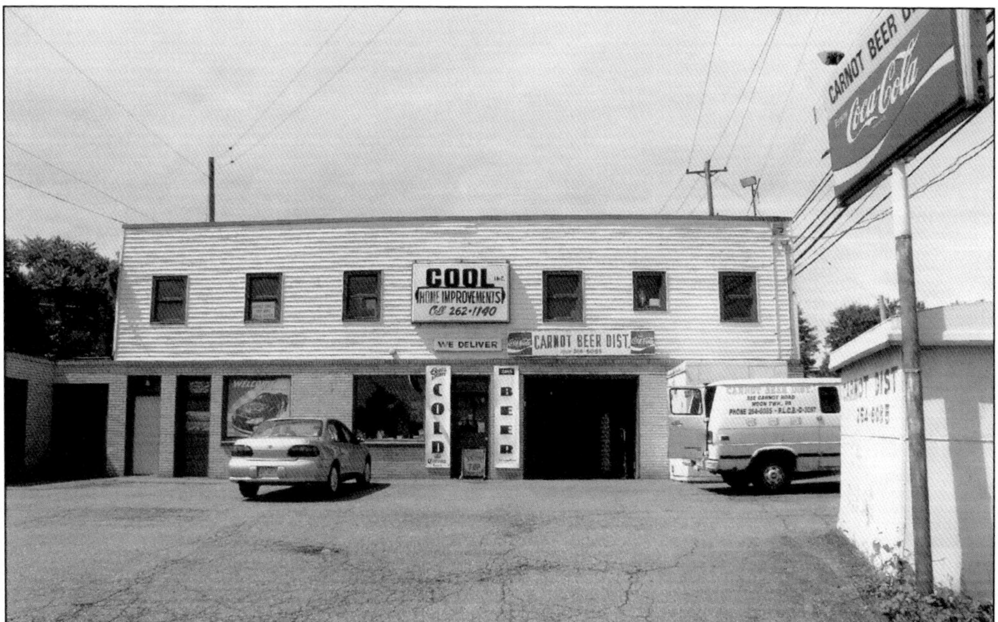

Today the Carnot Beer Distributor occupies a building where Carnot Elementary School once stood. Behind the building is Sharon Community Presbyterian Church. To its right are a Taco Bell and University Boulevard. In 1947, a log cabin would have stood to the left of the property along with several homes and garages. (Photograph by Mark Berton.)

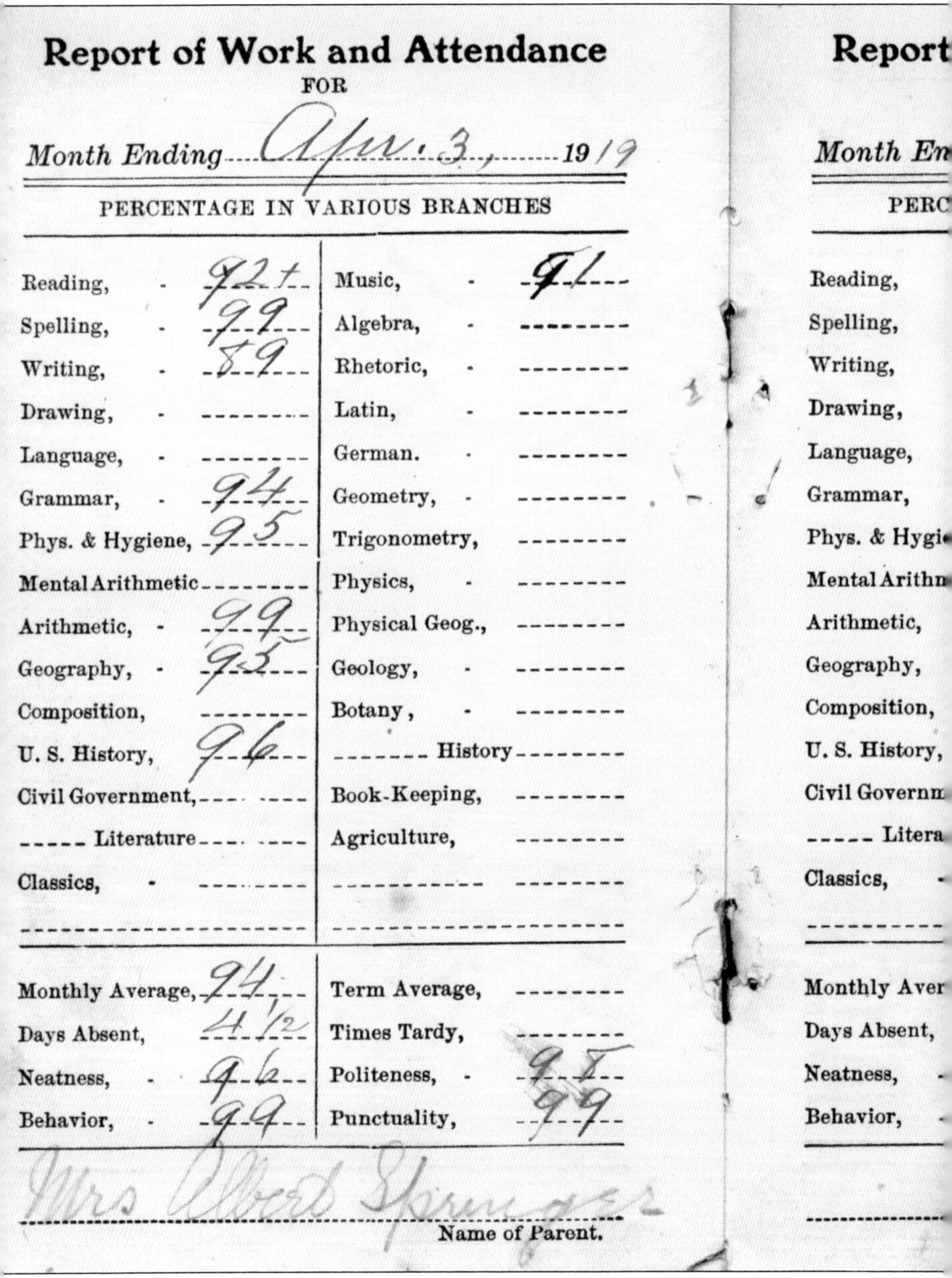

Report of Work and Attendance

FOR

Month Ending Apr. 3, 1919

PERCENTAGE IN VARIOUS BRANCHES

Reading,	92+	Music,	91
Spelling,	99	Algebra,	
Writing,	89	Rhetoric,	
Drawing,		Latin,	
Language,		German.	
Grammar,	94	Geometry,	
Phys. & Hygiene,	95	Trigonometry,	
Mental Arithmetic		Physics,	
Arithmetic,	99	Physical Geog.,	
Geography,	95	Geology,	
Composition,		Botany,	
U. S. History,	96	------- History	
Civil Government,		Book-Keeping,	
----- Literature		Agriculture,	
Classics,			

Monthly Average,	94	Term Average,	
Days Absent,	4 1/2	Times Tardy,	
Neatness,	96	Politeness,	95
Behavior,	99	Punctuality,	99

Mrs Albert Springer
Name of Parent.

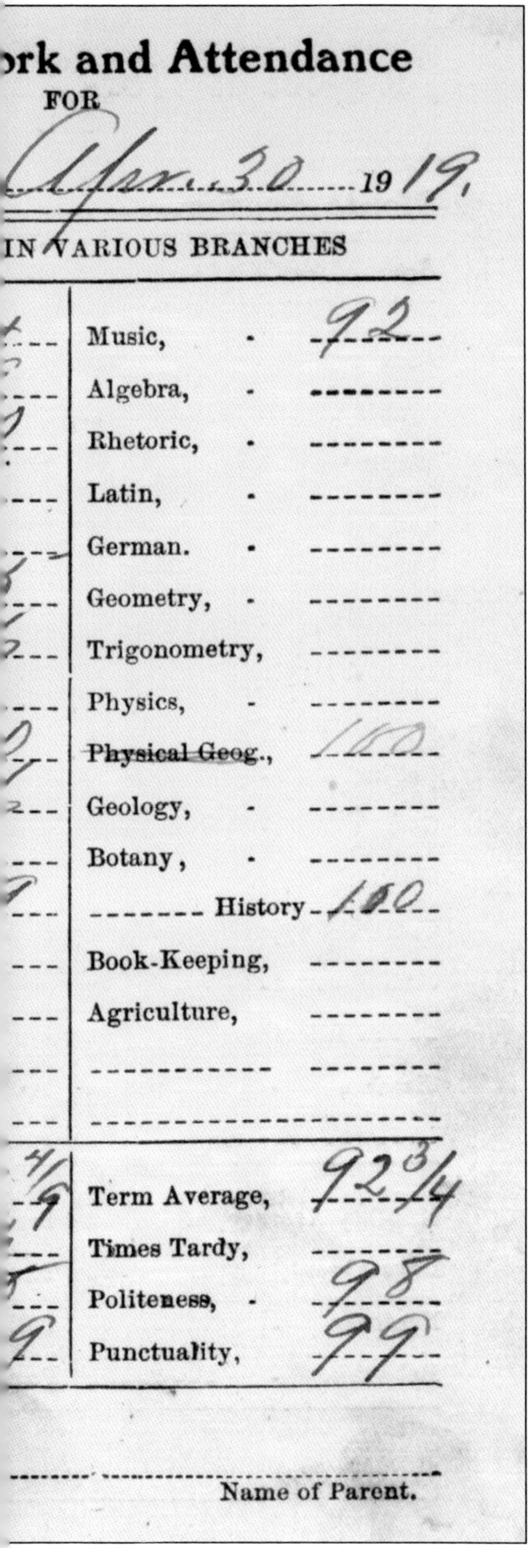

ork and Attendance

FOR

Apr. 30 1919.

IN VARIOUS BRANCHES

Music,	92
Algebra,	
Rhetoric,	
Latin,	
German.	
Geometry,	
Trigonometry,	
Physics,	
~~Physical Geog.~~,	100
Geology,	
Botany,	
History	100
Book-Keeping,	
Agriculture,	
Term Average,	92 3/4
Times Tardy,	
Politeness,	98
Punctuality,	99

Name of Parent.

In April 1919, students, including Nancy Springer whose report card is pictured here, were graded on a number of areas not necessarily related to getting an education in today's world. Categories such as hygiene and politeness are graded next to reading, spelling, and grammar. Students were evaluated monthly rather than quarterly as they are today. (Courtesy Nancy Mills.)

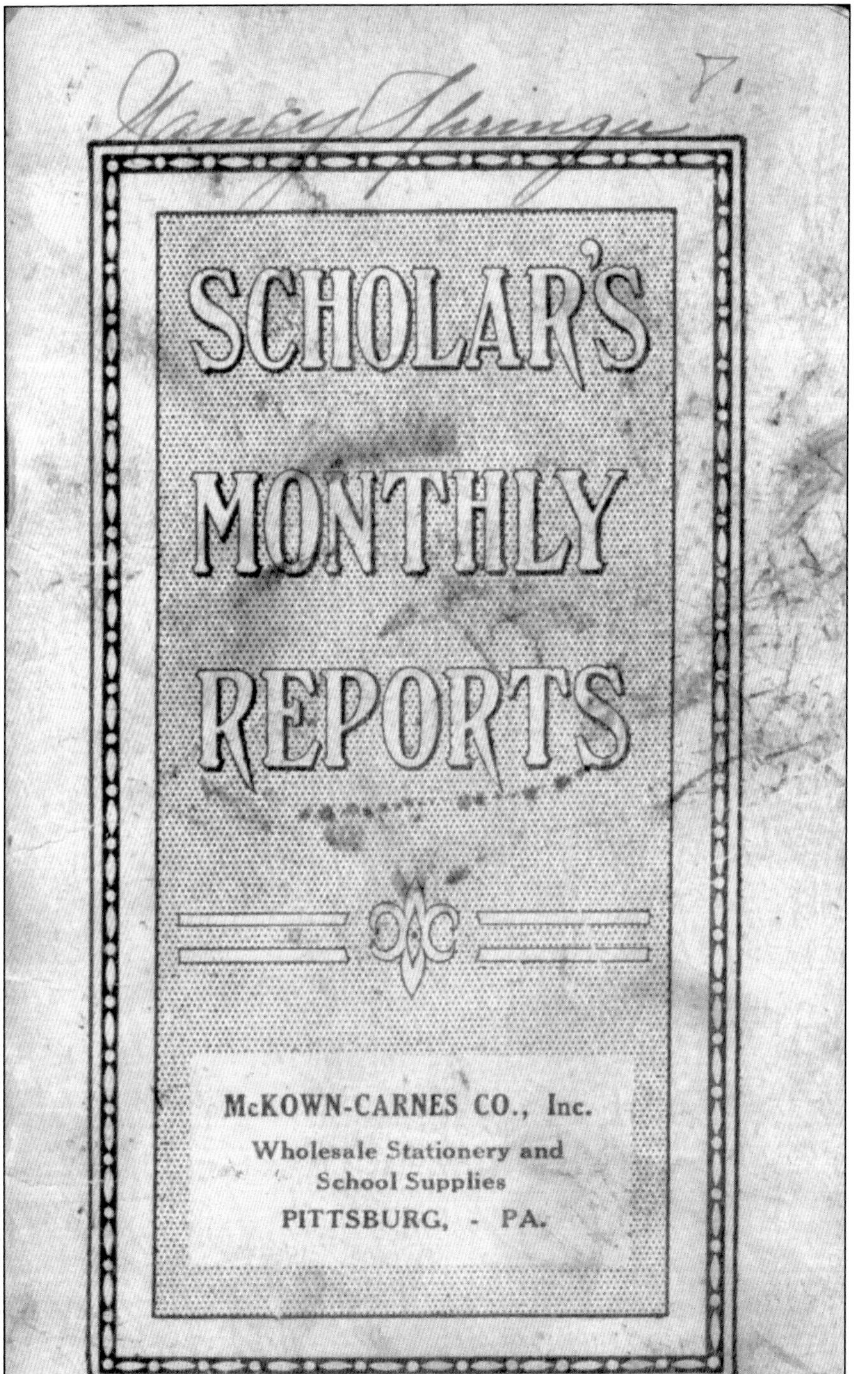

Nancy Springer was the daughter of Albert Springer. Shown here is the front of her report card for the year of 1919, just five years after Carnot Elementary School opened its doors to educate the students of Moon Township. Neighboring Crescent Township did not become part of the school district until 1952. (Courtesy Nancy Mills.)

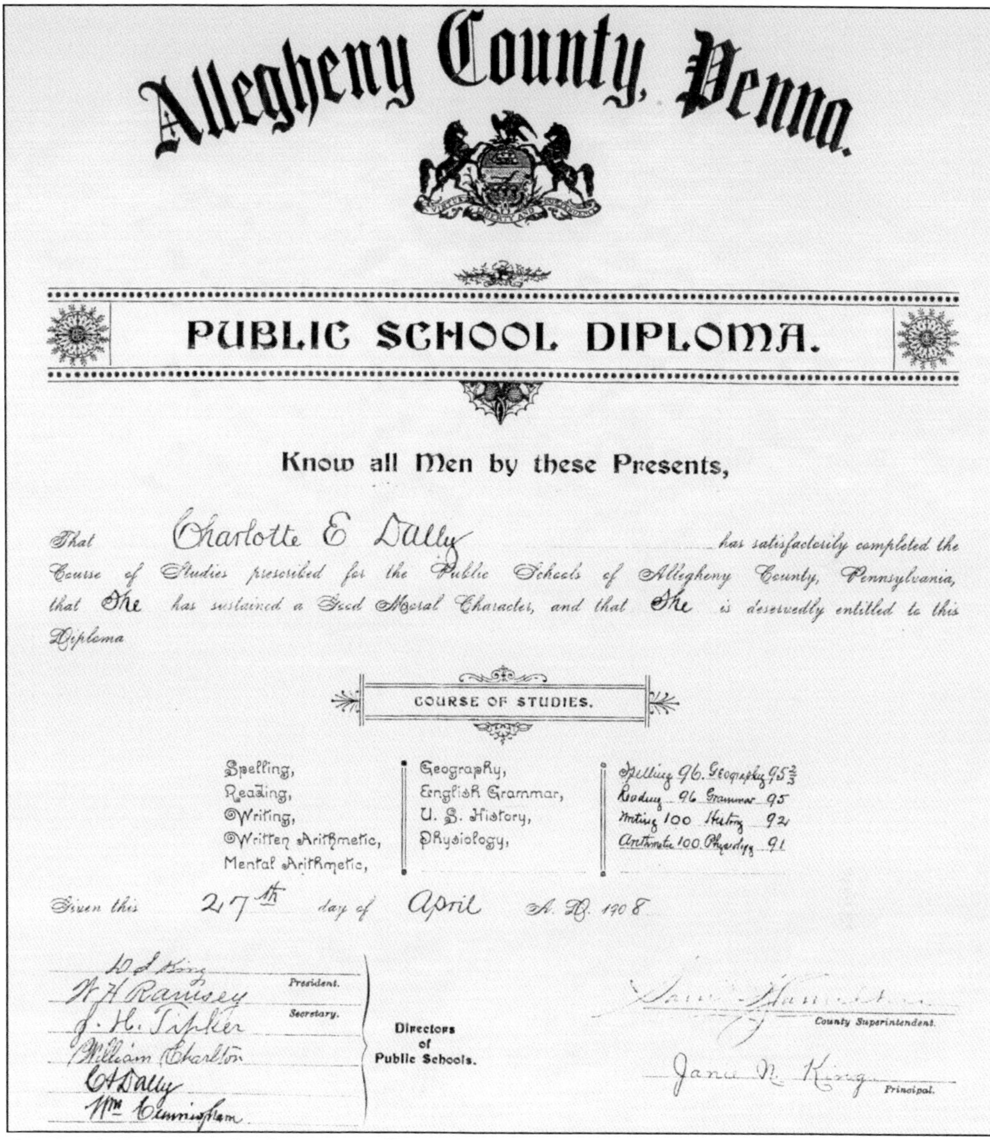
Allegheny County, Penna.

PUBLIC SCHOOL DIPLOMA.

Know all Men by these Presents,

That Charlotte E Dally has satisfactorily completed the Course of Studies prescribed for the Public Schools of Allegheny County, Pennsylvania, that She has sustained a Good Moral Character, and that She is deservedly entitled to this Diploma

COURSE OF STUDIES.

Spelling, Reading, Writing, Written Arithmetic, Mental Arithmetic,

Geography, English Grammar, U. S. History, Physiology,

Spelling 96. Geography 95 2/3
Reading 96 Grammar 95
Writing 100 History 92
Arithmetic 100 Physiology 91

Given this 27th day of April A. D. 1908

W H Ramsey President.
J. H. Tipker Secretary.
William Charlton
C A Dally
Wm Cunningham
Directors of Public Schools.

County Superintendent.
Jane N. King Principal.

On April 27, 1908, Charlotte E. Dally graduated from Moon schools with a diploma issued by the Public Schools of Allegheny County. Prior to 1936, many Moon students attended high school in neighboring communities with tuition billed to the home district. The new Carnot Elementary School later became the district high school. It later closed and was leased to U.S. Airways for a training facility. It now stands vacant. (Courtesy the Meanor family.)

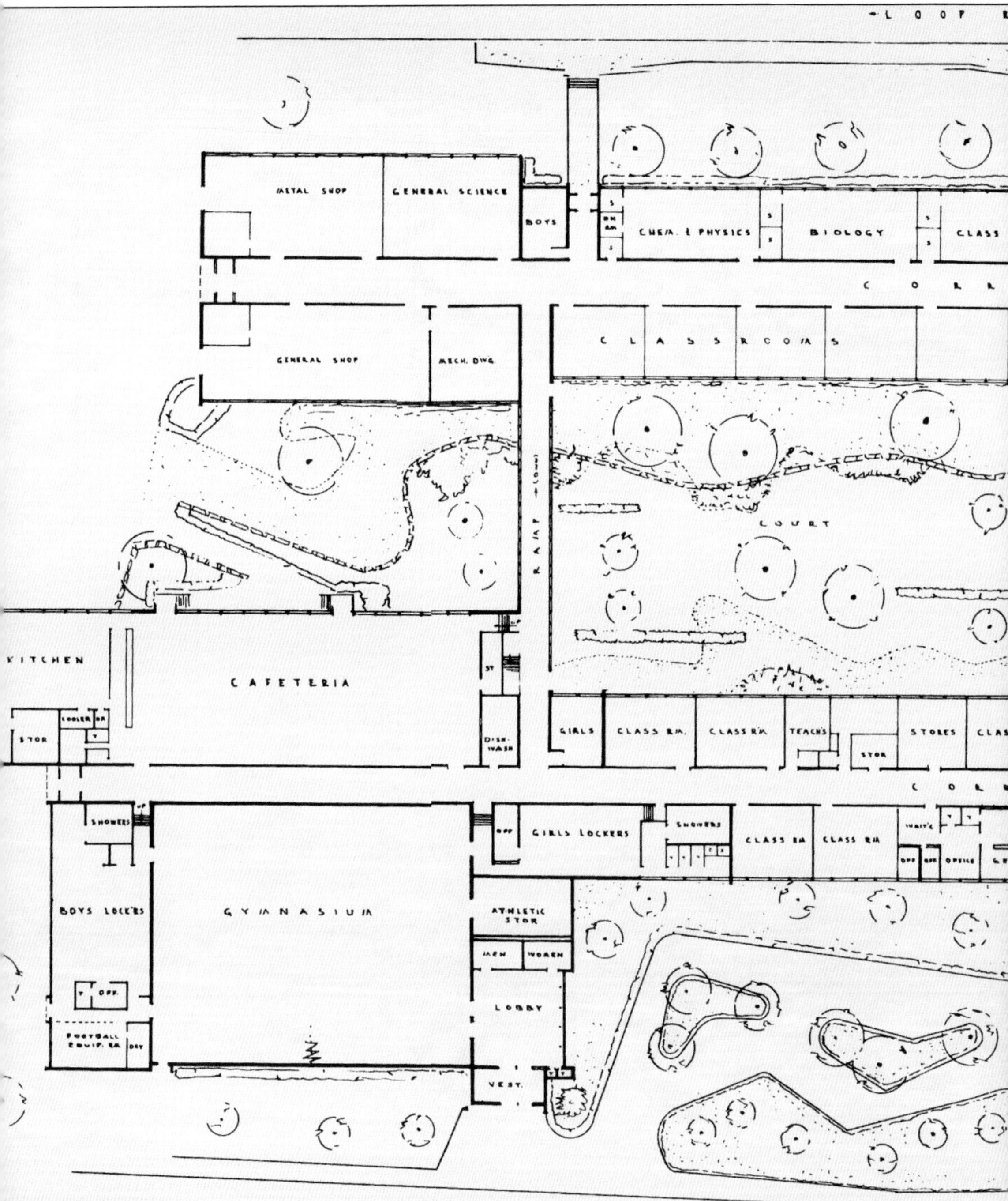

The new Moon High School was built on the principles of "Economy, beauty, safety and utility," at a cost of $2,308,627. District officials in the dedication booklet state that they expect 10,000 students to graduate from the school in the next 50 years. World War II was still fresh on everyone's mind as the cost of the school was considered a bargain when, "we think nothing

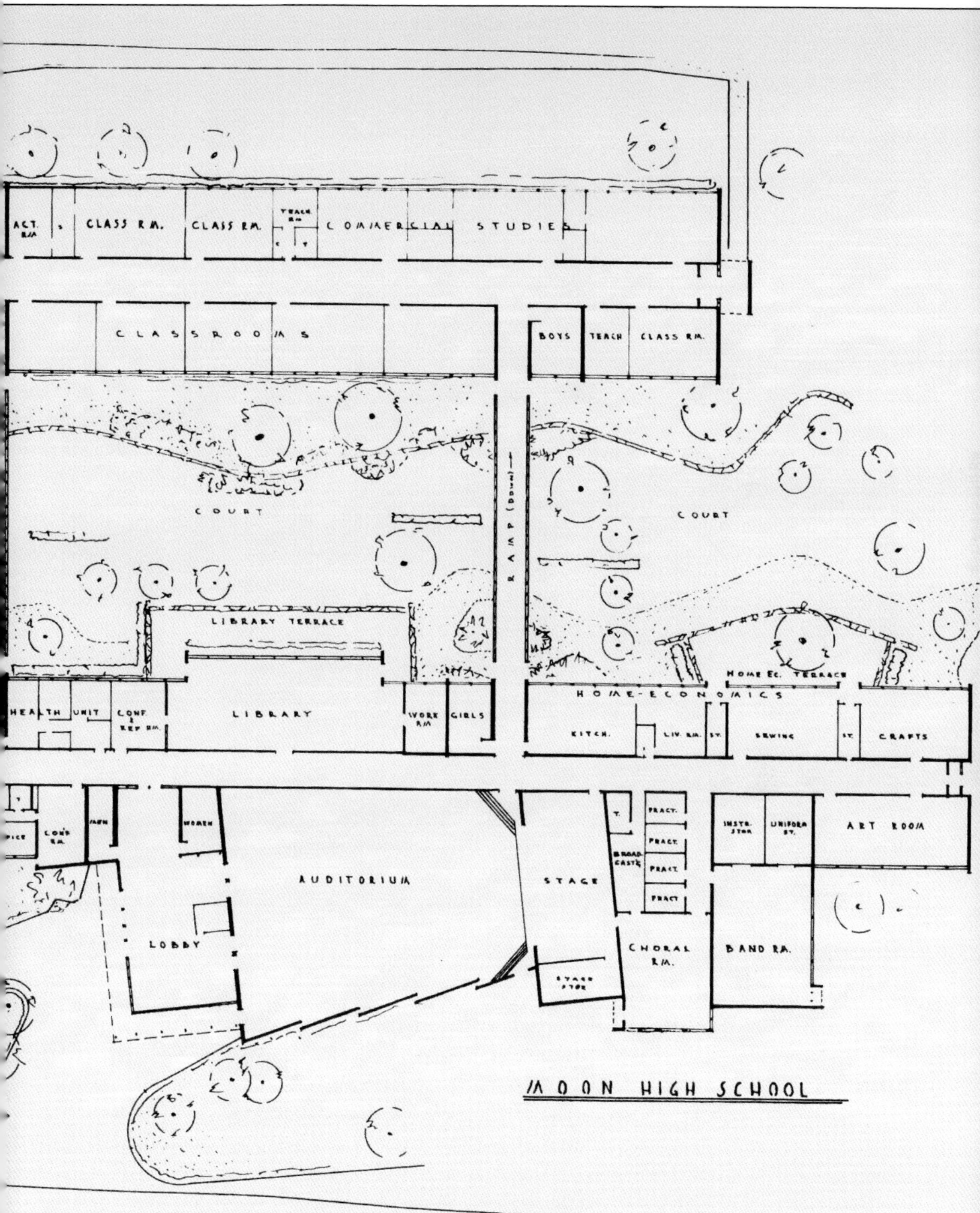

of spending $75,000,000 on a battleship which may last thirty years; $1,500,000 for each super Constellation with lifetime of 10 years; $450,000 for one Diesel locomotive which lasts about thirty years."

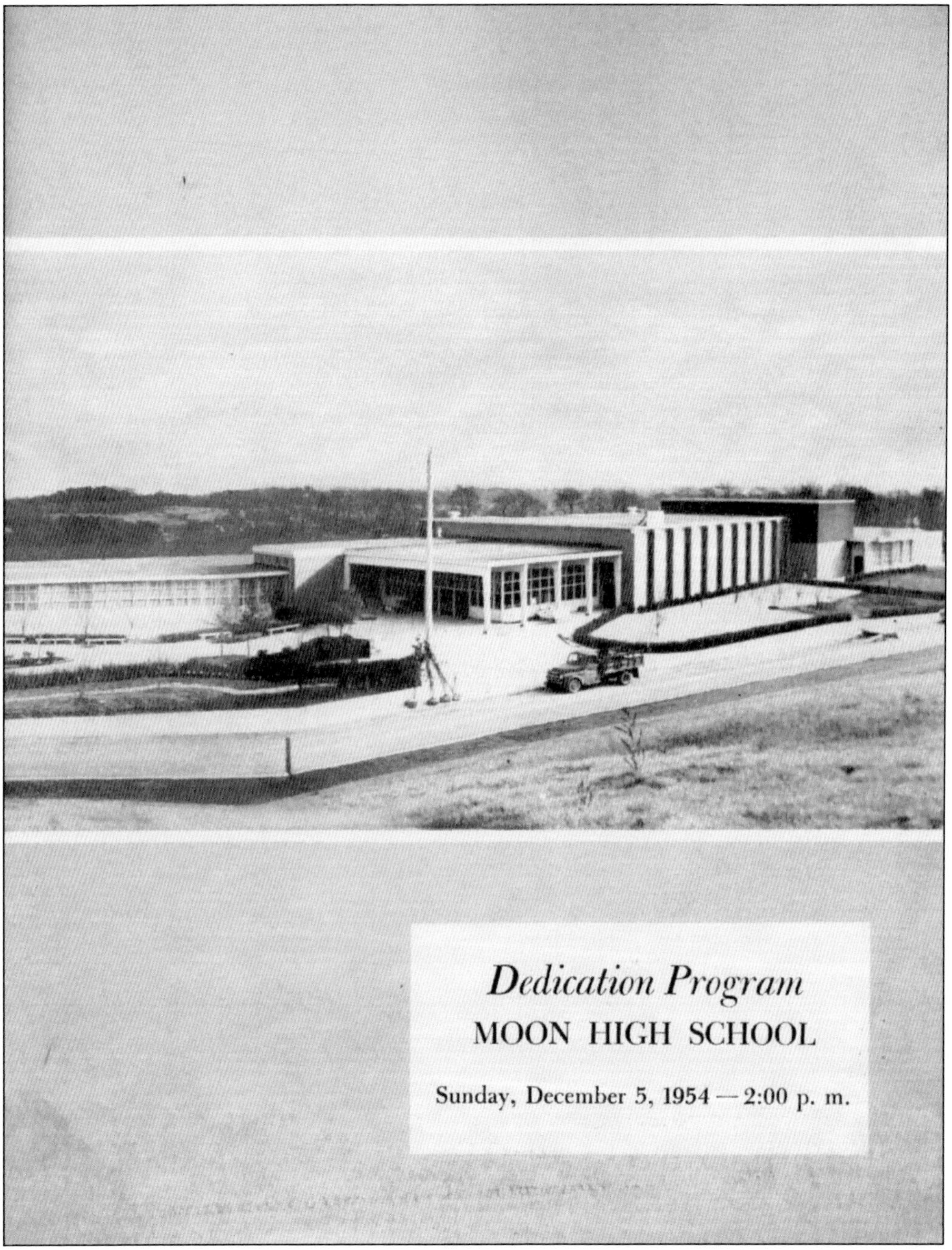

Less than 20 years after Carnot Elementary was converted to the Moon High School, the district dedicated a new, modern high school. The dedication ceremony opened to "Psyche and Eros" by Cesar Franck performed by the Moon High School band. The school opened on December 5, 1954. Open houses followed on December 6 and 7. The school's first athletic performance was a basketball game versus Sewickley High on December 7, 1954. (Courtesy Nancy Mills.)

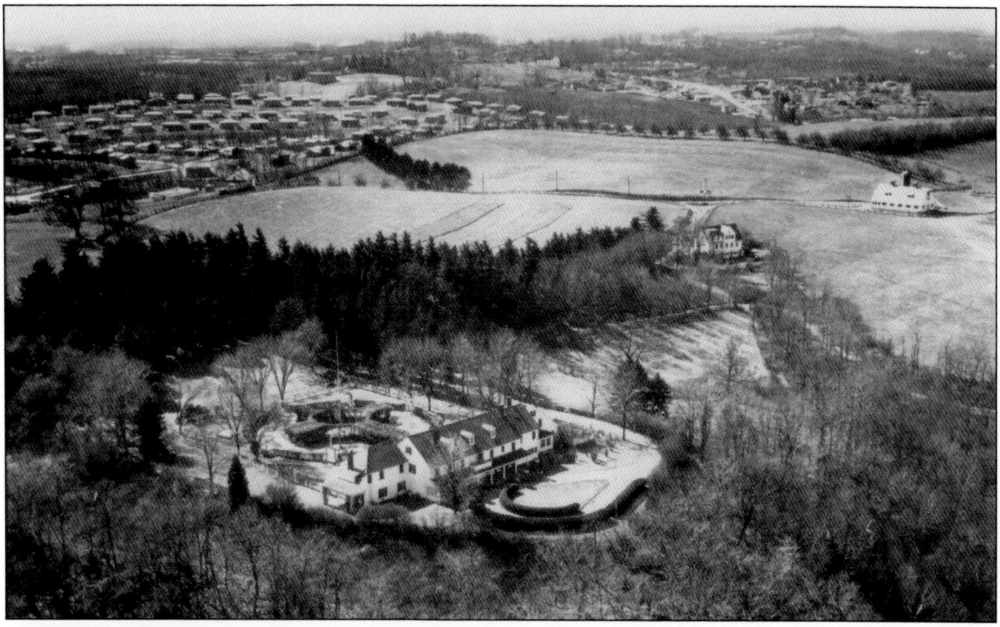

More than 230 acres in Moon were purchased to make room for a growing accounting school known as Robert Morris School. The 1962 purchase changed the site of the school's main campus from Pittsburgh to its new suburban home. Seven years later, the school changed its name to Robert Morris College. The farmland shown here was part of that 1962 purchase. (Courtesy Robert Morris University.)

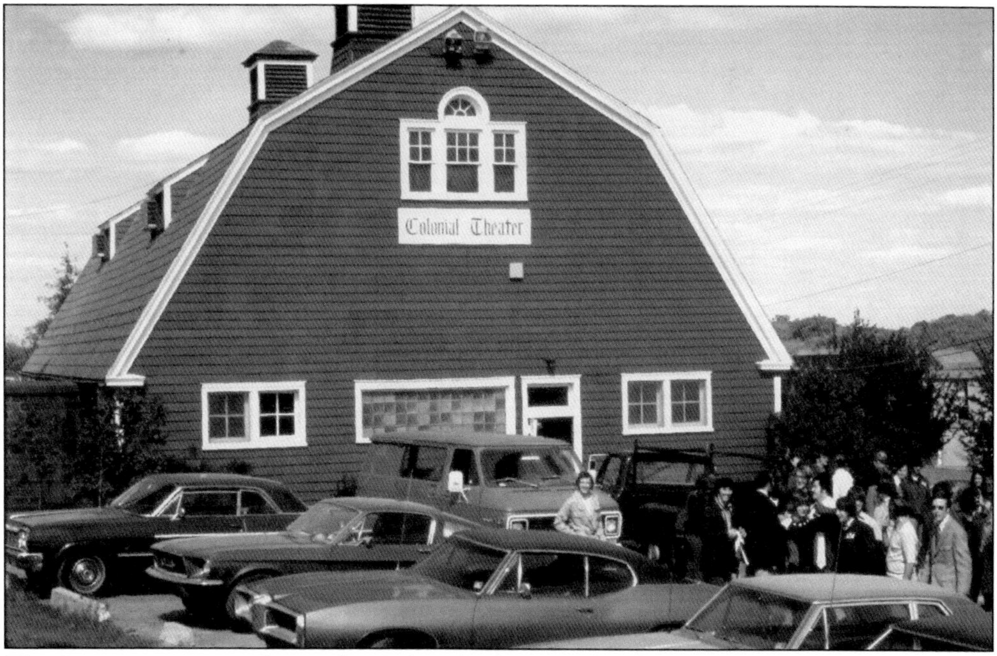

This barn was converted into the Colonial Theater. The theater burned to the ground in a fire and was lost. However, the school continued to grow and in 2002, Robert Morris College became Robert Morris University and now offers doctoral and master's degrees. The university has more than 30 undergraduate programs. (Courtesy Robert Morris University.)

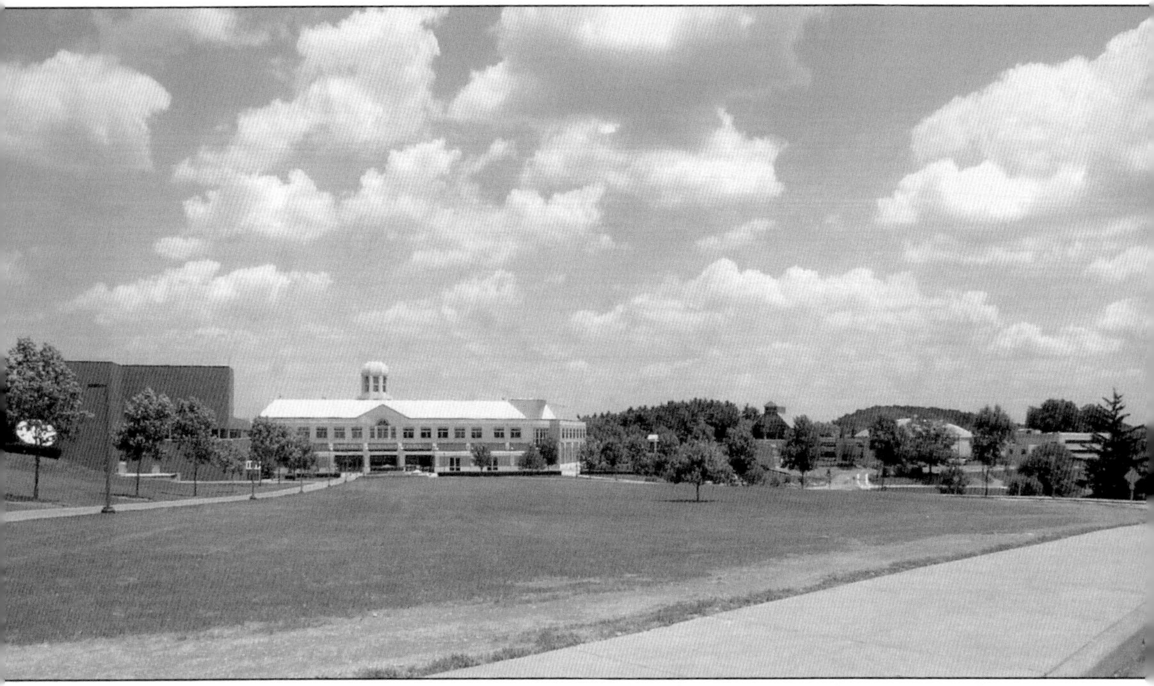

Today it can be argued that outside of the Pittsburgh International Airport, Robert Morris University has had the second-largest influence on Moon Township. Nearby communities such as Colony West, Forest Glen, and Fox Hollow are unofficial off-campus housing for the school. In 2006, Robert Morris University purchased and converted a former nursing facility into off-campus housing behind the Fox Hollow Condominium Association property. Enrollment for the school has been greater than 5,000 students. (Photograph by Mark Berton.)

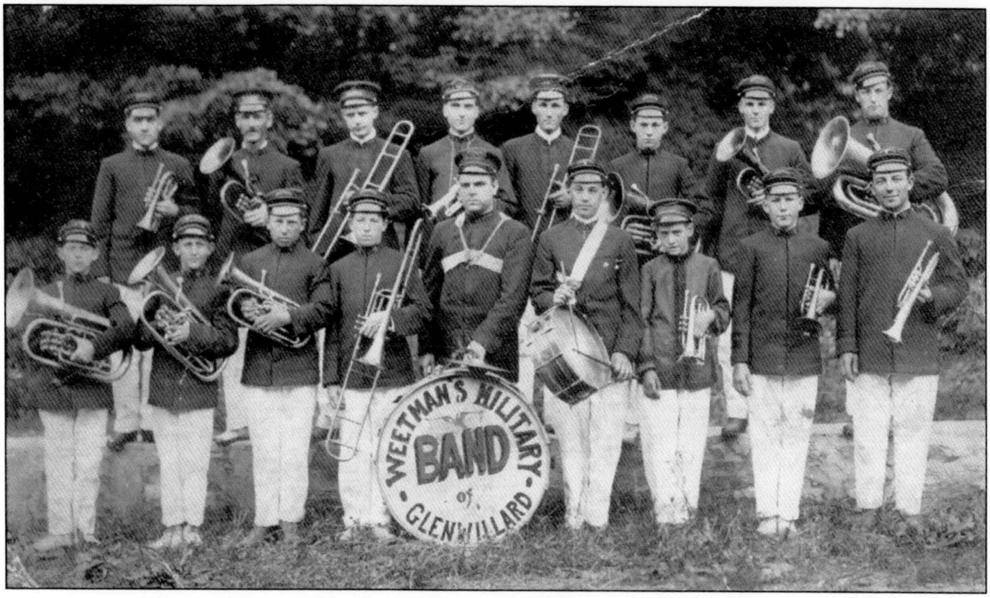

Weetman's Military Band of Glenwillard was a parade favorite in the early 1900s. While this photograph is undated, Shousetown's name was changed to Glenwillard in 1907. Crescent Township residents have always been patriotic. A World War II honor roll was erected and dedicated in Crescent on November 28, 1943. The monument was later moved to Honor Roll Park, and a Korean War monument was dedicated there in 1956. (Courtesy Eliot and Marjorie Johnson and the Crescent-Shousetown Area Historic Association.)

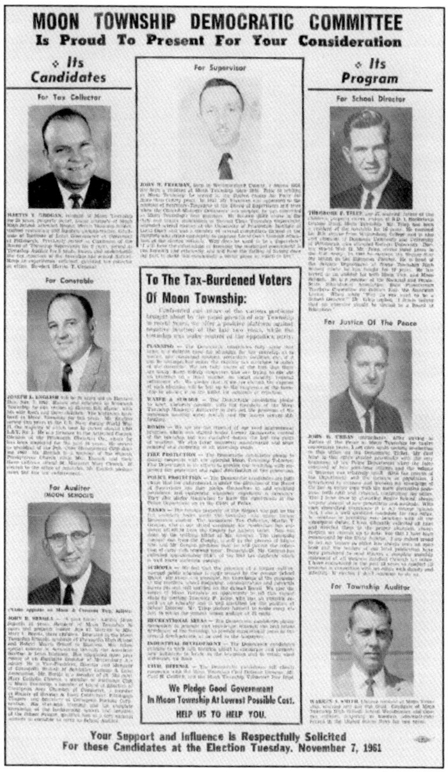

MOON TOWNSHIP DEMOCRATIC COMMITTEE
Is Proud To Present For Your Consideration

Its Candidates

Its Program

For Tax Collector

For Supervisor

For School Director

For Constable

To The Tax-Burdened Voters Of Moon Township:

For Justice Of The Peace

For Auditor (MOON SCHOOLS)

For Township Auditor

We Pledge Good Government
In Moon Township At Lowest Possible Cost.
HELP US TO HELP YOU.

Your Support and Influence is Respectfully Solicited
For these Candidates at the Election Tuesday, November 7, 1961

Politics in Moon have always been at the forefront of people's mind. This Moon Township Democratic Committee mailer from 1961 highlights the candidacy of John W. Freeman for Moon Township supervisor. Freeman was Moon Township's first manager. Freeman started his service to the township in 1957 as the board of supervisors' secretary-treasurer. (Courtesy Nancy Mills.)

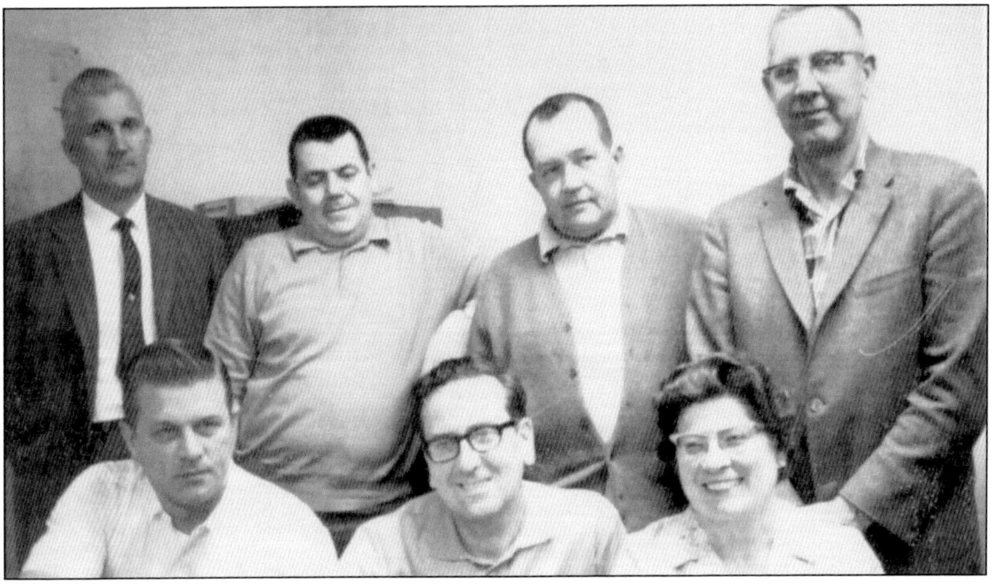

The first parks and recreation board in Moon Township was formed in 1963. Today Moon has more than 600 acres of parks, an amphitheater, and incentives in the planning code that give developers building credits if they include green space and trail systems in their developments. The parks department oversees not only the outdoor parks, but Robin Hill, a nature reserve donated to the township. In 2005, the township purchased the Bon Air Golf Course and now operates the Moon Golf Club.

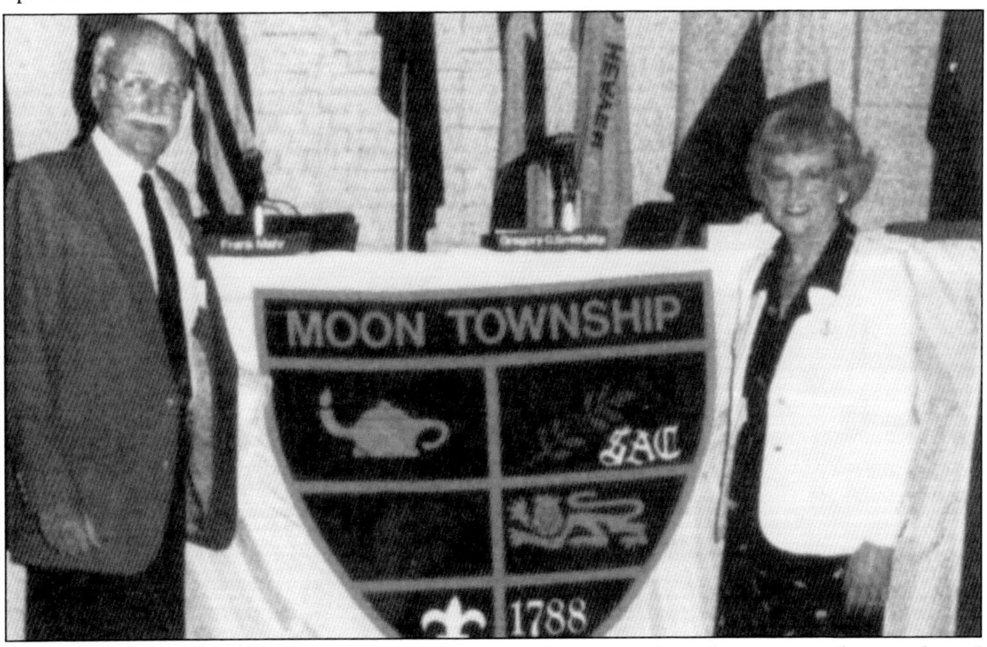

In 1972, the flag of Moon Township was designed after more than three years of research and effort by Janet Walsh and her father, William, who is pictured here with his wife, Ruth. The flag's symbols include a passant lion, a fleur-de-lis, a log fort, a lamp of learning, the 1788 date of erection of the township, and the Strategic Air Command logo. The flag is a white field with a black shield and gold trim. The flag became official on June 8, 1988.

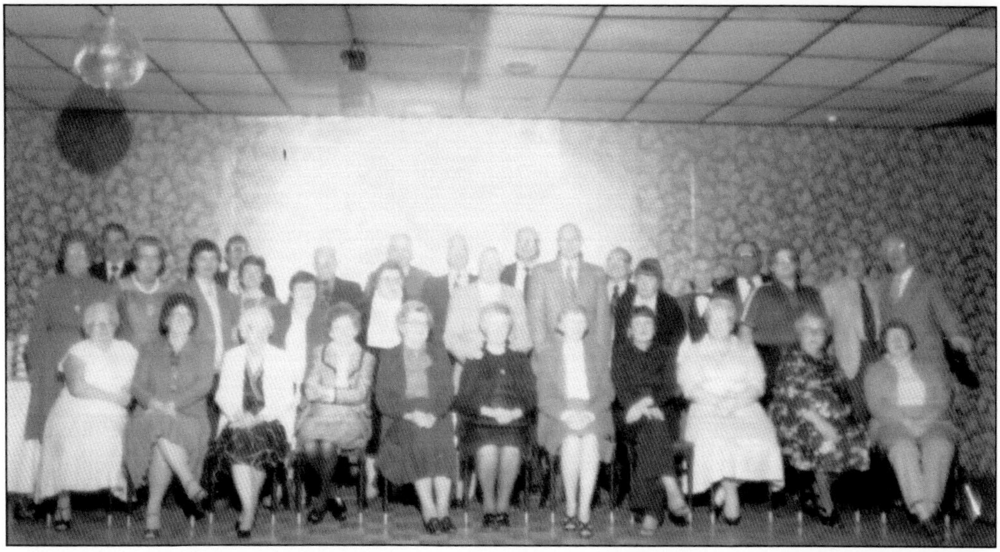

Pictured here are the members of the Crescent-Shousetown Area Historical Association, which is a very vibrant and enthusiastic group dedicated to preserving the history of their home. The group holds meetings at the Crescent Township Municipal Building. They are allotted an 8-foot-by-16-foot closet of space to hold their collection, which is all that can be afforded them. (Courtesy Eliot and Marjorie Johnson and the Crescent-Shousetown Area Historic Association.)

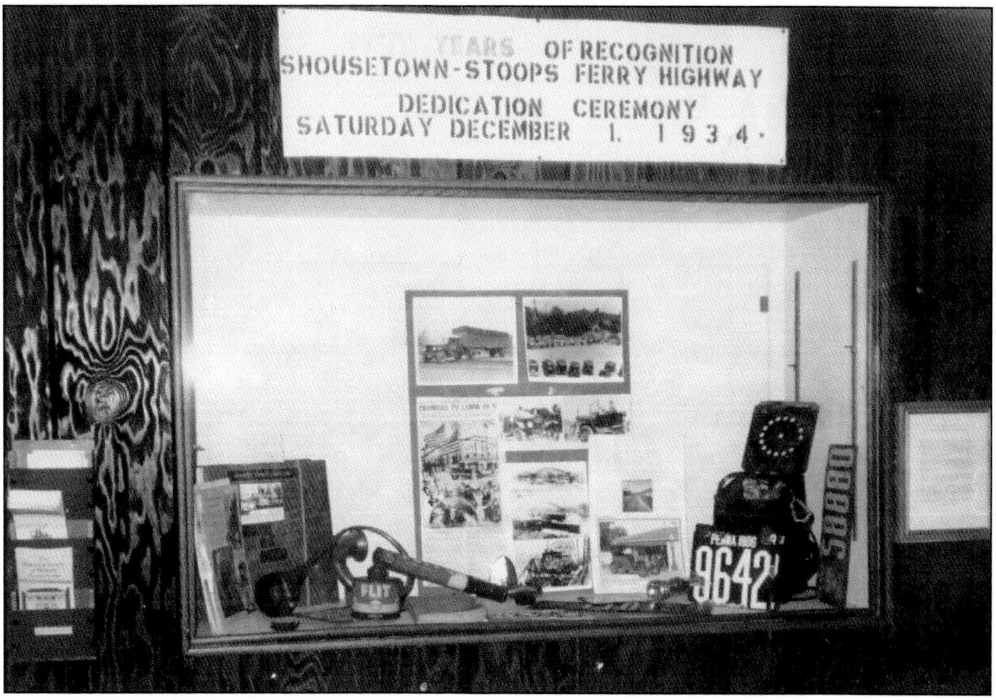

In 1982, this display in the Crescent Township Municipal Building was built by Earle Miller to show off the various artifacts the Crescent-Shousetown Area Historical Association has collected over the years. The display case contains items reflecting the early industries of the region, especially inland riverboat building. (Courtesy Eliot and Marjorie Johnson and the Crescent-Shousetown Area Historic Association.)

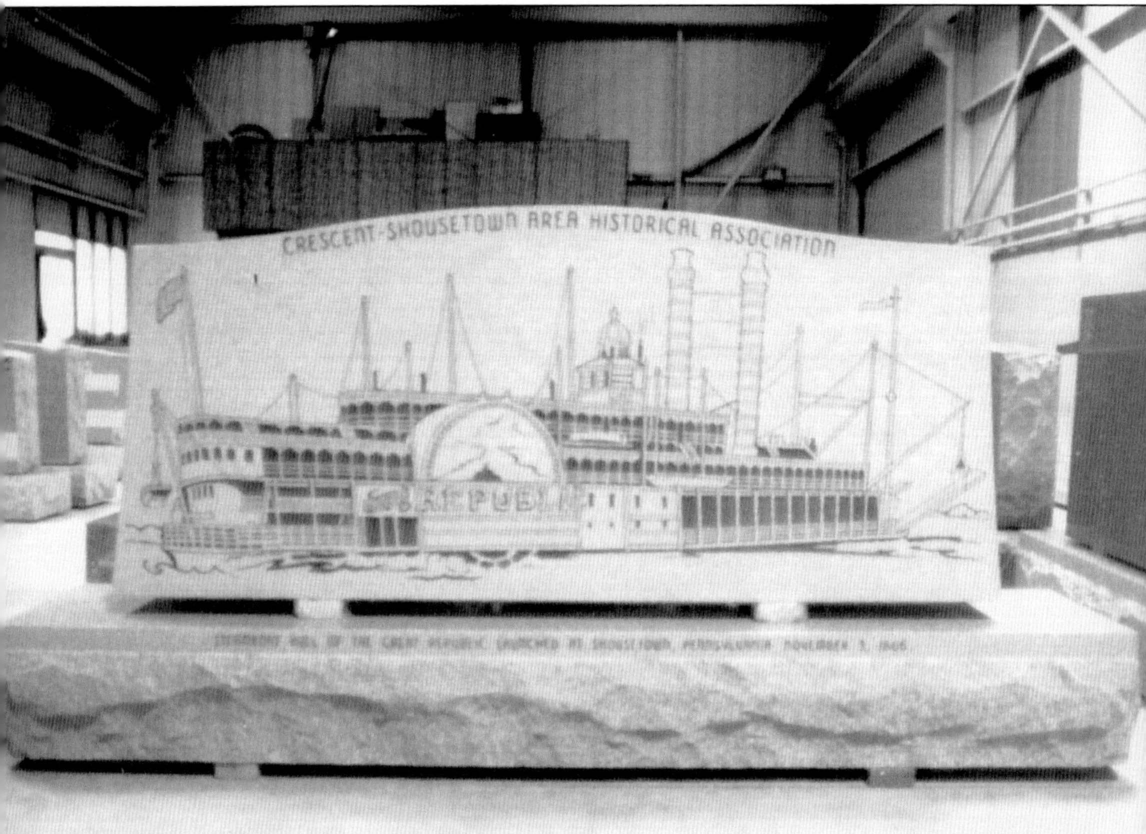

The Crescent-Shousetown Area Historical Association commissioned Moon Township's Rome Monument Company to create this monument/time capsule. The riverboat depicted is the *Great Republic*, which launched from Shousetown on November 3, 1866. Shousetown began building boats in 1827 when Peter Shouse started his business. The first boat launched was the *Kentuckian*. (Courtesy Eliot and Marjorie Johnson and the Crescent-Shousetown Area Historic Association.)

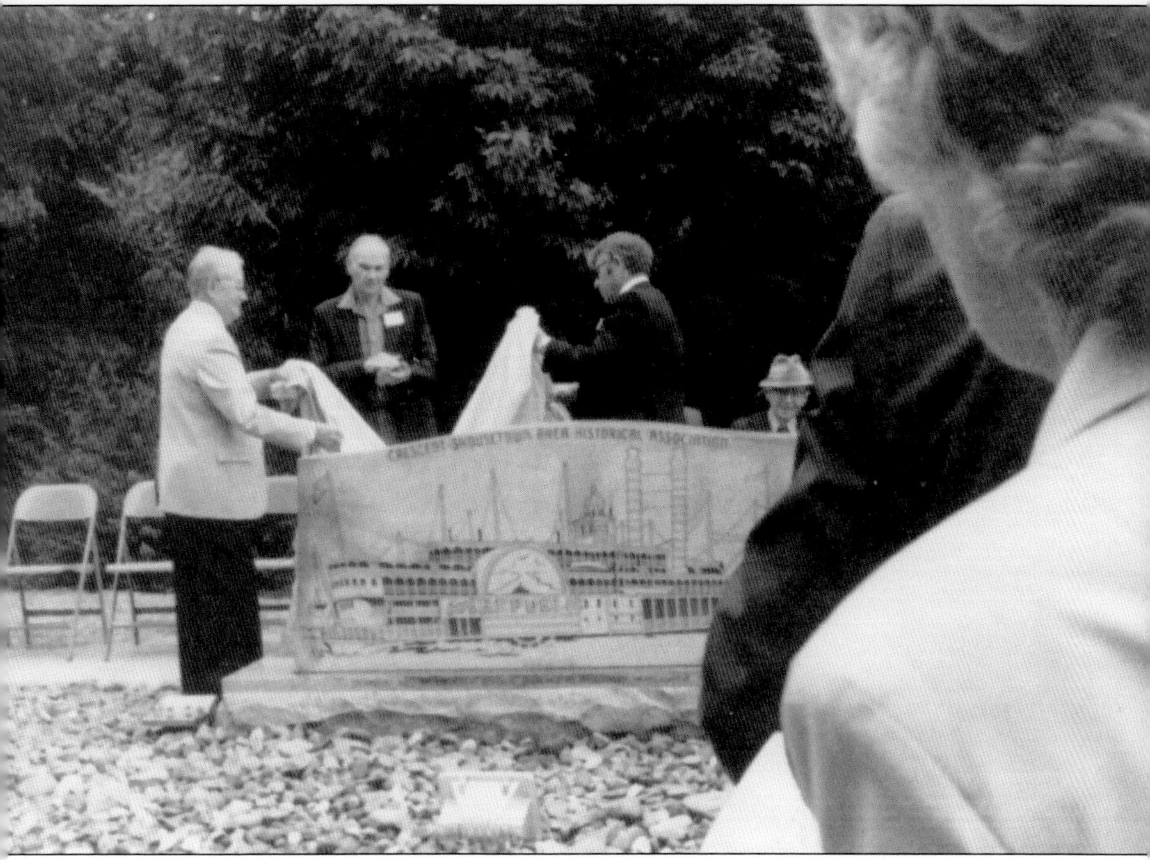

On May 28, 1984, the Shousetown Boatyard and Boatbuilders Memorial Monument was dedicated in Honor Roll Park. Pictured here from left to right are Harry Davis, Eliot Johnson, and Bill McCutcheon. A time capsule is embedded in the monument and will be opened in 2181, the 500th anniversary of the Commonwealth of Pennsylvania. (Courtesy Eliot and Marjorie Johnson and the Crescent-Shousetown Area Historic Association.)

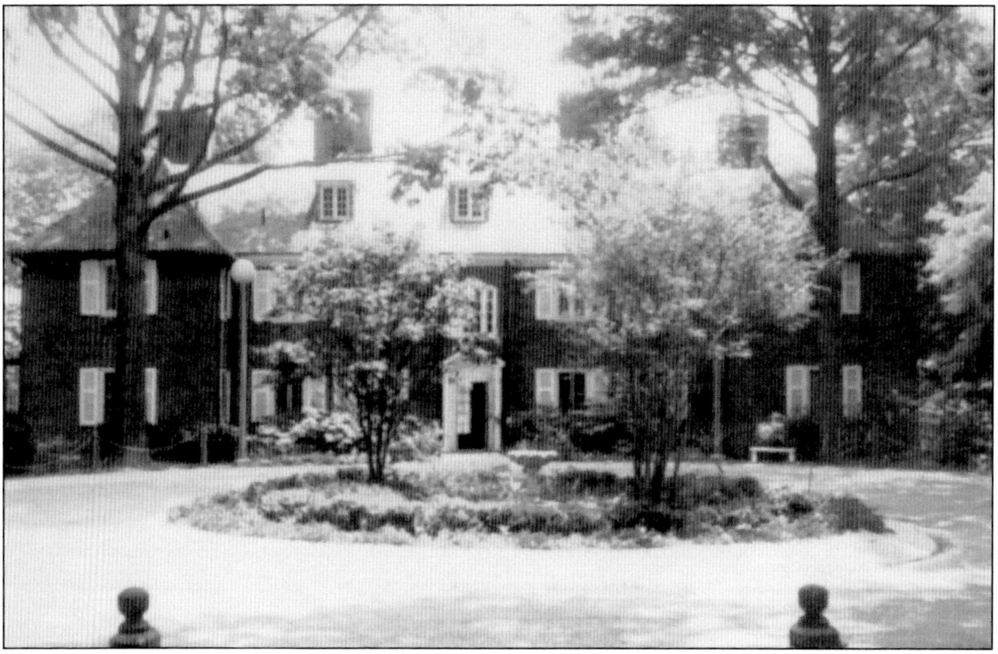

Robin Hill Park is home to this 24-room mansion that was donated to the township so long as it remained a nature preserve. The park has an herb garden, over two miles of trails, 200 acres of property, and a carriage house where the Moon Area Senior Citizens Center is based. Classes are offered to residents, and an annual Earth Day celebration is held on the premises.

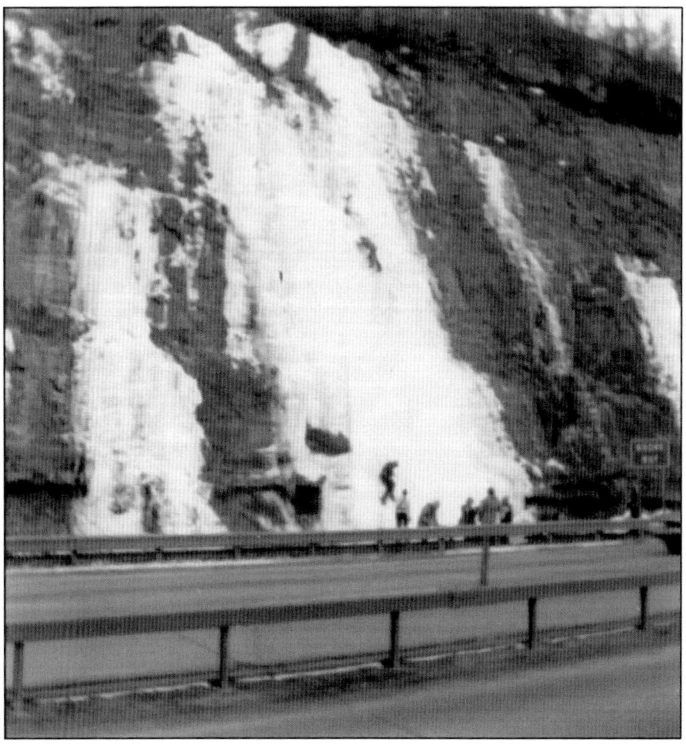

Here students from Robert Morris University climb the ice walls that form near the Ohio River banks. This photograph was taken in the mid-1980s. (Courtesy Eliot and Marjorie Johnson and the Crescent-Shousetown Area Historic Association.)

When the new Sewickley Bridge opened on October 21, 1981, an opening ceremony was held. Here the Moon Area School District High School Band is shown marching in a celebratory parade on the Moon side of the bridge. Moon Area School District combined Moon School District and Crescent School District in 1953. (Courtesy Eliot and Marjorie Johnson and the Crescent-Shousetown Area Historic Association.)

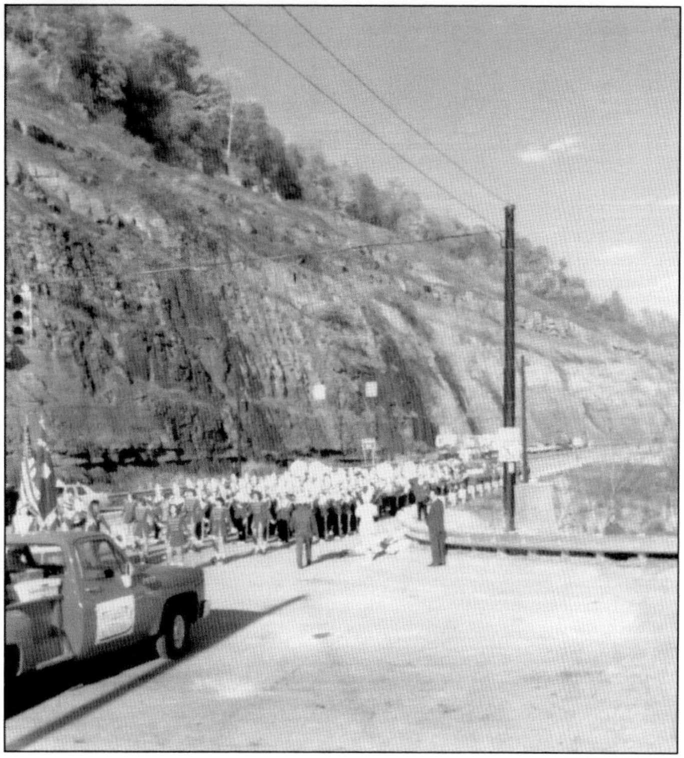

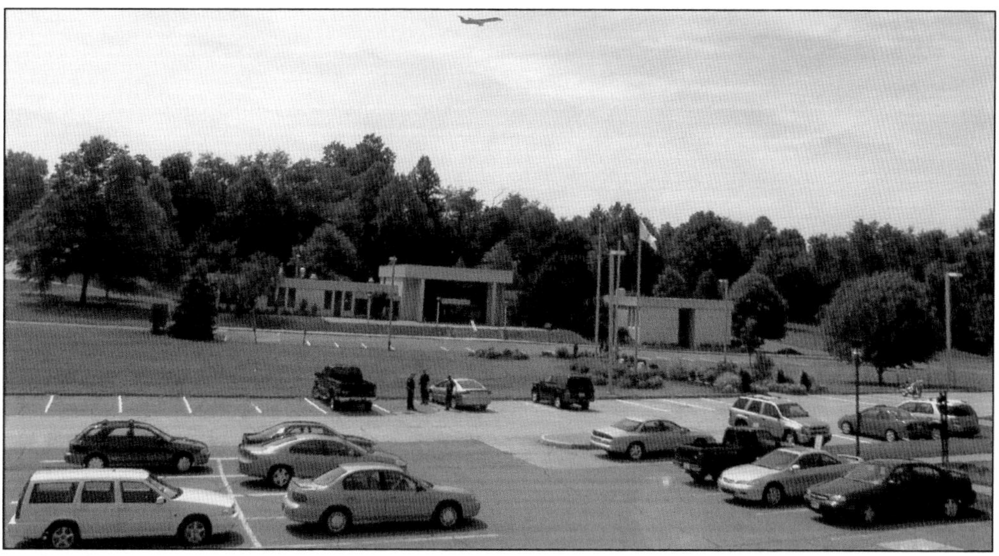

Today the Moon Township Municipal Building houses most administrative functions of the township. The township library, the cable access studio, and the tax office are in another building less than a mile away. Currently there are no plans to consolidate the two or expand the current municipal facilities. (Photograph by Mark Berton.)

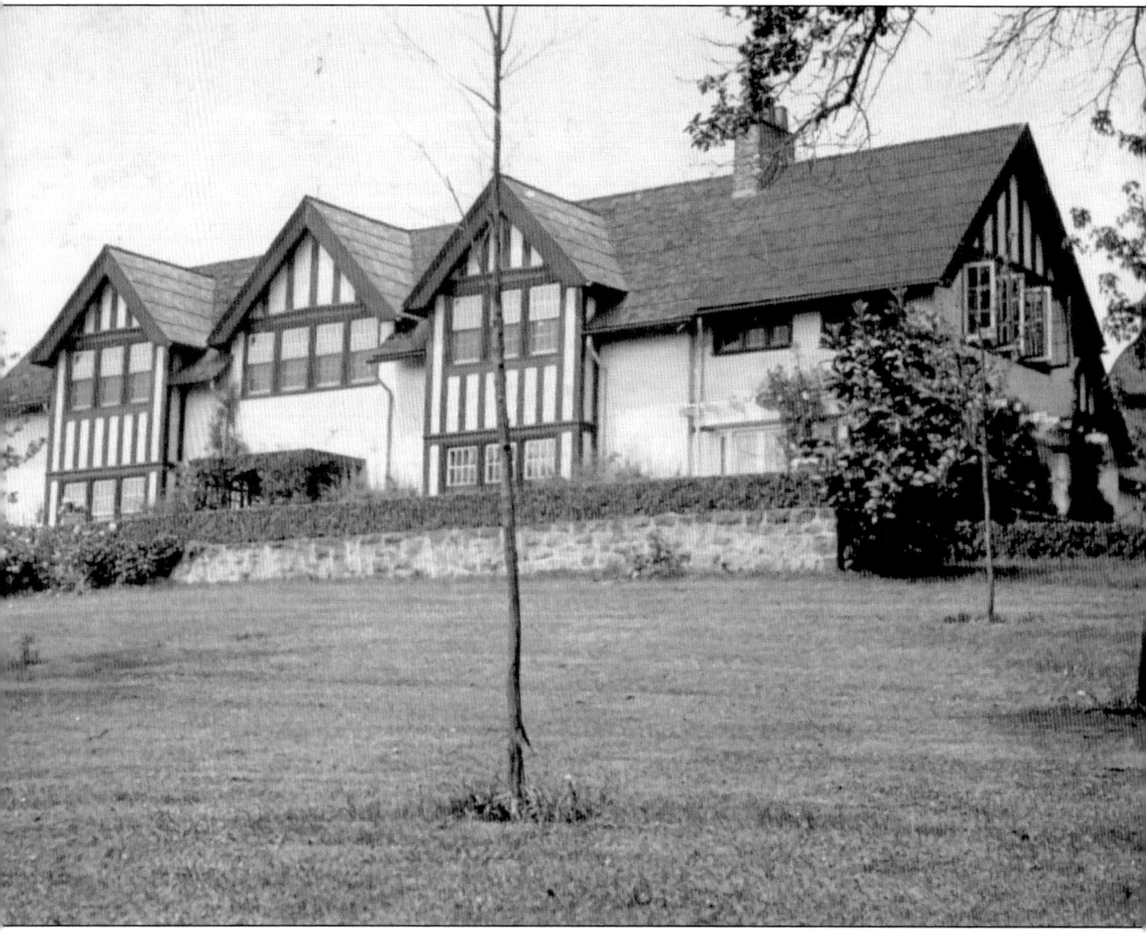

No history of Moon would be complete without mentioning Roselea Farm. Originally 123 acres, the farm is today approximately 3.5 acres. Much of the land was sold to Montour Heights Country Club, which is situated across Coraopolis Heights Road from Roselea. Once occupied by Locomotive Stoker Company president David Crawford, the farm was the home to a herd of award-winning Guernsey cattle. (Courtesy Nancy Mills.)

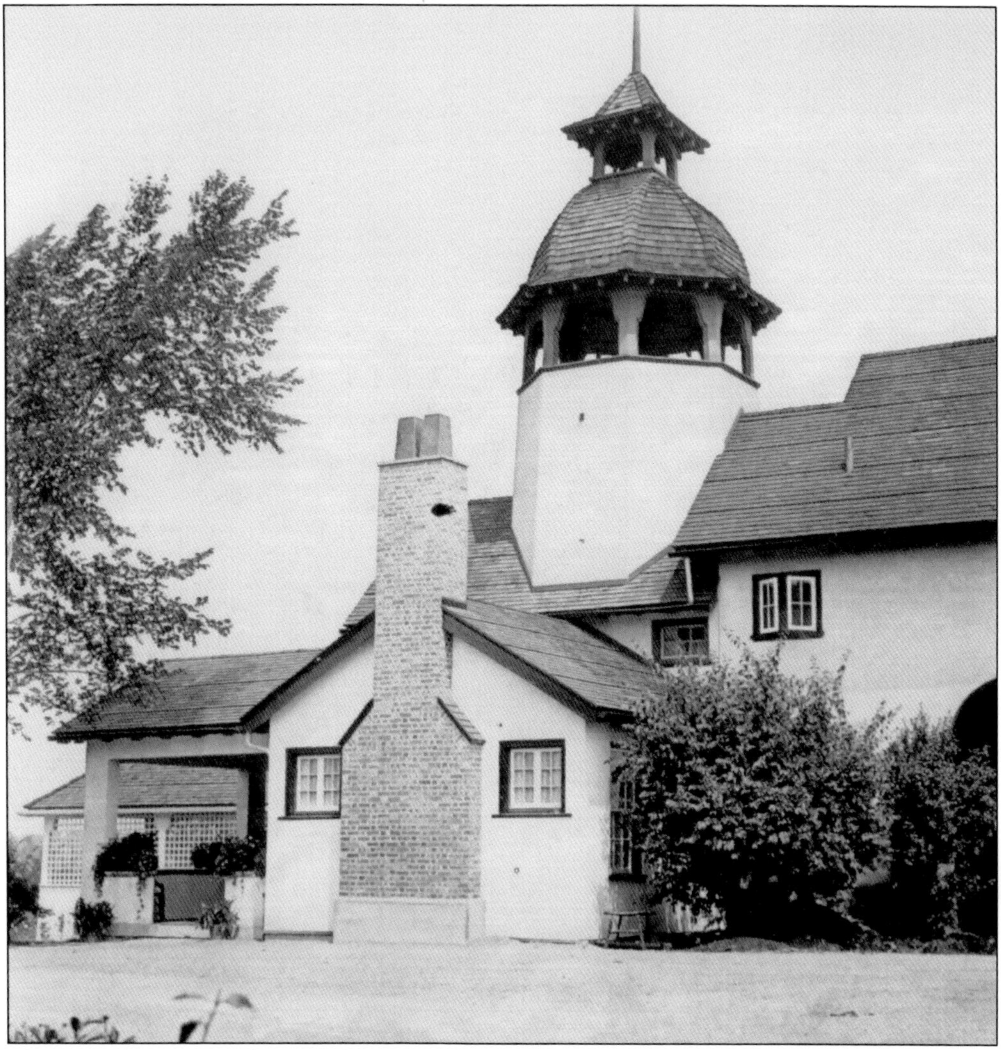

The "towerhouse" was the main house on the property and was attached to chauffeur's quarters. The property was sold to Russell and Nancy Springer Patton in 1950. During the Korean War, the house was seized by the government to be used for U.S. Air Force officers. Nearly 50 officers occupied the house, converting the east barn into an officers' club. The Pattons regained possession of the house in 1958. (Courtesy Nancy Mills.)

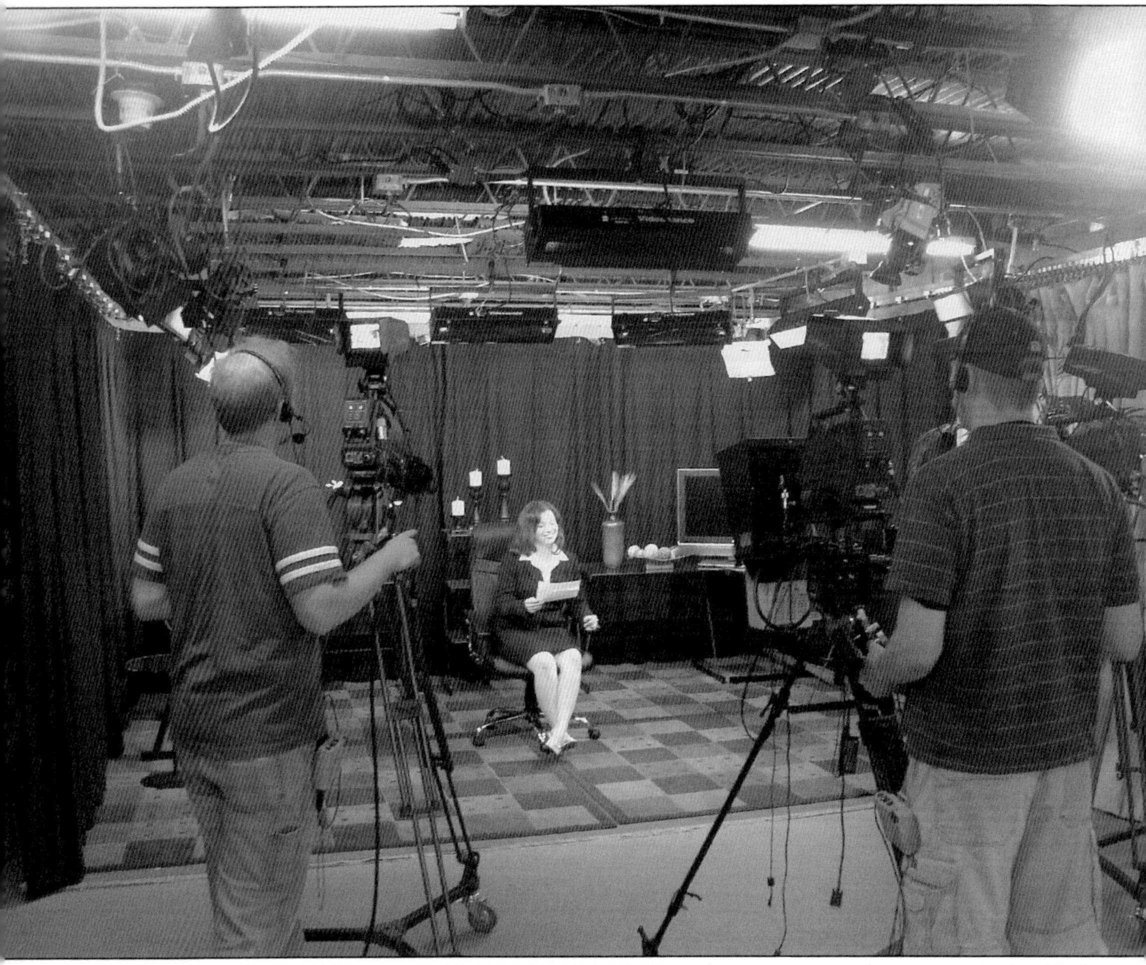

Moon Township's Public Access Channel, MCA-TV, broadcasts municipal meetings and publicly produced programs. A 2005 survey of the Moon residents revealed that 87.4 percent of those surveyed watch the channel at some point during the calendar year. More than 90 percent surveyed are aware of the channel and its programming. The station operates on cable franchise fees and costs the taxpayers nothing. Pictured here, Shannon Debes, chair of the Cable TV Advisory Board, records an introduction to a video report to the township board of supervisors. (Photograph by Mark Berton.)

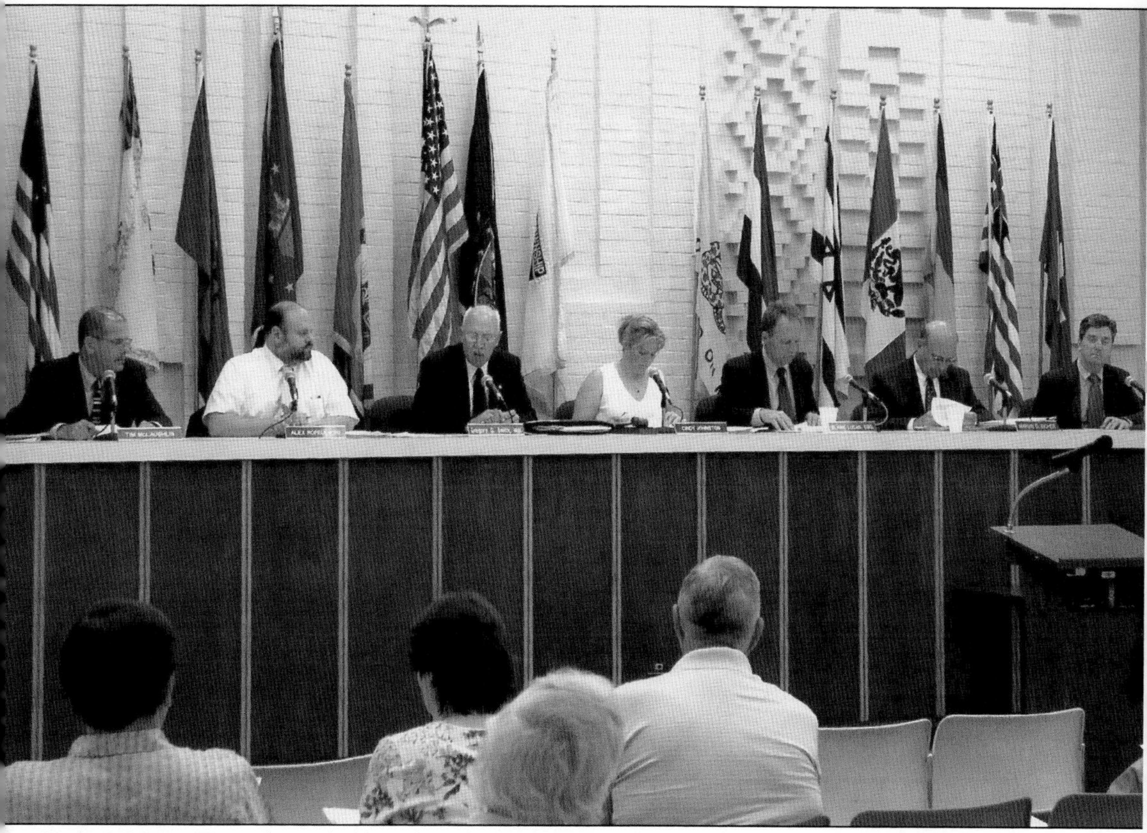

Today's Moon Township is led by a board of supervisors. Pictured here from left to right are the 2007 supervisors: Tim McLaughlin, Alex Ropelewski, township manager Gregory Smith, board president Cindy Johnston, solicitor Blaine Lucas, Marvin Eicher, and Michael Hopper. Both Johnston and Ropelewski chose not to run for reelection and finish their terms at the end of 2007. (Photograph by Mark Berton.)